INGLÉS IDIOMÁTICO
3

INGLÉS
IDIOMÁTICO
——3——

Eugene E. Long • William Buckwald

**EDITORIAL
TRILLAS**

México, Argentina, España,
Colombia, Puerto Rico, Venezuela

Catalogación en la fuente

Long, Eugene E.
    Inglés idiomático 3. -- 8a ed. -- México : Trillas,
1990 (reimp. 1995).
        372 p. : il. ; 21 cm.
        ISBN 968-24-4002-5

        1. Inglés - Estudio y enseñanza - Estudiantes
extranjeros. I. Buckwald, William. II. t.

        LC- PE1129.58'L6.5   D- 421'L245i   37

Derechos reservados
© 1960, Editorial Trillas, S. A. de C. V.,
División Administrativa, Av. Río Churubusco 385,
Col. Pedro María Anaya, C. P. 03340, México, D. F.
Tel. 6884233, FAX 6041364

División Comercial, Calz. de la Viga 1132, C. P. 09439
México, D. F. Tel. 6330995, FAX 6330870

Miembro de la Cámara Nacional de la
Industria Editorial. Reg. núm. 158

Segunda edición, 1960
(Primera publicada por Editorial Trillas, S. A. de C. V.)
Tercera edición, 1965
    Reimpresiones, 1966, 1967, 1968 y 1969
Cuarta edición, junio 1971
    Reimpresión, octubre 1971
Quinta edición, mayo 1972
    Reimpresiones, 1972, 1973, 1974, 1975, 1976, 1977 y 1978
Sexta edición, 1979 (ISBN 968-24-0734-6)
    Reimpresiones, mayo y noviembre 1980, 1981, 1983,
    1984, 1985, 1986, 1987 y 1988
Séptima edición, 1989 (ISBN 968-24-3168-9)
Octava edición, 1990 (ISBN 968-24-4002-5)
    Reimpresiones, 1991, 1992 y 1994

Cuarta reimpresión, julio 1995

Impreso en México
Printed in Mexico

Esta obra se terminó de imprimir y encuadernar
el 5 de julio de 1995,
en los talleres de Rotodiseño y Color, S. A. de C. V.
Se tiraron
3 000 ejemplares, más sobrantes de reposición.
AO 75

Índice de contenido

6

8

Lección 1

Vocabulary

1. **to complain (about), complained (about), complained (about)** quejarse (de)
2. **to introduce, introduced introduced** presentar(se) **introduction** presentación
3. **to promise, promised, promised** prometer
4. **to belong, belonged, belonged** pertenecer
5. **to raise, raised, raised** levantar, alzar; cultivar; criar
6. **to rise, rose, risen** levantarse; salir (*el sol*)
7. **suddenly** repentinamente
8. **informal** sin ceremonia
9. **glasses** lentes
10. **magazine** revista
11. **citizen** ciudadano
12. **lawyer** abogado
13. **soap** jabón
14. **cute** mono (*adj.*)
15. **package** paquete
16. **bundle** bulto
17. **beach** playa
18. **prize** premio
19. **war** guerra
20. **holiday** día de fiesta
21. **boss** jefe, patrón
22. **maid** criada
23. **human being** ser humano
24. **dry** seco
25. **dialogue** diálogo
26. **greeting** saludo

IDIOMS

1. **to miss, missed, missed a person or a thing** echar de menos a alguien o algo

I miss my girl. Echo de menos a mi novia.

She misses New York. Ella echa de menos Nueva York.

2. **to get a raise** aumentarle a uno el salario

   I got a raise. Me aumentaron (el salario).

3. **to say hello, good morning, good afternoon, good evening (to)** saludar (a)

   He said hello to me. Me saludó.

4. **What's new?** ¿Qué hay de nuevo? ¿Qué cuentas?

5. **How's everything?** ¿Cómo le va?

6. **whether** si (*dubitativo*)

   I don't know whether he'll come. No sé si venga.

7. **a friend of mine, of his, of hers, etc.** un amigo mío, suyo (de él), suyo (de ella), etc.

   a friend of John's, of my father's, etc. un amigo de Juan, de mi padre, etc.

8. **in advance** con anticipación, por adelantado

9. **Thanks a lot.** Muchísimas gracias.

10. **right now** (*used in the present*) en este momento

    just then (*used in the past*) en aquel momento

11. **My hands are cold.** Tengo las manos frías.

    My feet are warm. Tengo los pies calientes.

12. **Have you met...?** ¿Conoce Ud. a...?

13. **I want you to meet...** Te quiero presentar a...

    I'd like you to meet... Te quiero presentar a...

14. **How do you do.** Mucho gusto (en conocerlo).

    (*only used on being introduced*)

15. **It was nice meeting you.** Mucho gusto en haberlo conocido.

    I'm glad to have met you. Mucho gusto en haberlo conocido.

16. **It was nice seeing you.** Mucho gusto (en haberlo visto).

17. **I'll see you** (*familiar*). Ahí nos vemos.

    I'll be seeing you (*familiar*). Ahí nos vemos.

18. **Hi.** ¿Qué húbo(le)? ¿Qué pasó? Hola.

EXERCISE 1

Practice the following dialogue.

BEING INTRODUCED AND SAYING GOOD-BYE

Latin Americans should remember that North American introductions are very short and informal. When two older people are introduced or when a young person is introduced to an older person, a sincere **How do you do** is sufficient. When two young people are introduced, an informal **hello** or **hi** is all that is necessary. When saying good-bye to a person who you have just met, a good expression to remember is **It was nice meeting you** or **I'm glad to have met you.**

Bill: Come here, Tom. I want you to meet a friend of mine. Betty, this is Tom.
Tom: Hello, Betty.
Betty: Hi, Tom.

———

Tom: I have to go now. It was nice meeting you, Betty. Good-bye.
Betty: It was nice meeting you, Tom. Good-bye.

———

Bill: Mrs. Wood, this is Mr. Adams.
Mr. Adams: How do you do, Mrs. Wood.
Mrs. Wood: How do you do.

———

Mr. Adams: It was nice meeting you, Mrs. Wood.
Mrs. Wood: I'm glad to have met you too. Good-bye.

AFFIRMATIVE CONTRACTIONS WITH FORMS OF THE VERB BE AND A PRONOUN

Learn these contractions. The affirmative contractions are only used when followed by another word.

	Contraction	Contraction followed by not
I am	I'm	I'm not
you are	you're	you're not
he is	he's	he's not
she is	she's	she's not
it is	it's	it's not
we are	we're	we're not
you are	you're	you're not
they are	they're	they're not

11

EXERCISE 2

Read the following sentences. Change them to the negative using the contractions above.

1. I'm hungry.
2. They're over there.
3. We're leaving tomorrow.
4. He's singing.
5. You're tired.
6. She's angry.
7. It's a beautiful day.
8. I'm speaking English.
9. That's my father.
10. It's time to go.

EXERCISE 3

Translate the following sentences and practice reading them.

1. There's a ship.
2. There isn't a ship.
3. Is there a ship?
4. Isn't there a ship?
5. How many ships are there?
6. There was a window.
7. There wasn't a window.
8. Was there a window?
9. Wasn't there a window?
10. How many windows were there?
11. It's cold.
12. It isn't cold.
13. Is it cold?
14. Isn't it cold?
15. When is it cold?
16. It was hot.
17. It wasn't hot.
18. Was it hot?
19. Wasn't it hot?
20. When was it hot?
21. The children are sleepy.
22. The children aren't sleepy.
23. Are the children sleepy?
24. Aren't the children sleepy?
25. Why are the children sleepy?
26. The cat is hungry.
27. The cat isn't hungry.
28. Is the cat hungry?
29. Isn't the cat hungry?
30. Why's the cat hungry?

EXERCISE 4

Translate the following sentences. Change them to the negative interrogative and interrogative negative.

1. The dog misses me when I go to the office.
2. They'll miss you when you get married.
3. He's going to miss her a great deal.
4. She missed you while you were in the United States.
5. We missed you at Christmas time.
6. The baby has missed her mother.

12

7. Mr. Kelly is going to miss his oldest son.
8. Helen misses her friends when she's out of town.
9. The boys will miss you very much.
10. The children would miss me if I went to Cuernavaca.

EXERCISE 5

Give the past tense and past participle of the following verbs.

answer	agree	boil	belong
arrive (in, at)	appear	bother	call
ask	attack	breathe	change
add	avoid	burn	clean
admire	believe	bury	complain (about)

EXERCISE 6

Give the past tense and past participle of the following verbs.

be	buy	come	cost
become	bet	come back	do
begin	bleed	cut	drink
break	blow	catch	dig
bring	build	choose	draw

EXERCISE 7

Verb Practice *Expand the following verb practice using different tenses.*

1. My wife's boss has been complaining about me.
2. My wife's boss hasn't been complaining about me.
3. Has my wife's boss been complaining about me?
4. Hasn't my wife's boss been complaining about me?
5. Why has my wife's boss been complaining about me?

EXERCISE 8

Verb Practice *Make short sentences with forms of the verbs* introduce, get a raise, promise, belong, raise, rise, miss a person or a thing, say hello, good morning, good afternoon, good evening (to). *Expand each verb practice to include different tenses as in the exercise above. Use a*

13

different noun or pronoun with each verb. Use the interrogative words when it is possible.

EXERCISE 9

Translate into Spanish.

1. Do you think we'll get a raise the first of the year?
2. If your hands are cold, put on your gloves.
3. The sun rises about seven-thirty.
4. The students have been complaining because they have to pay in advance.
5. Thanks a lot for letting me know about the party.
6. I don't know whether the dog will miss the children or not.
7. I'm not doing anything right now.
8. How long has it been since you got a raise?
9. Robert, have you met my mother?
10. That looks like an interesting person over there. I'd like to meet him.
11. A friend of mine introduced me to my husband twenty years ago.
12. My feet are so cold that I can hardly walk.
13. Please raise your hand if you want to talk.
14. We had a wonderful time on the beach.
15. Do you plan to buy a new car this year?

EXERCISE 10

Translate into English.

1. Tengo las orejas frías.
2. ¿Cultiva Ud. legumbres en su jardín?
3. La criada no podrá cargar aquel bulto grande, ¿verdad?
4. Él la echó de menos tanto que parecía que no podía vivir sin ella.
5. Él no me haría caso.
6. Ellos se burlaron del traje de baño que ella llevaba en la playa.
7. Como de costumbre, llovió.
8. No hemos estado trabajando tan duro como trabajamos el año pasado.
9. ¿Conoce Ud. a la señora Ames?
10. Ella me presentó a su hermano (de ella), mas no me acuerdo de su nombre.

14

EXERCISE 11

Answer the following questions in the affirmative and in the negative, using the contractions.

1. Are you still working in the bank?
2. Is he still here?
3. Is she going to help you?
4. Are we ready?
5. Are they still living in Mexico?
6. Are you sick?
7. Is he going to the movies?
8. Is that your car?
9. Is she beautiful?
10. Are they going to eat here?
11. Is that your father?

Answer the following questions in the affirmative and in the negative.

12. Are your hands cold?
13. Are your feet cold?
14. Are your ears warm?
15. Is your face warm?
16. Do you miss her very much?
17. Do you expect to get a raise soon?
18. Are you going right now?
19. Do you like candy?
20. Is he a friend of yours?

Lección 2

Vocabulary

1. **to dream (about), dreamed (about), dreamed (about)** soñar (con)
2. **to dial, dialed, dialed** marcar el teléfono
3. **to owe, owed, owed** deber
4. **to kick, kicked, kicked** patear
5. **to lock, locked, locked** cerrar con llave
6. **to ring, rang, rung** sonar, tocar, timbrar
7. **meanwhile** mientras tanto
8. **extra** extra
9. **within** dentro de; a una distancia
10. **pleasant** agradable
11. **unpleasant** desagradable
12. **sunny** de sol (*día*); asoleado
13. **windy** de viento (*día*); ventoso
14. **quality** calidad
15. **quantity** cantidad
16. **deep** profundo, hondo
17. **middle** centro, en medio de
18. **shore** orilla, playa, ribera
19. **main** principal
20. **leather** cuero, piel
21. **receiver** audífono, bocina
22. **message** recado
23. **telephone book** directorio
    phone book directorio
24. **booth** caseta; vestidor
    telephone booth caseta telefónica
    phone booth caseta telefónica
25. **doorbell** timbre de la puerta

IDIOMS

1. **to miss (the train, boat, plane, etc.)** perder (el tren, barco, avión, etc.)

16

2. **to hang up** colgar
3. **to pick (a person or thing) up** pasar por o recoger (a una persona o una cosa)
4. **to phone** telefonear, hablar por teléfono
   to telephone telefonear, hablar por teléfono
5. **to be in** (*person*) estar (en casa), estar en la oficina, etc.
   Is he in now? ¿Está en este momento?
6. **to be out** (*person*) no estar (en casa), haber salido; no estar en la oficina, etc.
   He's out now. No está en este momento, Ha salido.
7. **long distance** larga distancia
8. **You have the wrong number.** Ud. está equivocado.
9. **The line is busy.** La línea está ocupada.
10. **You're wanted on the phone.** Le hablan por teléfono.
11. **I'll get it** (*in conversation*). Yo contesto (*el teléfono*).
12. **I'd love to.** Me encantaría (*se sobreentiende un verbo*).
13. **Who's calling please?** ¿De parte de quién? (*en el teléfono*)
14. **Is that you, John?** ¿Eres tú, Juan?
15. **This is John.** Soy Juan (*en el teléfono*).
16. **I'm going to make a phone call.** Voy a hablar por teléfono.

EXERCISE 1

Practice the following dialogue.

A TELEPHONE CONVERSATION

When the telephone rang, Mrs. Jones went to answer it.

Mrs. Jones:	Hello.
Tom:	Hello, Betty?
Mrs. Jones:	No, this isn't Betty. This is Betty's mother.
Tom:	I'd like to speak to Betty, please. Is she in?
Mrs. Jones:	No, she's out right now, but she should be back in a few minutes. Do you want me to tell her that you called?
Tom:	Yes, please tell her that Tom Brown called.
Mrs. Jones:	All right. Do you want to leave a message?
Tom:	No, thank you. Just tell her I called and that I'll call back later. Good-bye.
Mrs. Jones:	Good-bye.

After a while the telephone in the Jones house rang again. "I'll get it," Betty said to her mother, as she went to the phone.

Betty:	Hello.
Tom:	Hi, Betty. This is Tom.
Betty:	Hello, Tom. What's new?
Tom:	Nothing much. A few of us are having a little party at Ruth's house tonight, and I thought you might like to go.
Betty:	I'd love to.
Tom:	I'll pick you up around seven. Is that all right?
Betty:	That'll be fine.
Tom:	I have to call Ben and George too. Do you know their telephone numbers?
Betty:	Ben's phone number is 18-08-66. Wait just a minute. I think I gave you the wrong number. Yes, I did. It's 18-66-08. I don't have George's number, and I don't think it's in the phone book. You'll have to call information and ask them for it.
Tom:	O.K., Betty. Thanks a lot. I'll see you at seven. Good-bye.
Betty:	Good-bye.

AFFIRMATIVE CONTRACTIONS WITH FORMS OF THE VERB *HAVE* AND A PRONOUN

Learn these affirmative contractions. They are used almost exclusively with the past participle.

I have	I've
you have	you've
he has	he's
she has	she's
it has	it's
we have	we've
you have	you've
they have	the've

EXERCISE 2

Translate the following sentences and practice reading them.

1. I've been working all day.

2. You've had to work every Saturday.
3. We've eaten all the potatoes.
4. You've lived in Mexico a long time.
5. They've already seen that movie.
6. I've tried hard to help you.
7. You've been working too hard.
8. You've had to get up early.
9. You've been to Acapulco many times.
10. They've been waiting for you.
11. She's gone to Acapulco for her vacation.
12. He's written to her every day for a month.

EXERCISE 3

Translate the following sentences and practice reading them.

1. Hide it.
2. Don't hide it.
3. Let him hide it.
4. Don't let him hide it.
5. Let her hide it.
6. Don't let her hide it.
7. Let's hide it.
8. Let's not hide it.
9. Let me hide it.
10. Don't let me hide it.
11. Let them hide it.
12. Don't let them hide it.
13. Let's hide it.
14. Let's not hide it.
15. What are you complaining about?
16. What were you complaining about?
17. What did you complain about?
18. What have you complained about?
19. What have you been complaining about?
20. What had you complained about?
21. What had you been complaining about?

19

EXERCISE 4

Translate the following sentences. Change them to the negative, interrogative, and interrogative negative.

1. I missed the bus this morning.
2. We missed the train in Monterrey.
3. She misses the plane every time she goes to Chicago.
4. They miss the bus when they leave the house late.
5. You'll miss the ship when you go to Europe.
6. The soldiers have missed the boat.
7. He'd miss the bus if he didn't leave early.
8. The boys have been missing the train every morning.
9. My husband missed the nine o'clock plane.
10. His cousin missed the bus because she was late.

EXERCISE 5

Give the past tense and past participle of the following verbs.

close	clap	cry	die
complete	cook	dictate	die down
correct	count	drop	disappear
capture	cover	dance	dial
carry	cross	decide	dream (about)

EXERCISE 6

Give the past tense and past participle of the following verbs.

drive	feed	get	get thirsty
eat	fight	get angry (at)	get up
find	find out	get rich	give
forget	fly	get sleepy	give up
fall	freeze	get a raise	go

EXERCISE 7

Verb Practice *Expand the following verb practice, using different tenses.*

1. Elizabeth's sister dreamed about me, didn't she?

20

2. Elizabeth's sister didn't dream about me, did she?
3. Did Elizabeth's sister dream about me?
4. Didn't Elizabeth's sister dream about me?
5. Why didn't Elizabeth's sister dream about me?

EXERCISE 8

Verb Practice *Make short sentences with forms of the verbs* dial, owe, kick, lock, ring, hang up, pick (a person or thing) up, phone, telephone, be in, be out, miss a bus. *Expand each verb practice to include different tenses, as in the exercise above. Use a different noun or pronoun with each verb. Use the interrogative words when it is possible.*

EXERCISE 9

Transalate into Spanish.

1. I won't be able to pick you up before noon.
2. You're wanted on the telephone.
3. I'd love to spend two weeks in Acapulco in January.
4. You should dial after you pick the receiver up.
5. We told him not to lock the kitchen door, but he didn't pay any attention to us.
6. They won't get to Mexico City until Thursday because they missed the train in Dallas.
7. Tell him not to hang up. I want to say hello to him.
8. Long distance is calling Mr. J. M. Butler.
9. We couldn't keep from laughing at the way he pronounced our names.
10. You're lucky that the boss didn't come in while you were talking to Henry on the telephone.
11. It was very nice meeting you, George.
12. If it's raining in the morning, please pick me up when you go to work.
13. My ears were cold and my feet were frozen.
14. How long does it take to call long distance to San Francisco?
15. I wish the wind would die down.

EXERCISE 10

Translate into English.

1. ¿Está el Sr. Jackson? No, no está en este momento.

2. El jueves estuvo muy desagradable. Hizo mucho viento y llovió.
3. Si ya no me quieres, ¿por qué no me dejas en paz?
4. No podremos recogerlos en la mañana porque ya no habrá lugar en el coche.
5. Ud. marcó el número equivocado.
6. Cuelgue antes de volver a marcar.
7. ¿Quién tocó el timbre?
8. Ellos buscaron en el directorio, mas no encontraron el número.
9. ¿Quiere Ud. dejar algún recado?
10. Soñé contigo anoche.

EXERCISE 11

Answer the following questions in the affirmative and in the negative.

1. Did you miss the bus?
2. Did you miss the train?
3. Did you miss the plane?
4. Did you miss the boat?
5. Did you miss the ship?
6. Did you forget to hang up after speaking?
7. Can you pick me up about eight?
8. Did you dial the wrong number?
9. Did you say I was wanted on the phone?
10. The phone is ringing. Will you get it, please?

Answer the following questions.

11. How long does it take to make a suit?
12. How long did it take to read that book?
13. How long will it take to finish that work?
14. How long would it take to wash the car?
15. How long should it take to paint the house?
16. How long does it take to go to Europe by ship?
17. How long did it take to go to Chicago by plane?
18. How long will it take to go to New York by train?
19. How long is it going to take to go to Florida by car?
20. How long has it taken to walk to the market?
21. Is Mr. Jones in now?
22. Will he be in all afternoon?
23. Is he in all day?
24. Is she out to lunch?
25. Are they going to be out all day?

Lección 3

Vocabulary

1. **to arrest, arrested, arrested** arrestar
2. **to bite, bit, bitten** morder
3. **to whistle (at), whistled (at), whistled (at)** silbar
4. **to direct, directed, directed** dirigir
5. **to hold, held, held** sostener
6. **to fine, fined, fined** multar
7. **bus driver** chofer de camión
8. **bus stop** parada de camión
9. **police** cuerpo de policía
   policeman policía
   cop policía
10. **traffic** tránsito
    traffic cop agente de tránsito
11. **signal** señal
12. **traffic light** semáforo
    stop light alto, pare
    red light alto, pare
    green light siga, pase
13. **uniform** uniforme
14. **streetcar** tranvía
15. **pistol** pistola
16. **rifle** rifle
17. **bullet** bala
18. **speed limit** velocidad máxima
19. **fare** tarifa, pasaje
20. **law** ley
21. **trial** juicio por corte
22. **court** corte
23. **jury** jurado
24. **witness** testigo
25. **judge** juez
26. **passenger** pasajero
27. **stripe** franja; raya
28. **trade** oficio
29. **gutter** arroyo (*en la calle*)

IDIOMS

1. **to be missing** faltar (*de no estar*)
   Who's missing? ¿Quién falta?
   John is missing. Falta Juan.
   How many books are missing? ¿Cuántos libros faltan?
   There are three books missing. Faltan tres libros.
   Three books are missing. Faltan tres libros.
2. **to hit a car** chocar con un coche
   I hit a car. Choqué con un coche.
   A car hit me. Un coche chocó conmigo.
3. **The bus goes up (down) Madison Avenue.** El camión va por la Avenida Madison.
4. **Take the next bus.** Tome el próximo camión.
5. **He got a ticket for speeding.** Le levantaron infracción por exceso de velocidad.
6. **no right turn** no hay vuelta a la derecha
7. **no left turn** no hay vuelta a la izquierda
8. **one-way street** calle de un sentido
9. **because of** por; por causa de; por culpa de
   because of you por tí; por causa tuya, por culpa tuya
10. **due to** debido a, por causa de, por razón de
    due to the rain debido a la lluvia
11. **There is (are) enough.** Alcanza (n).
    There's enough time. Alcanza el tiempo.
12. **to have enough** alcanzarle a uno
    I don't have enough. No me alcanza (n).

EXERCISE 1

Practice the following dialogue.

A BUS TRIP

Passenger: Excuse me. Can you tell me where I can take a bus that goes down Madison Avenue?

Traffic Cop: I think those green buses with the red stripe that pass by here go down Madison Avenue, but I don't know how far down they go. There's a bus stop over there on the corner. Why don't you ask the bus driver?

Passenger: Thanks.

24

Passenger:	Does this bus go down Madison Avenue as far as Longview?
Bus Driver:	No, this bus doesn't go down Madison Avenue. It only crosses it. Take a bus marked Madison Avenue-Longview, and tell the driver to let you off at Longview.
Passenger:	Thank you very much.

Passenger:	Please tell me when we get to Longview. I want to get off there.
Bus Driver:	O. K. I'll let you know when we get there.
Passenger:	How much is the fare?
Bus Driver:	Fifteen cents.
Passenger:	Will I need a transfer?
Bus Driver:	No, this bus will take you within two blocks of Longview. When you get off, walk two blocks to the right.
Passenger:	Thank you.

EXERCISE 2

Learn these words.

NAMES OF TRADES AND PROFESSIONS

In English the indefinite article must be used after the verb be when referring to a profession or a trade. Example: He's a teacher.

1. **architect** arquitecto
2. **aviation** aviación
3. **biochemist** bioquímico
4. **biochemistry** bioquímica
5. **biologist** biólogo
6. **biology** biología
7. **botanist** botánico
8. **chemist** químico
9. **cook** cocinero, a
10. **dentistry** odontología
11. **agricultural engineer** ingeniero agrónomo
12. **chemical engineer** ingeniero químico
13. **electrical engineer** ingeniero electricista
14. **mechanical engineer** ingeniero mecánico
15. **metalurgical engineer** ingeniero metalúrgico

16. **mining engineer** ingeniero de minas
17. **fashion designing** diseño de modas
18. **fashion designer** diseñador de modas
19. **geologist** geólogo
20. **grocer** abarrotero
21. **historian** historiador
22. **interior decorating** decoración
23. **interior decorator** decorador
24. **law** derecho, leyes
25. **lawyer** licenciado, abogado
26. **mason** albañil
27. **mechanics** mecánica
28. **mechanic** mecánico
29. **mining** minería
30. **miner** minero
31. **modeling** el estudio para ser modelo
32. **model** modelo
33. **music** música
34. **nursing** enfermería
35. **nurse** enfermera
36. **ophthalmology** oftalmología
37. **ophthalmologist** oftalmólogo
38. **optician** óptico
39. **optometry** optometría
40. **optometrist** optometrista
41. **painter** pintor
42. **pharmacy** farmacia
43. **pharmacist** farmacéutico
44. **pianist** pianista
45. **pilot** piloto
46. **professor** profesor
47. **radio announcer** locutor de radio
48. **reporter** periodista
49. **TV announcer** locutor de televisión

AFFIRMATIVE CONTRACTIONS IN THE PAST PERFECT AND CONDITIONAL

Learn these contractions. Although this contraction is used for both the past perfect and the conditional, its meaning is clearly understood by its use in the sentence.

I had, I would	I'd
you had, you would	you'd
he had, he would	he'd
she had, she would	she'd
it had, it would	it'd
we had, we would	we'd
you had, you would	you'd
they had, they would	they'd

EXERCISE 3

Translate the following sentences and practice reading them.

1. I'd go if I had time.
2. We'd like to visit New York.
3. She'd work if she needed money.
4. They'd buy the vegetables if they were fresh.
5. It'd be late before we got home.
6. You'd be happy in Mexico.
7. I'd already left before he arrived.
8. He'd never been in the United States before.
9. She'd stopped talking when I hung up.
10. They'd lived in Mexico for several years.

EXERCISE 4

Translate the following sentences and practice reading them.

1. There'll be enough time.
2. There won't be enough time.
3. Will there be enough time?
4. Won't there be enough time?
5. Why won't there be enough time?
6. There's been enough time.
7. There hasn't been enough time.
8. Has there been enough time?
9. Hasn't there been enough time?
10. Why hasn't there been enough time?
11. It'll be hot.
12. It won't be hot.
13. Will it be hot?
14. Won't it be hot?
15. When will it be hot?
16. It's been cold.
17. It hasn't been cold.
18. Has it been cold?
19. Hasn't it been cold?
20. Why hasn't it been cold?
21. They'll be sleepy.
22. They won't be sleepy.
23. Will they be sleepy?
24. Won't they be sleepy?
25. Why won't they be sleepy?
26. They've been afraid.
27. They haven't been afraid.
28. Have they been afraid?
29. Haven't they been afraid?
30. Why have they been afraid?

EXERCISE 5

Translate the following sentences. Change them to the negative, interrogative, and interrogative negative.

1. There are three books missing.
2. A dollar is missing.
3. Two blankets are missing.
4. There are five chairs missing.
5. A silver spoon is missing.
6. His shoes and hat are missing.
7. A little money was missing.
8. There was a seat missing.
9. My watch was missing.
10. The policeman's pistol was missing.

EXERCISE 6

Give the past tense and past participle of the following verbs.

dress	examine	fill	fail
discover	expect	finish	follow
drown	explain	fix	help
direct	express	fine	hurry
dial	escape	form	hope

EXERCISE 7

Give the past tense and past participle of the following verbs.

go back	get better	get light	get on
go out	get dark	get lost	get out (of)
go to bed	get drunk	get off	get ready
go to sleep	get hurt	get married	get rid of
get away	get in	get old	get scared

EXERCISE 8

Verb Practice *Expand the following verb practice, using different tenses.*

1. The police will arrest them.
2. The police won't arrest them.

3. Will the police arrest them?
4. Won't the police arrest them?
5. Why won't the police arrest them?

EXERCISE 9

Verb Practice *Make short sentences with forms of the verbs* bite, whistle (at), direct, hold, fine, be missing, hit a car, there is (are) enough, have enough. *Expand each verb practice to include different tenses, as in the exercise above. Use a different noun or pronoun with each verb. Use the interrogative word when it is possible.*

EXERCISE 10

Translate into Spanish.

1. Turn on the lights as soon as it gets dark.
2. There are seven uniforms missing.
3. Thanks a lot for everything.
4. I hope you come back to work soon. We all miss you.
5. We expected him to be at the party, but we didn't see him.
6. What was your boss complaining about this morning?
7. You should have eaten before going out.
8. My hands were so cold that I could hardly drive.
9. Won't we have to buy our tickets in advance if we want good seats?
10. If you miss the train in the morning, let me know.
11. I wanted to tell her that I'd pick her up in the morning, but she hung up.
12. Did you see me looking out of the window?
13. We've been having a good time, haven't we?
14. They couldn't go because of the storm.
15. Is the money still missing?

EXERCISE 11

Translate into English.

1. La velocidad máxima en esta ciudad es de cuarenta millas por hora.
2. Él me multó con cinco dólares por exceso de velocidad.
3. Si Ud. no presta atención al agente de tránsito, lo arrestarán.
4. La tarifa en el tranvía es menos que la tarifa del camión.

5. ¿Quién está dirigiendo el tránsito en esta esquina?
6. Tenía miedo de que el perro me fuera a morder.
7. Necesitará Ud. dos testigos cuando se case.
8. Uds. pueden tomar el camión en la próxima parada.
9. Ojalá que dejaras de silbar.
10. Ud. debería tomar el tranvía que va por Insurgentes.

EXERCISE 12

Answer the following questions in the affirmative and in the negative.

1. Is it raining?
2. Are they here?
3. Is he sick?
4. Are we ready?
5. Is she going to work?
6. Have you seen this movie?
7. Have we been here before?
8. Have they worked all day?
9. Have you eaten yet?
10. Would you like to go with us?
11. Would he go if he could?
12. Did they think that he'd come?
13. Would she have gone if she'd had time?
14. Would you have come if it'd been raining?
15. Would they have studied if they'd had a book?

Answer the following questions.

16. Who's missing?
17. How many people are missing tonight?
18. Did he have a serious accident?
19. Did he get a ticket for speeding?
20. Is this a one-way street?
21. Can I make a right turn on this street?
22. Can I make a left turn on this street?
23. When will Mr. White be in?
24. Would you be in if I called at six?
25. Were you out all day yesterday?

Lección 4

Vocabulary

1. **to charge, charged, charged** cobrar
2. **to bore, bored, bored** aburrir
3. **to end, ended, ended** terminar
4. **to mix, mixed, mixed** mezclar
5. **to dry up, dried up, dried up** secarse (*plantas*)
6. **to taste, tasted, tasted** probar; saber
   to taste like, tasted like, tasted like saber a
7. **customer** parroquiano, cliente
8. **salesman** vendedor
   traveling salesman agente viajero
9. **tobacco** tabaco
   tobacco store tabaquería
10. **moist** húmedo
11. **cigar** puro
12. **cigarette** cigarro, cigarrillo
13. **cigarette holder** boquilla
14. **(cigarette) butt** colilla
15. **ashes** cenizas
16. **ashtray** cenicero
17. **pipe** pipa
    pipe cleaner limpiapipas
18. **odor** olor
19. **(cigarette) lighter** encendedor
20. **lighter fluid** combustible para encendedor
21. **filter** filtro; boquilla
22. **flint** piedra
23. **match** cerillo
    a book of matches una carterita de cerillos
24. **can** lata, bote
25. **lately** últimamente
26. **kind** marca
27. **king size** tamaño regio
28. **mild** suave (*tabaco*); templado
29. **strong** fuerte
30. **altogether** por todo
31. **slice** rebanada

31

IDIOMS

1. **to take place** tener lugar, suceder, ocurrir
2. **to borrow (something from someone)** pedir o tomar prestado (algo a alguien)
   He borrowed five dollars from me. El me pidió prestado cinco dólares.
3. **to light, lit, lit a match** encender un cerillo
   to strike, struck, struck a match encender un cerillo
4. **to be out of something** acabársele a uno algo, no tener más
   We're out of cigarettes. Se nos acabaron los cigarros.
   We were out of cigarettes. Se nos habían acabado los cigarros.
5. **Do you smoke?** ¿Fuma Ud.?
   Would you like a cigarette? ¿Quiere Ud. fumar?
6. **No, thank you. I don't smoke.** No gracias. No fumo.
7. **no smoking** no fumar, se prohíbe fumar
8. **a carton of cigarettes** un paquete de cigarros
9. **a pack of cigarettes** una cajetilla de cigarros
10. **to get bored, got bored, got bored** aburrirse
11. **Give me a cigarette.** Dame un cigarro.
    Give me a match. Dame un cerillo.
    Give me a light. Enciéndeme el cigarro.

EXERCISE 1

Practice the following dialogue.

AT THE TOBACCO SHOP

First Customer:	A pack of cigarettes, please—Camels—and some matches.
Salesman:	I'm out of Camels right now. Would you like Luckies or Philip Morris or Chesterfields?
First Customer:	Chesterfields. I also want a box of Corona cigars and a carton of Luckies. And will you let me see those cigarette holders, please?
Salesman:	Of course.
First Customer:	Hello, Ben. What are you doing here?
Second Customer:	My lighter won't (no quiere) work. I think it's out of fluid, and it might need a new flint. Give me a light, will you?

32

First Customer:	I thought you smoked a pipe.
Second Customer:	I used to, but I've been smoking cigarettes lately. My father still smokes a pipe. (*to salesman*) I want a small can of lighter fluid and a package of flints.
Salesman:	All right. Here you are. Anything else, sir?
Second Customer:	I need some pipe tobacco and some pipe cleaners. Give me a can of Prince Albert.
Salesman:	Do you want the half-pound or the pound can?
Second Customer:	Give me two half-pound cans. A pound dries up too quickly.
Salesman:	Why don't you put a few slices of apple in your tobacco? That will keep it moist, and it won't leave any odor. Is that all for now?
Second Customer:	Yes, that'll be all. How much is that?
Salesman:	Let's see. That's ten twenty-five altogether.
First Customer:	And how much do I owe you?
Salesman:	Thirteen ninety-five.

EXERCISE 2

Learn these words.

NAMES OF COLORS

1. **aquamarine** agua marina
2. **wine** guinda
3. **coral** coral
4. **dark blue, dark brown, etc.** azul oscuro, café oscuro, etc.
5. **gray** gris
6. **maroon** marrón
7. **light blue, light brown, etc.** azul claro, café claro, etc.
8. **navy blue** azul marino
9. **orange** anaranjado
10. **purple** morado
11. **beige** beige
12. **lavender** lila
13. **checked** a cuadros (*tela*)
14. **plaid** escocés (*tela*)
15. **polka dot** moteado
16. **striped** rayado
17. **pin-striped** de mil rayas

EXERCISE 3

Translate the following sentences and practice reading them.

1. Before raising corn, we raised beans.
2. After raising corn, we raised beans.

3. Instead of raising corn, we raised beans.
4. Besides raising corn, we raised beans.
5. They always complain, but I don't.
6. He always promised, but I didn't.
7. She's going to go, but he isn't.
8. We sometimes went, but he didn't.
9. You ate, but they didn't.
10. They're playing, but we aren't.
11. She was going swimming, but we weren't.
12. He can teach, but she can't.
13. He could dance, but she couldn't.
14. They don't ever complain, but I do.
15. They didn't usually promise, but I did.
16. She wouldn't laugh, but you would.
17. We won't laugh, but you will.
18. You shouldn't work, but he should.
19 You didn't like to eat, but he did.
20. I don't want to play, but she does.
21. You don't have to study, but they do.
22. I didn't want to dance, but she did.
23. They didn't have to come, but she did.
24. We aren't going to speak, but he is.
25. You don't want to go, but I do.
26. You didn't want to come, but I did.

EXERCISE 4

Translate the following sentences. Change them to the negative, interrogative, and interrogative negative.

1. The meeting will take place at ten o'clock.
2. The fight took place on Thursday.
3. The car race is going to take place next July.
4. The conference was going to take place in room No. 4.
5. The concert should take place on the second floor.
6. The contest has taken place in this park every year.
7. The basketball game can take place in the morning.

EXERCISE 5

Give the past tense and past participle of the following verbs.

34

hunt	join	laugh (at)	lift
invite	kill	learn	look alike
insist (on)	kiss	like	move
insult	knit	listen (to)	mix
jump	knock (on)	live	need

EXERCISE 6

Give the past tense and past participle of the following verbs.

get sick	go shopping	hang	know
get tired	go with	have a good time	keep
get wet	grow	have fun	leave
get worse	have	hide	let
get on	hear	hit	lie down

EXERCISE 7

Verb Practice *Expand the following verb practice, using different tenses.*

1. The salesman charged a lot.
2. The salesman didn't charge a lot.
3. Did the salesman charge a lot?
4. Didn't the salesman charge a lot?
5. Why did the salesman charge a lot?

EXERCISE 8

Verb Practice *Make short sentences with forms of the verbs* **end, bore, mix, borrow, taste, taste like, take place, strike a match, light a match, be out of something, dry up.** *Expand each verb practice to include different tenses, as in the exercise above. Use a different noun or pronoun with each verb. Use the interrogative words when it is possible.*

EXERCISE 9

Translate into Spanish.

1. We're out of sugar. Get some the next time you go to the store.
2. I can't light these matches because they're wet.

3. Is the telephone out of order?
4. The meeting won't take place until Wednesday.
5. How many books are missing?
6. How many books do we have left?
7. What kind of cigarettes do you smoke?
8. There was nothing left to eat when we got to the party.
9. I'm going to stop working at the bank if I don't get a raise soon.
10. This heavy coat will keep you from getting cold.
11. They went shopping after it stopped raining.
12. The teacher made me do my homework again.
13. We haven't been able to get rid of our old car yet.
14. This raincoat will keep you from getting wet.
15. Strike a match so I can see.

EXERCISE 10

Translate into English.

1. Pongamos todas las colillas en este cenicero.
2. Siempre me aburren las fiestas.
3. El cliente siempre tiene razón.
4. ¿Cuánto le cobró el vendedor por aquellos vestidos?
5. Estos dulces saben a jabón.
6. Él fuma como dos cajetillas de cigarros al día.
7. Yo fumo desde que cumplí veinte años.
8. No puedo salir porque está cerrada con llave la puerta.
9. Si alcanza el tiempo, iremos en coche (drive) a Cuernavaca.
10. ¿Te gusta el olor de tabaco?

EXERCISE 11

Answer the following questions in the affirmative and in the negative.

1. Did you miss me while I was gone?
2. Would you miss him if he went out of town?
3. Do you miss your teacher very much?
4. Does your wife miss you?
5. Did you miss the bus this morning?
6. Have you missed class this week?
7. Did you miss the movie?
8. Are there any books missing?

9. Is the money missing?
10. Are the letters missing?
11. Will the meeting take place tomorrow?
12. Did the contest take place last week?
13. Has the race taken place yet?
14. Should the game take place now?
15. Do the meetings always take place in this room?
16. Did he borrow ten dollars from you?
17. Did you borrow two books from me last week?
18. Did you borrow this pen from her?
19. Did you borrow my lighter?
20. Would you like to borrow some money from my brother?
21. Is the doctor in now?
22. Is he out for the day?

Lección

Vocabulary

1. **to guess, guessed, guessed** adivinar
2. **to swallow, swallowed, swallowed** tragar
3. **to chase, chased, chased** perseguir
4. **to destroy, destroyed, destroyed** destruir
5. **to joke, joked, joked** bromear
   joke broma
6. **to x-ray, x-rayed, x-rayed** sacar radiografía
   x-ray radiografía
7. **prescription** receta
8. **appointment** (*business*) cita
   date (*social and with the opposite sex*) cita
9. **fever** calentura, fiebre
10. **run-down** agotado
11. **check-up** examen médico general

12. **chest** pecho
13. **nurse** enfermera
14. **patient** paciente
15. **ambulance** ambulancia
16. **hospital** hospital, sanatorio
17. **disease** enfermedad (*infecciosa y trasmisible*)
    sickness enfermedad
18. **medicine** medicina
19. **arrangement** arreglo
20. **thermometer** termómetro
21. **normal** normal
22. **pill** píldora
    tablet tableta, pastilla
23 **vitamin** vitamina
24. **shot** inyección
25. **result** resultado
26. **bloodshot eyes** ojos enrojecidos o inyectados
27. **blood test** análisis de sangre

IDIOMS

1. **to take charge (of)** encargarse (de)
2. **to operate on someone or something** operar a alguien o algo
   They operated on him. Lo operaron.
   They operated on his arm. Lo operaron del brazo.
3. **to build you up** reconstituirle a Ud., reponerle a Ud.
   This will build you up. Esto le reconstituirá.
4. **to have your tonsils (appendix) taken out** operarse de las anginas
   (apéndice) (*sin indicar quien operó*)
   I had my tonsils taken out. Me operé de las anginas.
   to take someone's tonsils (appendix) out operar a alguien de las
   anginas (apéndice) (*indicando quien operó*)
   That doctor took my tonsils out. Aquel doctor me operó de las
   anginas.
5. **to take your pulse, temperature** tomar el pulso, la temperatura
6. **to take an x-ray** sacar una radiografía
7. **to take your blood pressure** tomar la presión
8. **to stick your tongue out** sacar (enseñar) la lengua
9. **Take a deep breath.** Respire profundamente.
10. **I hope so (not).** Espero que sí (no).
11. **Stand still.** Estése quieto.
12. **How are you getting along?** ¿Cómo sigue Ud.?
13. **I'm going to get a shot for a cold.** Voy a inyectarme para el catarro.
    Me van a poner una inyección para el catarro.
    The doctor gave me a shot. El doctor me inyectó.
14. **There's something wrong with my eyes, hand, etc.** Estoy mal de
    los ojos, la mano, etc.
15. **He has heart trouble, liver trouble, etc.** (*cronic and internal*) Pade-
    ce (Está mal) del corazón, del hígado, etc.

EXERCISE 1

Practice the following dialogue.

AT THE DOCTOR'S

Doctor: Good afternoon, Mrs. Macey. Come in. Your appointment
was at five-thirty, wasn't it?
Patient: Yes, doctor.

39

Doctor:	How have you been feeling?
Patient:	Just fine, thank you, except I feel a little run-down.
Doctor:	Is there anything wrong especially (en particular)?
Patient:	I hope not. I just came for my usual check-up.
Doctor:	Fine. I'll x-ray your chest first. Stand still and take a deep breath. Now sit down so I can take your blood pressure.
Patient:	I heard that Alice White was operated on for appendicitis. How's she getting along?
Doctor:	She's getting along fine. She'll be out of the hospital in a few days.
Patient:	Johnny wanted me to ask you when he could see you about having his tonsils taken out.
Doctor:	Tell him to come on Thursday before noon. I'll examine him then, and we'll make arrangements for him to go to the hospital for a few days. Your blood pressure is a little too high.
Patient:	I want you to test my heart again too.
Doctor:	Yes, I will. But first let me take your pulse and your temperature. Hold the thermometer in your mouth. Your pulse and temperature are normal. I want you to take some pills for your blood pressure and some vitamins to build you up. You're working too hard.
Patient:	If Mary's cold isn't better in the morning, I'm going to tell her to come in and get a shot.
Doctor:	All right. And if you'll come back on Wednesday at the same time, I'll give you the results of the x-ray and the blood test, and I'll examine your heart.
Patient:	Thank you very much, doctor. Good-bye.
Doctor:	Good-bye, Mrs. Macey.

EXERCISE 2

Learn these words.

NAMES OF DISEASES AND SICKNESSES

The words with an article must be used with that article when they follow verbs. Examples: He has the grippe. He had a heart attack.

1. **anemia** anemia
   anemic anémico

2. **appendicitis** apendicitis
3. **arthritis** artritis

4. **cancer** cáncer
5. **chicken pox** varicela, viruelas locas
6. **diphtheria** difteria
7. **dysentery** disentería
8. **the flu** influenza
9. **the grippe** gripa
10. **heart trouble** enfermedad del corazón
11. **a heart attack** ataque al corazón
12. **a hemorrhage** hemorragia
13. **malaria** paludismo
14. **the measles** sarampión
15. **German measles** rubéola
16. **the mumps** paperas
17. **pneumonia** pulmonía
18. **polio** polio
19. **a rash** erupción cutánea, salpullido; urticaria
20. **rheumatism** reumatismo
21. **scarlet fever** escarlatina
22. **smallpox** viruela negra
23. **a sore** llaga o úlcera
24. **tonsillitis** amigdalitis, anginas
25. **typhoid** tifoidea
26. **an ulcer** úlcera (*del estómago*)
27. **the whooping cough** tos ferina

EXERCISE 3

Translate the following sentences and practice reading them.

1. There'd been an accident.
2. There hadn't been an accident.
3. Had there been an accident?
4. Hadn't there been an accident?
5. How many accidents had there been?
6. There'd be a storm.
7. There wouldn't be a storm.
8. Would there be a storm?
9. Wouldn't there be a storm?
10. Why would there be a storm?
11. It'd be cold.
12. It wouldn't be cold.
13. Would it be cold?
14. Wouldn't it be cold?
15. He'd been hungry.
16. He hadn't been hungry.
17. Had he been hungry?
18. Hadn't he been hungry?
19. She'd be thirsty.

20. She wouldn't be thirsty.
21. Would she be thirsty?
22. Wouldn't she be thirsty?
23. Why wouldn't she be thirsty?

EXERCISE 4

Translate the following sentences. Change them to the negative, interrogative, and interrogative negative.

1. Mr. Evans is going to take charge of the business.
2. You'll take charge while I'm out of town.
3. He took charge on the first of the month.
4. She would take charge if she could.
5. We should take charge of the work in the office.
6. Mr. Logan was going to take charge if you didn't come back.
7. They have taken charge of everything.
8. Mrs. Lake wants Henry to take charge.
9. Mrs. Wilson can take charge.
10. We thought that Martha wanted to take charge.

EXERCISE 5

Give the past tense and past participle of the following verbs.

name	pick out	paint	punish
notice	pick up	play	push
open	place	prefer	reach
own	practice	prepare	reply
pass	pronounce	pull	rain

EXERCISE 6

Give the past tense and past participle of the following verbs.

lose	make fun of	put on	run away
lend	make money	pay	ride
make	meet	pay attention (to)	say
make a living	mean	read	see
make a mistake	put	run	sell

42

EXERCISE 7

Verb Practice *Expand the following verb practice, using different tenses.*

1. Mrs. Johnson's pupils will guess, won't they?
2. Mrs. Johnson's pupils won't guess, will they?
3. Will Mrs. Johnson's pupils guess?
4. Won't Mrs. Johnson's pupils guess?
5. Why won't Mrs. Johnson's pupils guess?

EXERCISE 8

Verb Practice *Make short sentences with forms of the verbs* **swallow, chase, destroy, joke, x-ray, operate on, take charge (of).** *Expand each verb practice to include different tenses, as in the exercise above. Use a different noun or pronoun with each verb. Use the interrogative words when it is possible.*

EXERCISE 9

Translate into Spanish.

1. The doctor says that I'll have to be operated on.
2. How long were you in the hospital when they took your tonsils out?
3. How are you getting along?
4. I'm going to get a shot for my cold.
5. We told him to call an ambulance, but he didn't pay any attention to us.
6. I feel a little run-down.
7. Take two of these pills before each meal.
8. My cigarette lighter won't work.
9. I stopped studying English because I got mad at the teacher.
10. Who will take charge of the clinic when Dr. Rogers leaves?
11. Do you have a date for tonight?
12. Don't get mad. They were only joking.
13. How do you plan to make a living now that you've lost your business?
14. I'd been living in Mexico for two years before I learned how to speak Spanish.
15. How long has it been since you were operated on?

EXERCISE 10

Translate into English.

1. Mi cita es a las tres, ¿verdad?
2. Le sacaron una radiografía de su pierna para ver si estaba rota.
3. ¿Cuánto tiempo ha tenido calentura?
4. La enfermera tomó el pulso al enfermo.
5. El doctor le dijo a ella que respirara profundamente.
6. Ya no voy a adivinar más. Me doy por vencido.
7. Mi papá está mal del corazón y tiene úlcera.
8. En esta parte del país se cultiva mucho trigo y maíz.
9. Había hecho mucho frío en Nueva York antes de que llegáramos, ¿verdad?
10. He estado trabajando muy duro este verano.

EXERCISE 11

Answer the following questions.

1. How long does it take to take his temperature?
2. How long will it take to take his tonsils out?
3. How long did it take to take his pulse?
4. How long should it take to get a raise?
5. How long is it going to take to call Chicago?
6. Who will take charge when you leave?
7. Who took charge of the class while the teacher was out?
8. When are they going to operate on him?
9. Why is she going to be operated on?

Answer the following questions in the affirmative and in the negative.

10. Did you make him stop smoking?
11. Have you made them give you a raise?
12. Does he make you take the medicine?
13. Will the doctor make you take the pills?
14. Were you going to make her get a shot?
15. Will you be able to keep (abstenerse) from smoking?
16. Can't you keep him from selling the car?
17. Did you keep him from borrowing the money?
18. Couldn't you keep them from complaining?
19. Have you kept her from leaving?

44

20. Have they operated on your father yet?
21. Do they have to operate on her leg?
22. Are they going to take your tonsils out soon?
23. Did he tell you to stand still?
24. Are you going to get a shot for your cold?
25. Will the doctor be in soon?
26. Are you going to be out this evening?

Lección

Vocabulary

1. **to deliver, delivered, delivered** entregar
2. **to develop, developed, developed** desarrollar
3. **to cause, caused, caused** causar
4. **to chew, chewed, chewed** masticar
5. **to cough, coughed, coughed** toser
6. **to drill, drilled, drilled** taladrar; perforar
   drill taladro
7. **to oversleep, overslept, overslept** quedarse dormido (*no despertar*)
8. **false teeth** dientes postizos
9. **wisdom tooth** muela del juicio
10. **toothpaste** pasta de dientes
    toothpowder polvo de dientes
11. **toothbrush** cepillo de dientes
    brush cepillo
12. **infection** infección
13. **cavity** muela picada, caries

14. **pain** dolor
15. **dentist** dentista
16. **steam** vapor
17. **lunch** comida ligera al mediodía
18. **valley** valle
19. **atmosphere** ambiente; atmósfera
20. **sand** arena
21. **juice** jugo
    juicy jugoso
22. **baggage** equipaje
23. **clinic** clínica
24. **swimming pool** piscina
25. **trouble** dificultad
26. **stairs** escaleras
    downstairs (*in a house*) abajo
    upstairs (*in a house*) arriba
27. **gums** encías
28. **brace** freno (*de dientes*)
29. **bridge** puente
30 **inlay** incrustación

46

IDIOMS

1. **to take a trip** hacer un viaje
   to make a trip hacer un viaje
   to go on a trip ir de viaje
2. **to pull a tooth** sacar una muela (*indicando quien la sacó*)
   They pulled my tooth. Me sacaron una muela.
   to have (get) a tooth pulled (*sacarse una muela sin indicar quien la sacó*)
   I had (got) a tooth pulled. Me saqué una muela.
3. **to fill a tooth** tapar una muela (*indicando quien la tapó*)
   They filled my tooth. Me taparon una muela.
   to have (get) a tooth filled taparse una muela (*sin indicar quien la tapó*)
   I had (got) a tooth filled. Me tapé una muela
   filling muela o diente tapado, empaste, obturación
   The dentist gave me a filling. El dentista me tapó una muela.
   One of my fillings fell out. Se me destapó una muela.
4. **to brush your teeth** lavarse los dientes
5. **to wash your mouth out** enjuagarse la boca
6. **to cut a tooth** salirle un diente
   He is cutting a tooth. Le está saliendo un diente.
7. **in good shape** en buen estado
   in bad shape en mal estado
8. **Do you mean _____?** ¿Quiere decir _____?

EXERCISE 1

Practice the following dialogue.

AT THE DENTIST'S

Dentist: What time is your appointment, Mr. Ellis?
Patient: At ten.
Dentist: It's almost ten now. Come in, please. How long has it been since I examined your teeth?
Patient: It's been almost a year, and I'm afraid I have another cavity or two by this time.
Dentist: Sit down, please. Now open your mouth. Wider, please. There's a cavity in one of your teeth. It's very small, but it should be filled now.

47

Patient:	Did you find only one cavity?
Dentist:	Yes, there's only one, but one of your wisdom teeth is in bad shape, and it should be pulled.
Patient:	Isn't there anything you can do to save it?
Dentist:	Yes, I can fill it and save it for a while, but it'd be much better if you let me pull it now. It might cause you a lot of trouble later. Anyway, you don't use it to chew.
Patient:	How long will it take?
Dentist:	It won't take long. I'll give you a shot to kill the pain. After that I'll use the drill on the tooth that I'm going to fill. Then I'll pull your wisdom tooth.
Patient:	Do you mean that I won't have to make another trip?
Dentist:	No, that'll be all. The rest of your teeth are in good shape. Do your gums bleed when you brush your teeth?
Patient:	A little, sometimes.

———————

Dentist:	Wash your mouth out with this medicine after each meal for a couple of days so there won't be any infection. And if the tooth that I filled hurts when you chew, come back to see me.
Patient:	Thank you. If you'll send me a bill at the end of the month, I'll come in and pay you then. Good-bye.
Dentist:	Good-bye.

EXERCISE 2

Learn these words.

(*Véase las páginas 49 y 50*)

COUNTRIES, NATIONALITIES, AND LANGUAGES

Country	Nationality (Nacionalidad)		Language (idioma)
	Noun	Adjective	
Alaska Alaska	an Alaskan alaskense		
Belgium Bélgica	a Belgian belga	Belgian belga	
Canada el Canadá	a Canadian canadiense	Canadian canadiense	
China China	a Chinese chino	Chinese chino	Chinese chino
Cuba Cuba	a Cuban cubano	Cuban cubano	
Denmark Dinamarca	a Dane danés	Danish danés	Danish danés
England Inglaterra	an Englishman inglés	English inglés	English inglés
	an Eskimo esquimal		
Finland Finlandia	a Finn finlandés	Finnish finlandés	Finnish finlandés
France Francia	a Frenchman francés	French francés	French francés
Germany Alemania	a German alemán	German alemán	German alemán
Greece Grecia	a Greek griego	Greek griego	Greek griego
Holland Holanda	a Dutchman holandés	Dutch holandés	Dutch holandés
India India	an Indian indio	Indian indio	
Ireland Irlanda	an Irishman irlandés	Irish irlandés	
Italy Italia	an Italian italiano	Italian italiano	Italian italiano
Israel Israel	an Israeli israelí	Israeli israelí	Hebrew hebreo
	a Jew judío	Jewish judío	Yiddish (dialecto judío-alemán)

49

English	Spanish		English	Spanish	English	Spanish	English	Spanish
Japan	el Japón	a **Japanese**	japonés	**Japanese**	japonés	**Japanese**	japonés	
Mexico	México	a **Mexican**	mexicano	**Mexican**	mexicano			
		a **Negro**	negro	**Negro**	negro			
Norway	Noruega	a **Norwegian**	noruego	**Norwegian**	noruego	**Norwegian**	noruego	
Portugal	Portugal	a **Portuguese**	portugués	**Portuguese**	portugués	**Portuguese**	portugués	
Russia	Rusia	a **Russian**	ruso	**Russian**	ruso	**Russian**	ruso	
Scotland	Escocia	a **Scotchman**	escocés	**Scotch**	escocés			
Spain	España	a **Spaniard**	español	**Spanish**	español	**Spanish**	español	
Sweden	Suecia	a **Swede**	sueco	**Swedish**	sueco	**Swedish**	sueco	
Switzerland	Suiza	a **Swiss**	suizo	**Swiss**	suizo			
The United States	Estados Unidos	an **American**	americano	**American**	americano			

English	Spanish	English	Spanish	English	Spanish	English	Spanish
Africa	Africa	an **African**	africano	**Atlantic Ocean**	Océano Atlántico	**Berlin**	Berlín
Asia	Asia	an **Asiatic**	asiático	**Pacific Ocean**	Océano Pacífico	**Geneva**	Ginebra
Australia	Australia	an **Australian**	australiano			**Florence**	Florencia
Europe	Europa	a **European**	europeo	**North Pole**	Polo Norte	**Havana**	La Habana
North America	América del Norte	a **North American**	norteamericano	**South Pole**	Polo Sur	**London**	Londres
				continent	continente	**Moscow**	Moscú
South America	América del Sur	a **South American**	sudamericano	**equator**	ecuador	**Paris**	París
				island	isla	**Rome**	Roma
						Tokyo	Tokio
						Vienna	Viena
						Venice	Venecia

EXERCISE 3

Translate the following sentences and practice reading them.

1. I can swim, can you?
2. I can't swim, can you?
3. He can swim, can she?
4. He can't swim, can she?
5. She can swim, can they?
6. She can't swim, can they?
7. They're going to swim, is he?
8. They aren't going to swim, is he?
9. You were going to swim, was she?
10. You weren't going to swim, was she?
11. He always works, and I do too.
12. He doesn't always work, and I don't either.
13. She's usually working, and he is too.
14. She isn't usually working, and he isn't either.
15. We were working, and they were too.
16. We weren't working, and they weren't either.
17. You always worked, and I did too.
18. You didn't always work, and I didn't either.
19. They have to work, and we do too.
20. They don't have to work, and we don't either.
21. She had to work, and you did too.
22. She didn't have to work, and you didn't either.
23. He's been working, and I have too.
24. He hasn't been working, and I haven't either.
25. He'd been working, and I had too.
26. He hadn't been working, and I hadn't either.
27. There should be a dentist here.
28. There shouldn't be a dentist here.
29. Should there be a dentist here?
30. Shouldn't there be a dentist here?

EXERCISE 4

Translate the following sentences. Change them to the negative, interrogative, and interrogative negative.

1. They take a trip every summer.
2. He took a trip last year.

3. We'll take a trip in March.
4. I have to make a trip to Mexico next week.
5. She's going to make a trip to Chicago.
6. They'd make a trip if they had time.
7. We should go on a trip when you get your vacation.
8. He went on a trip to San Francisco.
9. You were going to go on a trip.
10. I'll be able to go on a trip.

EXERCISE 5

Give the past tense and past participle of the following verbs.

rain	rest	study	smell
realize	return	satisfy	smile (at)
remember	show	save	smoke
rent	start	sew	snow
repeat	stop	shout (at)	sound

EXERCISE 6

Give the past tense and past participle of the following verbs.

set	stand up	shoot	take
set the table	steal	sing	teach
sit	send	spend	tell
sleep	shake	stand in line	think
speak	shine	swim	think of

EXERCISE 7

Verb Practice *Expand the following verb practice to include different tenses.*

1. The president of the bank would deliver those things.
2. The president of the bank wouldn't deliver those things.
3. Would the president of the bank deliver those things?
4. Wouldn't the president of the bank deliver those things?
5. How many things would the president of the bank deliver?

EXERCISE 8

Verb Practice *Make short sentences with forms of the verbs* develop, drill, oversleep, cause, chew, cough, take a trip, pull a tooth, fill a tooth, brush your teeth, cut a tooth, have (get) a tooth filled, have (get) a tooth pulled. *Expand each verb practice to include different tenses, as in the exercise above. Use a different noun or pronoun with each verb. Use the interrogative words when it is possible.*

EXERCISE 9

Translate into Spanish.

1. We took a long trip through South America after we got married.
2. He speaks English like an Englishman, but I think he's an American.
3. Is the North Pole colder than the South Pole?
4. I have an appointment with the dentist on Thursday. I'm going to have a tooth pulled.
5. Do you mean that you don't have any fillings?
6. The doctor told me to wash my mouth out after each meal.
7. He used the drill on my tooth, but it didn't hurt very much.
8. We missed American food when we lived in Mexico.
9. Did he mean that we won't have a vacation until March?
10. I got to school late this morning because I overslept.
11. I don't think she'd like to live among the Eskimos, and I wouldn't either.
12. The noise died down as soon as I went in the room.
13. We plan to study German before going to Europe.
14. I wish you'd stop making so much noise.
15. It may be a long time before I see you again.

EXERCISE 10

Translate into English.

1. No me gusta el ambiente de este lugar.
2. Debe haber jugo de naranja para el desayuno.
3. El dentista encontró algunas caries en sus dientes, ¿verdad?
4. No podremos cargar todo el equipaje.
5. Mastique bien la comida.
6. No hemos podido hacer un viaje este año, ni ellos tampoco.

7. Que tenga buen viaje.
8 No olvides lavarte los dientes antes de acostarte.
9. Dijo el dentista que quizá tendría que sacarme el diente.
10. No ha estado lloviendo toda la tarde, ¿verdad?

EXERCISE 11

Answer the following questions in the affirmative and in the negative.

1. Did the meeting take place yesterday?
2. Will he take charge of the clinic?
3. Are they going to take a trip?
4. Did you use to go to the dentist every six months?
5. Did you use to take a trip every summer?
6. Did you use to make a trip every summer?
7. Did you use to go on a trip every summer?
8. Did you use to take charge of the meetings?
9. Does he want you to stop working?
10. Did they want you to stop smoking?
11. Did you want them to stop talking?
12. Will he take care of the children?
13. Would they take care of the furniture?
14. Was he going to take care of the garden?
15. Is she taking care of her parents?
16. Did the dentist want to pull your wisdom tooth?
17. Is he going to have to pull that bad tooth?
18. Will he fill your tooth with gold?
19. Do you want a silver filling?
20. Does he brush his teeth after each meal?
21. Did you wash your teeth this morning?
22. Are your teeth in good shape?
23. Were her teeth in bad shape?
24. Did you have a tooth pulled?
25. Did one of your fillings fall out?
26. Did you oversleep this morning?
27. Were you late because you overslept?

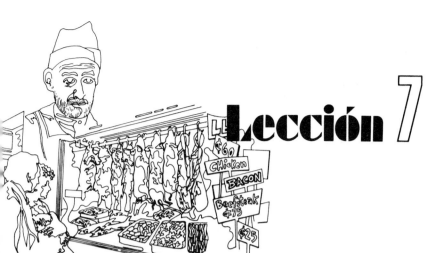

Lección 7

1. **to weigh, weighed, weighed** pesar
2. **to slice, sliced, sliced** rebanar
   slice rebanada, lonja
3. **to grind, ground, ground** moler
4. **to fry, fried, fried** freír
5. **to roast, roasted, roasted** asar
6. **to measure, measured, measured** medir
   measurement medida
7. **to bake, baked, baked** hornear
8. **super market** super mercado
9. **butcher** carnicero
10. **butcher shop** carnicería
11. **steak** bistec
12. **lean** limpio y sin grasa; magro
13. **meat loaf** albondigón
14. **hamburger** hamburguesa
15. **bacon** tocino
16. **bologna** mortadela
17. **ounce** onza
18. **tough** dura (*carne*)
19. **tender** suave (*carne*)
20. **cattle** ganado
21. **scales** báscula, balanza; escamas
22. **boring** aburrido (*ser*)
23. **alike** parecido; igual
24. **candle** vela
25. **bottle** botella
26. **weight** peso

IDIOMS

1. **to take a walk, ride** dar un paseo a pie, en coche
   to go for a walk, ride dar un paseo a pie, en coche

2. **to wait on** despachar, atender
   Is anybody waiting on you? ¿Lo están atendiendo?
3. **May I help you?** ¿Qué se le ofrece?
   Can I help you? ¿Qué se le ofrece?
4. **to be fattening** engordar (*impersonal*)
   Candy is fattening. Los dulces engordan.
5. **to make someone fat** engordar o hacer engordar a alguien
   Candy makes you fat. (*impersonal*) Los dulces engordan.
   That will make him fat. Eso le hará engordar.
6. **to get fat** engordar (*personal*)
   She got very fat. Engordó mucho.
7. **How much is steak?** ¿Cuánto vale el bistec?
   Seventy cents a pound. Setenta centavos la libra.
   How much is ground meat? ¿Cuánto vale la carne molida?
   Thirty-nine cents a pound. Treinta y nueve centavos la libra.
   How much are eggs? ¿Cuánto valen los huevos?
   Eighty cents a dozen. Ochenta centavos la docena.
   How much is milk? ¿Cuánto vale la leche?
   Twenty-five cents a bottle. Veinticinco centavos la botella.
8. **a half pound** media libra
   a pound and a half libra y media
   two, three, etc. pounds and a half dos, tres, etc. libras y media

EXERCISE 1

Practice the following dialogue.

AT THE BUTCHER SHOP

Butcher: Have you been waited on?
Customer: No, not yet. How much is steak?
Butcher: Seventy cents a pound.
Customer: I want a pound and a half of steak and a half pound of hamburger.
Butcher: What else?
Customer: A pound of bologna and some bacon, please.
Butcher: Do you want it sliced?
Customer: Yes, sliced very thin, please. Don't you have any lean bacon? This seems very fat.
Butcher: No, that's all we have today.
Customer: Are you sure the steak is tender? The last time I bought

steak here it was a little tough. Maybe it would be better if you ground it.

Butcher: All right. Do you want the ground meat and the hamburger too?

Customer: Yes, I want to make a meat loaf.

Butcher: Will that be all?

Customer: No, I want a chicken to bake. How much are they a pound?

Butcher: Seventy-five cents a pound.

Customer: How much does that large one weigh?

Butcher: That one weighs four pounds.

Customer: It's a little too big. Pick out one that weighs about three pounds.

Butcher: Here's one. How's this?

Customer: That's fine.

Butcher: Is there anything else?

Customer: No, that's all for today.

EXERCISE 2

Learn these words.

MEATS AND FISH

1. **beef** carne de res
2. **cold cuts** carnes frías
3. **frankfurters** salchichas
4. **ham** jamón
5. **lamb** cordero
6. **lamb chops** chuletas de cordero
7. **lard** manteca
8. **liver** hígado
9. **beef liver** hígado de res
10. **calf liver** hígado de ternera
11. **meat ball** albóndiga
12. **mutton** carnero
13. **pork** carne de puerco
14. **pork chops** chuletas de puerco
15. **roast** asado
16. **sausage** salchicha de puerco
17. **spareribs** costillas de puerco
18. **veal** carne de ternera
19. **veal cutlet** chuleta de ternera
20. **caviar** caviar
21. **crab** cangrejo
22. **herring** arenque
23. **lobster** langosta
24. **octopus** pulpo
25. **oyster** ostión
26. **salami** salami
27. **salmon** salmón, salmones
28. **sardine** sardina
29. **sea food** mariscos
30. **shrimp** (*sing.*) camarón, camarones
31. **trout** trucha, truchas
32. **tuna** atún, atunes

EXERCISE 3

Translate the following sentences and practice reading them.

1. It should be cold.
2. It shouldn't be cold.
3. Should it be cold?
4. Shouldn't it be cold?
5. Why should it be cold?
6. They should be hungry.
7. They shouldn't be hungry.
8. Should they be hungry?
9. Shouldn't they be hungry?
10. Why shouldn't they be hungry?
11. There's a market.
12. There isn't a market.
13. Is there a market?
14. Isn't there a market?
15. How many markets are there?
16. There were two buses.
17. There weren't two buses.
18. Were there two buses?
19. Weren't there two buses?
20. How many buses were there?
21. It's rarely hot.
22. It isn't ever hot.
23. Is it sometimes hot?
24. Isn't it usually hot?
25. Why is it always hot?
26. It was never cold.
27. It wasn't ever cold.
28. Was it always cold?
29. Wasn't it often cold?
30. Why was it seldom cold?

EXERCISE 4

Translate the following sentences. Change them to the negative, interrogative, and interrogative negative.

1. He wants to go for a walk.
2. They went for a walk.
3. She goes for a walk every Sunday.
4. We'll go for a ride tomorrow.
5. He's going to go for a ride.
6. He'd like to take a ride.
7. We should take a ride this morning.
8. They have taken a walk every day.
9. She'll be able to take a walk this afternoon.
10. You took a walk yesterday.

EXERCISE 5

Give the past tense and past participle of the following verbs.

slice	talk	test	turn
spill	translate	tie	turn over

stay	try	touch	use
suffer	turn on	travel	visit
surprise	turn off	try hard	weigh

EXERCISE 6

Give the past tense and past participle of the following verbs.

take a bath	take a trip	wake up	weave
take away	take a walk	wear	be
take a shower	throw	win	become
take care of	throw away	write	begin
take off	understand	wear out	break

EXERCISE 7

Verb Practice *Expand the following verb practice, using different tenses.*

1. The butcher should weigh the meat.
2. The butcher shouldn't weigh the meat.
3. Should the butcher weight the meat?
4. Shouldn't the butcher weigh the meat?
5. Why shouldn't the butcher weigh the meat?

EXERCISE 8

Verb Practice *Make short sentences with forms of the verbs* **slice, grind, fry, bake, roast, measure, take a walk (ride), go for a walk (ride), wait on, be fattening, make someone fat, get fat.** *Expand each verb practice to include different tenses, as in the exercise above. Use a different noun or pronoun with each verb. Use the interrogative words when it is possible.*

EXERCISE 9

Translate into Spanish.

1. Do you want me to go for a walk with you?
2. Have you been waited on?
3. Whose book is this?

4. This hamburger meat isn't worth buying.
5. Would you rather have sausage or bacon with your eggs?
6. I'd rather have sausage than bacon.
7. The butcher said that he was out of pork.
8. She is making fun of my cooking.
9. Are his eyes blue or brown?
10. We told him that he would have to get rid of those scales.
11. How far is it from here to the butcher shop?
12. How long will it take to grind this meat?
13. There isn't any meat left.
14. After standing in line for more than an hour, we gave up and went home.
15. I like steak better than anything else.

EXERCISE 10

Translate into English.

1. Me gustaría hacer un pastel para tu cumpleaños.
2. El tocino vale treinta centavos la libra.
3. Los huevos estrellados engordan.
4. He estado atendiendo a los clientes toda la mañana.
5. Quiero media libra de jamón y dos libras y media de carne de puerco.
6. ¿Cuándo te operaron de las amígdalas?
7. ¿Sabe Ud. de quién es este sombrero?
8. Ojalá que no esté dura la carne.
9. No me diga que se le acabaron otra vez los huevos.
10. Pesemos este jamón otra vez.
11. ¿Cuál es tu peso? Pesé ciento cincuenta libras ayer.

EXERCISE 11

Answer the following questions.

1. How much is steak?
2. How much is pork?
3. How much are eggs?
4. Whose cigarettes are these?
5. Whose matches are these?
6. Whose coat is this?

Answer the following questions in the affirmative and in the negative.

7. Are your hands cold?
8. Are your feet cold?
9. Are your eyes blue?
10. Is your hair long?
11. Are your hands dirty?
12. If you had seen him, would you have spoken to him?
13. If you had had time, would you have gone to the market?
14. If the meeting had taken place at ten o'clock, would you have gone?
15. If you had been sick, would you have worked yesterday?
16. Would you like to take a walk?
17. Would you like to take a ride?
18. Is anybody waiting on you?
19. Does candy make you fat?
20. Did she get very fat?

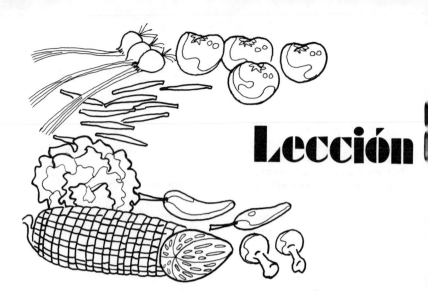

Lección

Vocabulary

1. **to serve, served, served** servir
2. **to can, canned, canned** envasar, enlatar; hacer conservas de alimento
3. **to melt, melted, melted** derretir
4. **to climb, climbed, climbed** escalar, subir (*trepando*)
5. **to sink, sank, sunk** hundir (se)
6. **to hate, hated, hated** odiar
7. **groceries** abarrotes
   grocery store tienda de abarrotes
8. **clerk** dependiente
9. **applicant** solicitante
10. **ripe** maduro (*fruta*)
11. **wealth** caudal, riqueza (s)
    wealthy rico
12. **fresh** fresco, del día
13. **string beans** ejotes
    green beans ejotes
14. **spinach** espinacas
15. **watermelon** sandía
16. **jar** frasco
17. **clay** barro, arcilla
18. **century** siglo
19. **stain** mancha
20. **damp** húmedo
21. **daily** diariamente
22. **tear** lágrima
23. **magazine** revista
24. **bulb** foco; bulbo
25. **curious** curioso
26. **vegetable store** recaudería
27. **garden** huerta; jardín

IDIOMS

1. **to run a business, boardinghouse, school, etc.** manejar un negocio, casa de huéspedes, escuela, etc.

62

2. **to open a business** poner un negocio
   He opened a school downtown. Puso una escuela en el centro.
3. **to get up early** madrugar.
   I got up early this morning. Madrugué esta mañana.
4. **to go to bed late** desvelarse, acostarse tarde
   I went to bed late. Me acosté tarde, estoy desvelado.
5. **to get excited** excitarse, emocionarse
6. **a little bit** un poquitín
7. **in that case** en tal caso
8. **in any case** en cualquier caso
9. **How much are tomatoes?** ¿A cómo son los jitomates?
   Tomatoes are fifteen cents a pound. Los jitomates son a quince centavos la libra.
   How much are potatoes? ¿A cómo son las papas?
   Potatoes are ten cents a pound. Las papas son a diez centavos la libra.
   How much are oranges? ¿A cómo son las naranjas?
   Oranges are five cents apiece. Las naranjas son a cinco centavos cada una.
10. **a head of cabbage, lettuce** una col, lechuga
11. **two pounds of tomatoes** dos libras de jitomate
12. **room and board** cuarto con asistencia

EXERCISE 1

Practice the following dialogue.

AT THE VEGETABLE STORE

Clerk:	May I help you?
Customer:	I want some tomatoes to can. How much are they?
Clerk:	They're fifteen cents a pound.
Customer:	Can you deliver them to my house before noon?
Clerk:	Of course. Do you want anything else?
Customer:	Yes, I want some potatoes and some onions. Are those string beans fresh?
Clerk:	Yes, they were brought in this morning.
Customer:	Then give me about two pounds. Do you have any spinach?
Clerk:	Only in cans. We have no fresh spinach today. Would you like another watermelon? We have some nice ones today.

Customer:	How much are they?
Clerk:	The small ones are fifty cents apiece, and the large ones are seventy-five.
Customer:	Are you sure they're ripe? The one I got here last week was a little green.
Clerk:	Yes, they're ripe.
Customer:	I'll take a small one.
Clerk:	What else?
Customer:	I want a large head of lettuce and a small head of cabbage.
Clerk:	Is that all?
Customer:	Yes, that's all.

EXERCISE 2

Learn these words.

VEGETABLES

1. **artichoke** alcachofa
2. **asparagus** (*sing.*) espárragos
3. **avocado** aguacate
4. **beet** betabel
5. **Brussels sprouts** colecitas de Bruselas
6. **cantaloupe** melón
7. **carrot** zanahoria
8. **cauliflower** coliflor
9. **celery** apio
10. **corn** elote, maíz
11. **corn (on the cob)** elote **cob** olote, mazorca
12. **cucumber** pepino
13. **eggplant** berenjena
14. **garlic** ajo
15. **herb** hierba
16. **honeydew melon** melón valenciano
17. **mushroom** hongo
18. **parsley** perejil
19. **peanuts** cacahuates
20. **peas** chícharos
21. **pepper** pimiento
22. **pickle** pepino encurtido
23. **pumpkin** calabaza
24. **radish** rábano
25. **rhubarb** ruibarbo
26. **rice** arroz
27. **sauerkraut** col agria
28. **squash** calabacita (s)
29. **sweet potato** camote
30. **turnip** nabo
31. **water cress** berro

EXERCISE 3

Translate the following sentences and practice reading them.

1. They were always sleepy.

2. They weren't usually sleepy.
3. Were they ever sleepy?
4. Weren't they ever sleepy?
5. Why were they sleepy?
6. Let him spend that money.
7. Don't let him spend that money.
8. Let's spend that money.
9. Let's not spend that money.
10. Spend that money.
11. Don't spend that money.
12. What are you looking for?
13. What are you laughing at?
14. Who are you going to go with?
15. Who were you talking to?
16. What are you putting on?
17. Who are you living with?
18. Who are you waiting for?
19. What are you doing that for?
20. Who are you going to give it to?

EXERCISE 4

Translate the following sentences. Change them to the negative, inter-rogative, and interrogative negative.

1. He runs his father's business.
2. You'd like to run a boardinghouse.
3. They ran a school for girls for many years.
4. Mr. Williams runs that grocery store on the corner.
5. We have been running this business for ten years.
6. Jack should run the hotel while his father is away.
7. That young man is running the business very well.
8. She'll be able to run the business by herself.
9. I'm going to run this business next year.
10. She ran a boardinghouse for men.

EXERCISE 5

Give the past tense and past participle of the following verbs.

wait (for)	watch	answer	agree
walk	wish	arrive (in, at)	appear

want	worry (about)	ask	attack
wash	wrap	add	avoid
work	arrest	admire	belong

EXERCISE 6

Give the past tense and past participle of the following verbs.

bite	be worth	come back	do
bring	bleed	cut	drink
buy	blow	catch	dig
be born	build	choose	draw
bet	come	cost	draw interest

EXERCISE 7

Verb Practice *Expand the following verb practice, using different tenses.*

1. Mrs. Turner's maid should serve the soup.
2. Mrs. Turner's maid shouldn't serve the soup.
3. Should Mrs. Turner's maid serve the soup?
4. Shouldn't Mrs. Turner's maid serve the soup?
5. At what time should Mrs. Turner's maid serve the soup?

EXERCISE 8

Verb Practice *Make short sentences with forms of the verbs* **can, melt, climb, sink, hate, get excited, run a business, open a business, get up early, go to bed late.** *Expand each verb practice to include different tenses, as in the exercise above. Use a different noun or pronoun with each verb. Use the interrogative words when it is possible.*

EXERCISE 9

Translate into Spanish.

1. Don't get excited. Everything will be all right.
2. How much do you pay a month for room and board?
3. Do you remember which clerk waited on you?
4. There is a little bit of water left.

5. In any case, he should help you run the business.
6. There are two glasses missing.
7. Are you sure that these eggs are fresh?
8. Did the boss promise you a raise?
9. You have the wrong number. Please hang up and dial again.
10. Does this bus go down Lincoln Street?
11. Give me a light. My lighter won't (no quiere) work.
12. If the meeting takes place tomorrow, I won't be able to go.
13. Do you think the doctor can keep him from smoking?
14. I wish you wouldn't tell them that they have to pay in advance.
15. Maybe they won't have to operate on him.

EXERCISE 10

Translate into English.

1. Ya se derritió la nieve.
2. Ayer envasé cincuenta libras de jitomate.
3. ¿Por qué no madrugaste esta mañana? Porque anoche me desvelé.
4. ¿Cuántas gentes se ahogaron cuando se hundió el barco?
5. Si comes esas manzanas verdes, puede que te dé dolor de estómago.
6. Tengo catarro, pero no tengo (any) temperatura.
7. ¿Cultivó Ud. estos ejotes en su huerta?
8. ¿A qué hora te recogieron ayer?
9. Debe haber verduras frescas en el mercado.
10. ¿Cuánto pesa Ud.? Peso más de sesenta kilos.

EXERCISE 11

Answer the following questions.

1. Did the sun rise earlier today than yesterday?
2. Did the telephone ring?
3. Did that dog bite you?
4. Did he hold your hat?
5. Did the butcher grind the meat?
6. Did the ship sink?
7. Did the children get excited?
8. Did you get rid of your cold?
9. Did they get rid of all the books?
10. Did they get rid of their old clothes?

11. How far is it from here to the doctor's office?
12. How far is it from here to the grocery store?
13. How far is it from here to the hospital?
14. How far is it from here to the clinic?
15. How far is it from here to the dentist's office?
16. What kind of a business did he open?
17. Do you like to get up early?
18. Is it hard for you to get up early?
19. Did you go to bed late last night?
20. Are you sleepy because you went to bed late?

Leccion 9

Vocabulary

1. **to spoil, spoiled, spoiled** echar (se) a perder; consentir
2. **to go up, went up, gone up** subir (se) (*yendo hacia arriba*) **to come up, came up, come up** subir(se) (*viniendo hacia arriba*)
3. **to go down, went down, gone down** bajar (se) (*yendo hacia abajo*) **to come down, came down, come down** bajar (se) (*viniendo hacia abajo*)
4. **to sign, signed, signed** firmar
5. **to describe, described, described** describir
6. **to rot, rotted, rotted** pudrirse
7. **sense** sentido
8. **price** precio
9. **gallon** galón
10. **bunch** racimo, manojo; montón
11. **syrup** jarabe; almíbar
12. **citrus fruits** frutas cítricas
13. **sauce** salsa **apple sauce** puré de manzana **tomato sauce** puré de jitomate
14. **jelly** jalea **jam** mermelada
15. **seed** semilla **seedless** sin semilla
16. **vine** vid, parra; enredadera
17. **bush** arbusto, matorral
18. **walnut** nuez de Castilla
19. **wormy** agusanado
20. **shipment** embarque
21. **rotten** podrido (*estar*)
22. **grape** uva
23. **grapefruit** toronja
24. **banana** plátano
25. **strawberry** fresa

IDIOMS

1. **to run out of** agotársele a uno, acabársele a uno
   We ran out of money. Se nos acabó (agotó) el dinero.
2. **to get burned** quemarse
   to burn your hands, arms, etc. quemarse las manos, los brazos, etc.
3. **to describe (something to someone)** describir (algo a alguien)
   Please describe that to me. Por favor, descríbame eso.
4. **for instance** por ejemplo
5. **the only time** la única vez
6. **a bunch of grapes** un racimo (manojo) de uvas
7. **two dozen oranges** dos docenas de naranjas
8. **around the block** a la vuelta de la cuadra
9. **on hand** en existencia

EXERCISE 1

Practice the following dialogue.

AT THE FRUIT STORE

Clerk: Is anyone waiting on you?
Customer: No. How much are bananas?
Clerk: Bananas are nineteen cents a pound.
Customer: I want about two pounds.
Clerk: What else?
Customer: About a dozen of the sweetest oranges you have and about a dozen seedless grapefruits—large ones, please.
Clerk: All right. Anything else?
Customer: I'd like some apples if you're sure they aren't wormy. The last ones I bought here were, and two of them were rotten.
Clerk: No, these apples aren't wormy. They're much better than the ones I had last week. We just received this shipment yesterday.
Customer: All right. How much are they?
Clerk: They're thirty cents a pound.
Customer: Just give me four pounds. I don't want them to spoil. Prices are still going up, aren't they?
Clerk: On some things, yes. But on other things they're going down. We're going to have to raise the price of tomatoes. Will there be anything else?

70

Customer: I want a gallon of canned peaches in syrup, a jar of strawberry jam, a bottle of grape juice, and two cans of orange juice.
Clerk: Is that all?
Customer: Yes, I think so.

EXERCISE 2

Learn these words.

FRUITS AND NUTS

1. **apricot** albaricoque, chabacano
2. **cherry** cereza
3. **cranberry** arándano
4. **date** dátil
5. **fig** higo
6. **lemon** limón
7. **lime** limón (*verde de color*)
8. **olive** aceituna
9. **pear** pera
10. **pineapple** piña
11. **plum** ciruela
12. **pomegranate** granada
13. **prune** ciruela pasa
14. **raisin** pasa
15. **tangerine** mandarina
16. **almond** almendra
17. **cashew nut** nuez de la India
18. **coconut** coco
19. **pecan** nuez encarcelada
20. **hazelnut** avellana
21. **filbert** avellana
22. **chestnut** castaña
23. **nutmeg** nuez moscada
24. **pistachio** pistache

EXERCISE 3

Verb Practice

1. There'll be some fruit.
2. There won't be any fruit.
3. Will there be any fruit?
4. Won't there be any fruit?
5. How much fruit will there be?
6. There have been some peaches.
7. There haven't been any peaches.
8. Have there been any peaches?
9. Haven't there been any peaches?
10. Why haven't there been any peaches?
11. It's been hot.
12. It hasn't been hot.

13. Has it been hot?
14. Hasn't it been hot?
15. Maybe he'll work.
16. Maybe he won't work.
17. Maybe he's going to work.

EXERCISE 4

Translate the following sentences. Change them to the negative, interrogative, and interrogative negative.

1. His car ran out of gas.
2. He'll have to work when he runs out of money.
3. We've run out of water.
4. They ran out of food before the party was over.
5. She came back early because she ran out of money.
6. I was cooking breakfast when I ran out of gas.
7. You're running out of food.
8. They were going to run out of milk.
9. We run out of bread every day.
10. We wrote until we ran out of paper.

EXERCISE 5

Give the past tense and past participle of the following verbs.

bore	bother	charge	can
borrow	breathe	chase	climb
bake	burn	cause	call
believe	bury	chew	change
boil	complain (about)	cough	clean

EXERCISE 6

Give the past tense and past participle of the following verbs.

drive	fall in love (with)	find out	get
eat	feed	fly	get mad (at)
find	feel	freeze	get rich
forget	feel at home	go up	get sleepy
fall	fight	go down	get to (here, there)

72

EXERCISE 7

Verb Practice *Expand the following verb practice, using different tenses.*

1. The tomatoes are going to spoil.
2. The tomatoes aren't going to spoil.
3. Are the tomatoes going to spoil?
4. Aren't the tomatoes going to spoil?
5. Why are the tomatoes going to spoil?

EXERCISE 8

Verb Practice *Make short sentences with forms of the verbs* go up, come up, go down, come down, sign, describe, rot, get burned, burn your hands, describe (something to someone). *Expand each verb practice to include different tenses, as in the exercise above. Use a different noun or pronoun with each verb. Use the interrogative words when it is possible.*

EXERCISE 9

Translate into Spanish.

1. Don't eat those bananas. They'll make you sick.
2. I'm late because the bus ran out of gas this morning.
3. We took a walk around the block.
4. She fell in love with a married man.
5. We have a lot of nice apples on hand at this time.
6. These rotten bananas aren't worth anything.
7. I've changed my mind. I'm not going.
8. I hope prices don't go up any more.
9. That was the only time I saw him.
10. If we run out of gas before dinner is ready, we won't have anything to eat.
11. Is Walter still here? No, he just left.
12. We always feel at home among American people.
13. Do Mexicans always shake hands with their friends whenever they say good-bye?
14. She ran away because she got scared.
15. He insisted on telling the truth about everything.

EXERCISE 10

Translate into English.

1. Recibimos un embarque de manzanas podridas.
2. Por favor, firme en la parte inferior de la página.
3. La carne se echó a perder porque hacía mucho calor.
4. Debe haber fresas en el mercado ahora.
5. Se nos acabó el dinero y tuvimos que regresar a casa.
6. ¿Le gustaría describirnos lo que vio en el zoológico?
7. Si los precios no bajan, no podré comprar todos estos abarrotes, ¿y tú?
8. Por favor, descríbenos lo que pasó anoche.
9. Ella dijo que se había quemado mientras estaba haciendo conservas de frutas.
10. Dos racimos de uvas deberían ser suficientes para la comida, ¿verdad?

EXERCISE 11

Answer the following questions in the affirmative and in the negative.

1. Do you run a boardinghouse?
2. Does he run a shool?
3. Did he run his father's business?
4. Did you run out of money?
5. Has the car run out of gas?
6. Will they run out of water?
7. Do you know what time it is?
8. Do you know what day this is?
9. Do you know what month this is?
10. Do you know what year this is?
11. Do you know where we are?
12. Do you know where they went?
13. Do you know how old I am?
14. Do you know how tall he is?
15. Do you know how big this room is?

Lección 10

Vocabulary

1. **to comb your hair, combed your hair, combed your hair** peinarse
2. **to shave, shaved, shaved** rasurar (se)
   to shave (something off), quitarse con navaja (bigote, barba, etc.)
3. **to sharpen, sharpened, sharpened** sacar punta, afilar
4. **to wet, wet, wet** mojar, humedecer
5. **to step on, stepped on, stepped on** pisar
6. **to lean back, leaned back, leaned back** recargarse
   to lean (against, on), leaned (against, on), leaned (against, on) apoyarse (en), recargarse (en)
7. **barber** peluquero
   barber shop peluquería
8. **razor** navaja; rastrillo

electric razor rasuradora eléctrica
razor blade hoja de afeitar

9. **shaving soap** jabón para afeitar
   shaving cream crema para afeitar
   shaving lotion loción para después de afeitar
10. **oil** aceite
    hair oil grasa para el cabello
11. **sideburns** patillas
12. **shoe polish** grasa para los zapatos
13. **clippers** maquinilla para cortar el pelo
14. **mustache** bigote (s)
15. **beard** barba
    whiskers barbas
16. **shampoo** champú
17. **towel** toalla
18. **dull** sin filo

75

19. **twice** dos veces	23. **company** compañía
20. **century** siglo	24. **pile** montón
21. **barrel** barril	25. **dandruff** caspa
22. **raw** crudo	26. **heavy beard** barba cerrada

IDIOMS

1. **to run around** pasearse, salir a pasear; andar juntos; recorrer
2. **to get a haircut** cortarse el pelo, cortarle a uno el pelo
   I got a haircut. Me corté el pelo, Me cortaron el pelo.
3. **to get a trim** emparejarse el pelo, empárejarle a uno el pelo
   I got a trim. Me emparejé el pelo, Me emparejaron el pelo.
4. **to get a shave** rasurarse, rasurarle a uno
   I got a shave. Me rasuré, Me rasuraron.
   Do you want a close shave? ¿Quiere que le descañone?
5. **to get a shine** bolearle a uno (los zapatos)
   I go⁺ a shine. Me bolearon (los zapatos).
   Give me a shine. Boléeme los zapatos.
   I'd like a shine. Quiero que me boleen.
6. **to part your hair** hacerse la raya
   I part my hair on the left side. Me hago la raya a la izquierda.
7. **to trim your mustache, beard** emparejarse el bigote, la barba
   I trimmed my mustache, beard. Me emparejé el bigote, la barba.
8. **to be sharp** tener filo
9. **to be through** terminar, haber terminado (*personal*)
   I'm through. Terminé. He terminado. Ya acabé.
10. **Who's next?** ¿Quién sigue?
11. **crewcut** corte de cepillo (brocha)
12. **all over** por todas partes, por todo

EXERCISE 1

Practice the following dialogue.

AT THE BARBER SHOP

Barber: Who's next?
Customer: I believe I am. I'd like a shave and a haircut.
Barber: How do you want your hair cut?
Customer: Cut it a little short. Don't take too much off the top. And don't shave off my mustache.

76

Barber:	Do you want me to use the clippers on the sides?
Customer:	Yes, but not too high. And leave sideburns, but not too long.
Shoe Shine Boy:	How about a shine?
Customer:	O. K. But be careful not to get polish on my socks.
Barber:	How's that?
Customer:	Cut a little more off the top, please.
Barber:	Is this short enough?
Customer:	Yes, that's all right.
Barber:	I'll shave your neck now and we'll be through. Where do you part your hair—on the side or in the middle?
Customer:	On the left side.
Barber:	Your hair is very dry. Would you like a shampoo?
Customer:	No, not today. I don't have time.
Barber:	Do you want me to wet your hair?
Customer:	No, comb it dry. And when you shave me, be sure to trim my mustache.
Barber:	Now lean back in the chair, and I'll put a hot towel on your face.

EXERCISE 2

Learn these words.

SUPPLEMENTARY VOCABULARY

1. **complaint** queja
2. **introduction** presentación
3. **promise** promesa
4. **raise** aumento
5. **dream** sueño
6. **kick** patada
7. **lock** candado; cerradura; chapa
8. **arrest** arresto
9. **bite** mordida
10. **whistle** chiflido; silbato
11. **direction** dirección
12. **fine** multa
13. **charge** cargo, acusación
14. **bore** (*noun*) aburrido, aburrición
15. **boring** (*adj.*) aburrido
16. **end** término, fin
17. **mixture** mezcla
18. **taste** gusto; sabor
19. **guess** conjetura
20. **swallow** trago
21. **destruction** destrucción
22. **joke** chiste
23. **x-ray** radiografía
24. **delivery** entrega
25. **development** desarrollo

26. **drill** taladro
27. **cause** causa
28. **cough** tos
29. **weight** peso
30. **slice** rebanada
31. **baker** panadero
32. **service** servicio
33. **servant** sirviente (a)
34. **can** lata
35. **mountain climber**

alpinista, montañista
36. **signature** firma
37. **sign** letrero
38. **description** descripción
39. **rotten** (*adj.*) podrido
40. **comb** peine
41. **shave** rasurada
42. **sharp** (*adj.*) filoso
43. **step** paso; escalón

EXERCISE 3

Translate the following sentences and practice reading them.

1. There had been a complaint.
2. There hadn't been a complaint.
3. Had there been a complaint?
4. Hadn't there been a complaint?
5. How many complaints had there been?
6. It'll be warm.
7. It won't be warm.
8. Will it be warm?
9. Won't it be warm?
10. When will it be warm?
11. It's going to be cold.
12. It isn't going to be cold.
13. Is it going to be cold?
14. Isn't it going to be cold?
15. When is it going to be cold?
16. She was seldom hungry.
17. She wasn't usually hungry.
18. Was she often hungry?
19. Wasn't she always hungry?
20. Why wasn't she ever hungry?

EXERCISE 4

Translate the following sentences. Change them to the negative, interrogative, and interrogative negative.

1. We ran around all over town.

78

2. He's running around with his cousin.
3. They run around with their boss.
4. You like to run around.
5. We ran around in Paris.
6. They've been running around all day.
7. I'm going to run around with those boys.
8. You should run around with those boys.
9. He'll run around a lot when he gets to New York.
10. She had time to run around last week.

EXERCISE 5

Give the past tense and past participle of the following verbs.

close	change your mind	cross	destroy
complete	clap	cry	deliver
correct	cook	dream (about)	drill
capture	count	dial	describe
carry	cover	direct	dictate

EXERCISE 6

Give the past tense and past participle of the following verbs.

get thirsty	go back	get better	get light
get up	go out	get dark	get a haircut
give	go to bed	get drunk	get a trim
give up	go to sleep	get hurt	get a shave
go	get away	get in	get a shine

EXERCISE 7

Verb Practice *Expand the following verb practice, using different tenses.*

1. That boy has to comb his hair.
2. That boy doesn't have to comb his hair.
3. Does that boy have to comb his hair?
4. Doesn't that boy have to comb his hair?
5. Why does that boy have to comb his hair?

79

EXERCISE 8

Verb Practice *Make short sentences with forms of the verbs* shave, shave off, sharpen, wet, step on, lean back, lean (against, on), get a shave, get a haircut, get a shine, get a trim, part your hair, be sharp, be through. *Expand each verb practice to include different tenses, as in the exercise above. Use a different noun or pronoun with each verb. Use the interrogative words when it is possible.*

EXERCISE 9

Translate into Spanish.

1. Who is she running around with?
2. I had to stand in line to get a haircut.
3. Will you have time to give me a shine before the train leaves?
4. My hair is too short. The barber took too much off the top when he cut it.
5. I want a pack of razor blades and a pack of cigarettes.
6. Who runs this barber shop?
7. We've looked all over town for you. Where have you been?
8. What are you going shopping today for?
9. I'm late because I had to go with my father to the barber shop.
10. Do you make a good living running this kind of business?
11. These two barber shops look alike. Which one were we in yesterday?
12. She ran away because she got scared.
13. Who took my chair away?
14. I like to take a warm bath before going to bed.
15. We threw away everything that we didn't need.

EXERCISE 10

Translate into English.

1. No te recargues en la pared. Todavía no está seca la pintura.
2. Ayer me cortaron el pelo. Solamente me emparejaron el pelo.
3. Este barril de manzanas se va a pudrir.
4. Voy a que me rasuren y a que me boleen los zapatos.
5. ¿Cuántas toallas faltan?
6. Esta navaja no tiene filo. Tendré que afilarla antes de afeitarlo.
7. ¿Qué clase de grasa usa Ud. para el cabello?

8. Él no se ve bien cuando se hace la raya en medio (in the middle).
9. Viajamos por todo México en nuestro último viaje.
10. Él me pisó mientras estábamos bailando.

EXERCISE 11

Answer the following questions.

1. Is this book worth reading?
2. Is this movie worth seeing?
3. Is this suit worth keeping?
4. Is this candy worth buying?
5. Are these paintings worth selling?
6. How long ago did you come to Mexico?
7. How long ago did you see him?
8. How long ago did you live in London?
9. How long ago did you study English?
10. How long ago did they visit you?
11. Would you rather have milk or water?
12. Would you rather live in Taxco or Cuernavaca?
13. Would you rather be tall or short?
14. Would you rather eat now or later?
15. Would you rather go to the movies or to a party?

Answer the following questions in the affirmative and in the negative.

16. Did you run around all day?
17. Do you expect to get a haircut tomorrow?
18. Would you like a trim?
19. Did he get a close shave?
20. Do you part your hair on the left side?
21. Did you get a shine?
22. Did the barber trim your mustache?
23. Does he look good in a crewcut?
24. Are you going to get a crewcut?
25. Are you next?

Lección 1

Vocabulary

1. **to match, matched, matched** hacer juego (con)
2. **to spread, spread, spread** extender (se), aplicar
3. **to recommend, recommended, recommended** recomendar
4. **to remove, removed, removed** quitar (se)
5. **to rub, rubbed, rubbed** frotar; aplicar (*frotando*)
6. **to neglect, neglected, neglected** descuidar
7. **to brush, brushed, brushed** cepillar (se)
   brush cepillo
8. **beauty shop** salón de belleza
   beauty parlor salón de belleza
9. **beauty operator** cultor (a) de belleza
10. **cosmetics** cosméticos
11. **powder** polvo
12. **lipstick** lápiz de labios
    a tube of lipstick un tubo de labios, lápiz labial
13. **cleansing cream** crema limpiadora
    cold cream cold cream
    a jar of cold cream un frasco de cold cream
14. **rouge** colorete
15. **eyebrow pencil** lápiz de ceja
    mascara rímel
    eye shadow sombra para los ojos
16. **powder base** base de polvo
17. **facial** masaje facial
18. **cheek** mejilla
19. **blemish** mancha (*de la piel*)
    blackhead espinilla
    pimple grano, barro
    freckle peca
20. **liquid** líquido
21. **reasonable** razonable
22. **indelible** indeleble
23. **shiny** brillante, brilloso
24. **clear** claro
25. **size** tamaño

26. **job** empleo, puesto
27. **dark-complexioned** de piel morena
    light-complexioned de piel clara; güero
28. **shade** tono; matiz
29. **hair dresser** peinador (a)
30. **oily skin** cutis grasoso
31. **tissue** kleenex; pañuelo desechable

IDIOMS

1. **to run after** correr detrás de; perseguir
2. **to put on make-up** ponerse maquillaje
3. **to pluck your eyebrows** depilarse las cejas
4. **to remove the stale make-up** quitarse el maquillaje anterior
5. **What can we do for you?** ¿En qué podemos servirlo?
6. **Can you take me right away?** ¿Puede atenderme inmediatamente?
7. **Come this way, please.** Por aquí, por favor.
8. **I can recommend it (him, her) highly.** Se lo (lo, la) recomiendo mucho.
9. **It doesn't cake.** No se apelmaza.
10. **finger tip** yema, punta del dedo

EXERCISE 1

Practice the following dialogue.

AT THE BEAUTY SHOP

Beauty Operator: Good morning, Miss Young. What can we do for you today?

Customer: I'd like a facial. Can you take me right away?

Beauty Operator: Yes, we can. Come this way, please. We have a new line of cosmetics that's very good. This week we're having a special (oferta especial). Would you like to try it? They have some beutiful shades of powder and lipstick.

Customer: Yes, if you think it's good.

Beauty Operator: I can recommend it highly. The price is reasonable and it's good quality. First you remove the stale make-up with this cleansing cream. It's good (sirve) for either dry or oily skin. At night you remove the cream with a tissue and leave the rest on until morning.

83

Customer:	It feels good.
Beauty Operator:	There are three shades of liquid powder base that you can use. Which do you prefer—light, rosy, or dark?
Customer:	I prefer the light one. I don't like the rosy shades.
Beauty Operator:	Liquid make-up doesn't cake on the face, although it covers blemishes and pimples.
Customer:	I need a bottle of liquid powder base. This seems nice. How much does it cost?
Beauty Operator:	The small bottle is $1.25; but the large, economical size is only $2.00.
Customer:	I'll take the small one to see if I really like it.
Beauty Operator:	The cream rouge is very nice too. Just rub a little on your finger tips and spread it high up on your cheek bones and under the eyes. It's the most natural rouge I've ever seen.
Customer:	Isn't that too much?
Beauty Operator:	No, it won't be after you put the powder on. I believe Rachel is the best shade for you.
Customer:	Yes, I always use that shade.
Beauty Operator:	I believe we'd better pluck your eyebrows. They're very heavy.
Customer:	Yes, I have to pluck them every day.
Beauty Operator:	Now we can apply the powder. It's really lovely, and it lasts for hours. You don't have to worry about your face being shiny. Do you use eyebrow pencil?
Customer:	No, I don't. My eyebrow are naturally dark.
Beauty Operator:	That's true, but it looks better. Mascara and eye shadow are also often neglected, and yet they are very important. Blue eye shadow goes lovely with your blue eyes. Try it and you'll see the difference. Now what shade of lipstick do you prefer—clear red or pink?
Customer:	As the dress I'm going to wear to the party tonight is lavender, I think I'll use the pink shade. Is it indelible?
Beauty Operator:	Yes, it is. Do you use a lipstick brush?
Customer:	No, I don't.
Beauty Operator:	To do a really professional job you must use a brush. It takes practice, but the results are much better.
Customer:	It looks nice. It's very natural-looking make-up,

but I think I'll only take the powder base, a box of powder, and a large tube of bright red lipstick. How much will that be?

Beauty Operator: It's $4.25, including the facial.
Customer: That's very reasonable.
Beauty Operator: Thank you. Come again soon.

EXERCISE 2

Learn these words.

NAMES OF RELATIONS

1. **in-laws** pariente políticos
2. **father-in-law** suegro
3. **mother-in-law** suegra
4. **stepfather** padrastro
5. **stepmother** madrastra
6. **stepbrother** hermanastro
7. **stepsister** hermanastra
8. **half brother** medio hermano
9. **half sister** media hermana
10. **second cousin** primo segundo
11. **foster parents** padres adoptivos
12. **adopted child** hijo adoptivo
13. **adopted children** hijos adoptivos
14. **adopted son** hijo adoptivo
15. **adopted daughter** hija adoptiva
16. **grandchild** nieto
17. **grandchildren** nietos
18. **grandson** nieto
19. **granddaughter** nieta
20. **great-grandchild** bisnieto
21. **great-grandchildren** bisnietos
22. **great-grandson** bisnieto
23. **great-granddaughter** bisnieta
24. **great-grandfather** bisabuelo
25. **great-grandmother** bisabuela
26. **great-grandparents** bisabuelos
27. **son-in-law** yerno
28. **daughter-in-law** nuera
29. **godfather** padrino
30. **godmother** madrina
31. **godson** ahijado
32. **goddaughter** ahijada
33. **godparents** padrinos
34. **twins** gemelos
35. **triplets** triates

EXERCISE 3

Translate the following sentences and practice reading them.

1. There should be a barber shop here.
2. There shouldn't be a barber shop here.
3. Should there be a barber shop here?
4. Shouldn't there be a barber shop here?
5. How many barber shops should there be here?

6. It's going to be hot.
7. It isn't going to be hot.
8. Is it going to be hot?
9. Isn't it going to be hot?
10. When is it going to be hot?
11. He's going to be hungry.
12. He isn't going to be hungry.
13. Is he going to be hungry?
14. Isn't he going to be hungry?
15. When is he going to be hungry?
16. She might often study.
17. She might not often study.
18. She may sleep now.
19. She may not sleep now.
20. Maybe she'll sleep now.

EXERCISE 4

Translate the following sentences. Change them to the negative, interrogative, and interrogative negative.

1. That dog is running after the chickens.
2. He ran after his hat.
3. We've been running after the cows.
4. The hunter is going to run after the dogs.
5. The policeman should run after those thieves.
6. He is running after me.
7. They ran after the bus.
8. You should run after those animals.
9. Mrs. Riley was running after the children.
10. She ran after her sister.

EXERCISE 5

Give the past tense and past participle of the following verbs.

drop	disappear	dial	develop
dance	discover	dream	drill
decide	dress	(about)	deliver
die	drown	dry up	escape
die down	describe	destroy	examine
			expect

EXERCISE 6

Give the past tense and past participle of the following verbs.

get lost	get out	get tired	go with
get off	get ready	get up early	grow
get married	get rid of	get wet	grind
get old	get scared	get worse	go up
get on	get sick	go on	go down
		go shopping	go to bed late

EXERCISE 7

Verb Practice *Expand the following verb practice, using different tenses.*

1. These colors match, don't they?
2. These colors don't match, do they?
3. Do these colors match?
4. Don't these colors match?
5. Why don't these colors match?

EXERCISE 8

Verb Practice *Make short sentences with forms of the verbs* **spread, recommend, remove, rub, brush, run after, neglect, put on make-up, pluck your eyebrows.** *Expand each verb practice to include different tenses, as in the exercise above. Use a different noun or pronoun with each verb. Use the interrogative words when it is possible.*

EXERCISE 9

Translate into Spanish.

1. He comes highly recommended to us, and I highly recommend him to you.
2. You should pluck your eyebrows every other day.
3. It takes me half an hour to put on my make-up in the morning.
4. Who runs that beauty shop in the next block?
5. Why didn't you pay attention to what the beauty operator said?
6. Did the dentist say he would have to pull your tooth?
7. Which bus goes down Insurgentes?
8. I'm out of rouge and lipstick.

9. How are you getting along?
10. Do you part your hair on the right side or on the left side?
11. How often do you go to the beauty shop?
12. My hands are cold.
13. The bus had an accident at the corner of Juarez and San Juan, and three people were killed.
14. We might go to Acapulco during Easter Week.

EXERCISE 10

Translate into English.

1. Antes de pintar la mesa, debes quitarle toda la pintura vieja.
2. El Sr. Tracy no recomendará a este joven, pero el señor Hervey sí.
3. Tiene el pelo brillante porque se lo cepilla todas las mañanas.
4. Tus zapatos y bolsa no hacen buen juego, ¿verdad?
5. Ha de haber un salón de belleza en aquel hotel.
6. Quiero un frasco de cold cream, del mismo tamaño que éste.
7. Se pone demasiado maquillaje, ¿no es verdad?
8. Dimos una vuelta a la manzana.
9. ¿Quién prendió ese cerillo?
10. Le hablan a Ud. por teléfono. Creo que es larga distancia.

EXERCISE 11

Answer the following questions.

1. Would you rather have cake or fruit?
2. Would you rather have coffee or tea?
3. Would you rather live in Cuernavaca or Taxco?
4. Would you rather take the bus or the street car?
5. Would you rather walk or ride?
6. How often do you go to the beauty shop?
7. How often do you go to the barber shop?
8. How often do you get a haircut?
9. How often do you go to the movies?
10. How often do you pluck your eyebrows?
11. Did you pay attention to what he said?
12. Did you pay attention to what I told you?
13. Did you pay attention to what he was doing?
14. Did you pay attention to what I was reading?
15. Did you pay attention to what I wrote?

Lección 12

1. **to smear, smeared, smeared** embarrar, rayar (se) (*pintura fresca*)
2. **to rinse, rinsed, rinsed** enjuagar
3. **to polish, polished, polished** sacar brillo; bolear
4. **to soak, soaked, soaked** remojar; empapar
5. **to dye, dyed, dyed** teñir, pintar
   to bleach, bleached, bleached teñir, pintar; blanquear
6. **to braid your hair, braided your hair, braided your hair** hacerse trenzas
7. **to curl, curled, curled** rizar
   curl rizo
   curly hair pelo chino o rizado
   straight hair pelo lacio
8. **wave** onda

wavy ondulado
9. **mirror** espejo
10. **model** modelo
11. **dryer** secador
12. **(finger) nail** uña de la mano
13. **(finger) nail file** lima para las uñas
    nail clipper cortauñas
    emery board lima de cartón
14. **(finger) nail polish** barniz para las uñas
15. **cuticle** cutícula
16. **hangnail** padrastro
17. **half-moons** medias lunas
18. **length** (*noun*) largo; longitud
19. **lotion** loción
    hand lotion crema (*líquida*) para las manos
    a bottle of hand lotion un frasco de crema (*líquida*) para las manos
20. **hair-do** peinado
21. **bobby pin** pasador

22. **perfume** perfume	27. **loose** suelto, flojo
a bottle of perfume	28. **bangs** fleco
un frasco de perfume	29. **hair net** red para el pelo
23. **complexion** cutis	30. **bun** chongo
24. **deodorant** desodorante	31. **toupee** bisoñé, peluca
25. **peroxide** agua oxigenada	32. **wig** peluca (*de ornato*)
26. **blond, blonde** rubio (a)	33. **iodine** yodo
brunet, brunette moreno (a)	

IDIOMS

1. **to run over** atropellar
   to get run over ser atropellado
   He got run over. Lo atropellaron.
2. **to get a permanent (a cold wave)** hacerse el permanente (en frío)
3. **to get a manicure** hacerse el manicure
4. **to get a tan** broncearse
5. **to get sunburned** quemarse (*por el sol*)
6. **to put your hair up** hacerse anchoas
7. **to take a sun bath** tomar un baño de sol
   to take a steam bath tomar un baño de vapor
8. **to file your (finger) nails** limarse las uñas
9. **to set your hair** arreglarse el pelo
10. **Whose turn is it?** ¿A quién le toca?
    It's my (your, his, etc.) turn. Me (te, le, etc.) toca a mí, (ti, él, etc.).
11. **It makes the time pass faster.** Hace que se pase el tiempo volando.

EXERCISE 1

Practice the following dialogue.

AT THE BEAUTY SHOP

Beauty Operator: Good morning.

Customer: Good morning. I'd like to make an appointment for a permanent.

Beauty Operator: We can take you at eleven-thirty. Would you like to wait or come back?

Customer: I think I'll wait. It's only twenty-five minutes.

Beauty Operator:	It's your turn now, Miss Smith. Go to the third booth, please. I'll be there in just a minute.
Customer:	All right.
Beauty Operator:	What kind of permanent do you want?
Customer:	A cold wave.
Beauty Operator:	Do you want your hair cut?
Customer:	Not very much.
Beauty Operator:	Cold waves are only good for short hair.
Customer:	All right. Cut it then.
Beauty Operator:	We'll have to cut all the old permanent off.
Customer:	Don't cut it too short. I want it to look nice this week.
Beauty Operator:	Let's go into the other booth so I can shampoo your hair. How hot do you like the water?
Customer:	I like it very hot.
Beauty Operator:	Is your hair dyed?
Customer:	No, it isn't. I dyed it once, but I didn't like it.
Beauty Operator:	Your hair should take a good permanent then. It isn't too fine.
Customer:	Yes, I've always had good luck with permanents, but my hair grows so fast that I'm always getting a new one.
Beauty Operator:	It's better that way.
Customer:	How long will it take?
Beauty Operator:	About an hour. I'll make a test curl. Do you want it very tight?
Customer:	No, I prefer a loose curl. It doesn't last as long, but it's much prettier.
Beauty Operator:	Would you like a manicure while you're sitting under the dryer?
Customer:	Yes, I would. It makes the time pass faster.
Beauty Operator:	Your nails are long, but one is broken. Shall I file them all down to the same length?
Customer:	Yes, please do.
Beauty Operator:	Do you want the cuticle cut or just pushed back?
Customer:	Just pushed back. I don't want to have hangnails. What can I do to keep nail polish on? It doesn't last more than a day.
Beauty Operator:	That's unusual. It stays on most people's nails for a whole week.
Customer:	I know, but not on mine.

Beauty Operator:	We can put an iodine base on. It generally helps. Let your left hand soak while I work on your right hand. What color of polish do you prefer? Here they are. Pick out the shade you want.
Customer:	I'd like Cherries in the Snow, because it goes with my lipstick.
Beauty Operator:	Shall I paint the whole nail, or do you want half-moons?
Customer:	Paint the whole nail.
Beauty Operator:	Be careful. Don't smear the polish before it dries. Your hair took a nice curl. I'll rinse it and then set it. How would you like it set? Here are a few models to choose from.
Customer:	I like this one. My hair looks better parted on the side.
Beauty Operator:	It's so easy to keep your hair nice when it's short. Shall I put some oil on it?
Customer:	Just a little bit. Not much. My hair is naturally oily.
Beauty Operator:	I won't put much on. Here's a mirror so you can see the sides and back.
Customer:	Thank you. How much is it?
Beauty Operator:	It's eleven twenty-five, counting the manicure.
Customer:	I'd like to make an appointment for a shampoo next week.
Beauty Operator:	What day?
Customer:	Next Thursday morning.
Beauty Operator:	Would ten-thirty be all right?
Customer:	No, that's too early.
Beauty Operator:	I could take you at eleven forty-five.
Customer:	That's fine. I'll be in next week.
Beauty Operator:	Thank you. Good-bye.

EXERCISE 2

Learn these words.

SCHOOL TERMS

1. **algebra** álgebra
2. **architecture** arquitectura
3. **arithmetic** aritmética
4. **biology** biología
5. **blackboard** pizarrón
6. **bookcase** librero

7. **bookstore** librería
8. **botany** botánica
9. **calculus** cálculo
10. **chalk** gis (gises)
    a piece of chalk un gis
11. **chemistry** química
12. **classroom** sala de clase
13. **college** universidad; facultad
14. **dramatics** el estudio de drama
15. **drawing** dibujo
16. **dormitory** dormitorio
17. **economics** economía
18. **elementary school** primaria
19. **engineering** ingeniería
20. **eraser** borrador; goma
21. **geology** geología
22. **geometry** geometría
23. **handwriting** letra
24. **grade** año escolar;
    calificación
25. **high school** escuela
    secundaria
26. **ink** tinta
27. **library** biblioteca
28. **literature** literatura
29. **mathematics** matemáticas
30. **physical education**
    educación física
31. **physics** física
32. **primary** primaria
33. **principal** director
34. **reading** lectura
35. **roommate** compañero
    de cuarto
36. **scholarship** beca
37. **science** ciencia
38. **sociology** sociología
39. **spelling** ortografía
40. **trigonometry** trigonometría
41. **university** universidad

EXERCISE 3

Translate the following sentences and practice reading them.

1. She was going to be hungry.
2. She wasn't going to be hungry.
3. Was she going to be hungry?
4. Wasn't she going to be hungry?
5. Why was she going to be hungry?
6. We studied before going to the movies.
7. We studied after going to the movies.
8. Besides going to the movies, we studied.
9. We studied instead of going to the movies.
10. We went to the movies in spite of being sick.
11. He worked all day without getting tired.
12. She can cook, and I can too.
13. She can't cook, and I can't either.
14. She should cook, and I should too.
15. She shouldn't cook, and I shouldn't either.
16. She'll cook, and I will too.
17. She won't cook, and I won't either.

93

18. I like to cook, and she does too.
19. I don't like to cook, and she doesn't either.
20. I want to cook, and she does too.
21. I don't want to cook, and she doesn't either.
22. I wanted to cook, and she did too.
23. I didn't want to cook, and she didn't either.
24. I've cooked, and she has too.
25. I haven't cooked, and she hasn't either.

EXERCISE 4

Translate the following sentences. Change them to the negative, interrogative, and interrogative negative.

1. That car is going to run over you.
2. He was run over by a bus.
3. The horses ran over the little boy.
4. That driver has run over two children.
5. The streetcar will run over that old man.
6. I thought he was going to get run over.
7. Four people got run over during the holidays.
8. He said he didn't want to get run over.
9. They'll get run over.
10. We can get run over very easily.

EXERCISE 5

Give the past tense and past participle of the following verbs.

explain	fix	fine	hurry
express	form	file your	hope
end	fail	(finger) nails	hunt
fill	follow	guess	hate
finish	fry	help	invite
			insist (on)

EXERCISE 6

Give the past tense and past participle of the following verbs.

get a haircut	get old	get a manicure	have
get a shave	get a shot	get a tan	hear

get a shine	get excited	get a permanent	hang
get run over	get sunburned	go on a trip	have a good time
get burned	get a trim	go for a walk, ride	have fun

EXERCISE 7

Verb Practice *Expand the following verb practice, using different tenses.*

1. The painter smeared the paint, didn't he?
2. The painter didn't smear the paint, did he?
3. Did the painter smear the paint?
4. Didn't the painter smear the paint?
5. Why did the painter smear the paint?

EXERCISE 8

Verb Practice *Make short sentences with forms of the verbs* rinse, polish, soak, dye, bleach, braid, curl, run over, get run over, get a permanent, get a manicure, get a tan, get sunburned, take a sun bath, take a steam bath, file your (finger)nails, set your hair, put your hair up. *Expand each verb practice to include different tenses, as in the exercise above. Use a different noun or pronoun with each verb. Use the interrogative words when it is possible.*

EXERCISE 9

Translate into Spanish.

1. What are you polishing the silver for?
2. I'm going to read a book while I'm on the train. It makes the time pass faster.
3. How can you keep from getting sunburned in Acapulco?
4. She came back from Cuernavaca with a beautiful tan.
5. She is going to dye her hair when she gets a new permanent.
6. This nail polish isn't worth buying.
7. Let me borrow your nail file. I broke one of my finger nails.
8. Be careful when you take a sun bath, or you'll get sunburned.
9. Does she make a living running that beauty shop?

10. She says she makes about $100.00 (dollars) a week.
11. I wish the barber would stop putting so much oil on my hair.
12. Why don't you let the beauty operator wash your hair?
13. I hope it's your turn next (después).
14. Why don't you pay attention to what you're doing?
15. There are two bottles of fingernail polish missing.

EXERCISE 10

Translate into English.

1. He estado tan ocupada que no he tenido tiempo de hacerme anchoas.
2. Ud. debe enjuagarse el pelo en agua fría.
3. Ella tiene un cutis bonito, ¿verdad?
4. ¿Es rubia natural, o tiene el pelo pintado?
5. Remoja esa ropa vieja antes de lavarla.
6. Yo me trencé el pelo, pero Elena no.
7. Margarita tiene el pelo chino, pero Isabel no.
8. Tomemos un baño de sol en la azotea.
9. Me hice el permanente en frío anteayer.
10. Debe haber un frasco de perfume en mi bolsa.

EXERCISE 11

Answer the following questions.

1. How long has it been since you lived in Mexico?
2. How long has it been since you visited New York?
3. How long has it been since you saw your brother?
4. How long has it been since you studied English?
5. How long has it been since you got a haircut?
6. Did you pay attention to the teacher?
7. Do you pay attention to your parents?
8. Will you pay attention to the music?
9. Have you paid attention to the conversation?
10. Shouldn't you pay attention to the speaker?
11. Have you been working all day?
12. Have you been reading that book?
13. Have you been talking to John?
14. Have you been watching TV?
15. Have you been studying English?

Answer the following questions in the affirmative and in the negative.

16. Did he get run over?
17. Did the truck driver run over the cat?
18. Was he run over?
19. Are you going to get a permanent?
20. Do you often get a permanent?
21. Do you want a manicure?
22. Did he get a manicure at the barber's?
23. Do you usually get so sunburned?
24. Do you always file your nails so short?
25. Is it your turn?
26. Is it Helen's turn?

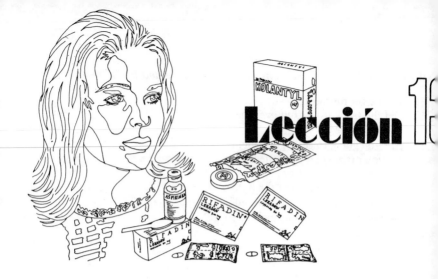

Vocabulary

1. **to arrange, arranged, arranged** arreglar, acomodar
2. **to sterilize, sterilized, sterilized** esterilizar
3. **to poison, poisoned, poisoned** envenenar
   poison veneno
4. **to commit suicide, committed suicide, committed suicide** suicidarse, matarse
   to kill yourself, killed yourself, killed yourself suicidarse, matarse
5. **to heal, healed, healed** sanar, cicatrizar
   to cure, cured, cured curar
6. **to mention, mentioned, mentioned** mencionar
7. **drugstore** botica, farmacia
8. **druggist** farmacéutico
9. **drug** droga, medicamento
10. **narcotics** narcóticos
    dope narcóticos
11. **health** salud
    healthy saludable; sano

12. **bandage** venda
13. **gauze** gasa
14. **adhesive tape** tela adhesiva
    a roll of adhesive tape un rollo de tela adhesiva
15. **disinfectant** desinfectante
16. **aspirin** aspirina
    a bottle of aspirins un frasco de aspirinas
17. **sleeping pills** pastillas para dormir
18. **instrument** instrumento
19. **hoarse** ronco
20. **band-aid** curita
21. **salve** ungüento
22. **nervous** nervioso
23. **illness** enfermedad
24. **crowd** multitud, gentío
25. **blister** ampolla
26. **mole** lunar
27. **delivery boy** mensajero, mandadero

IDIOMS

1. **to feel sorry for** sentir pena por; compadecer (se)
2. **to blow your nose** sonarse
3. **to get well** mejorarse; aliviarse
4. **to fill a prescription** surtir una receta
5. **in stock** en existencia
6. **Would you mind (gerund)** _____? ¿No le molesta (infinitivo)_____? ¿Tiene inconveniente en que _____?
   Would you mind helping me? ¿No le molesta ayudarme?
   Would you mind if I don't go? ¿Tiene Ud. inconveniente en que yo no vaya?
7. **a twenty-dollar bill** un billete de a veinte dólares
8. **Don't mention it.** No hay por qué.
9. **God bless you.** (*al estornudar*) Salud.
10. **Here you are.** Aquí tiene Ud., Aquí lo(s) tiene.

EXERCISE 1

Practice the following dialogue.

AT THE DRUGSTORE

Druggist: Have you been waited on?

Customer: No, not yet. Do you have this list of medicine on hand?

Druggist: Yes, we have this medicine in stock, but I can't sell you these sleeping pills without a doctor's prescription. Get a prescription from your doctor, and I'll fill it for you.

Customer: Oh, I have a doctor's prescription. Here it is.

Druggist: All right. Would you mind waiting for a few minutes, or would you like to come back later? The medicine will be ready in about fifteen minutes.

Customer: Could you deliver it to my house?

Druggist: I'm sorry, but our delivery boy just left for the day.

Customer: Then I'll wait.

———————

Druggist: I've filled your prescription. The medicine is ready. Do you need anything else now?

Customer: I want a bottle of aspirins, a roll of adhesive tape, and some gauze.

Druggist: Will there be anything else?
Customer: No, thank you. That'll be all. Can you change a twenty-dollar bill?
Druggist: I think so. That is, if you don't mind taking all one-dollar bills. I don't have any big bills left.
Customer: No, that's all right. And give me some change. I have to make some calls.
Druggist: Here you are, and thank you.

EXERCISE 2

Learn these words.

PARTS OF THE BODY

1. **ankle** tobillo
2. **big toe** dedo gordo (*del pie*)
3. **calf** pantorrilla
4. **elbow** codo
5. **eyebrow** ceja
6. **eyelash** pestaña
7. **fist** puño
8. **forehead** frente
9. **hip** cadera
10. **instep** empeine
11. **intestines** intestinos
12. **jaw** mandíbula
13. **joint** articulación, coyuntura
14. **kidneys** riñones
15. **knee** rodilla
16. **knuckles** nudillos
17. **little finger** dedo meñique
18. **little toe** dedo meñique (*del pie*)
19. **lungs** pulmones
20. **muscle** músculo
21. **ribs** costilla
22. **shin** espinilla
23. **skeleton** esqueleto
24. **skull** cráneo
25. **spine** espina dorsal
26. **thigh** muslo
27. **thumb** pulgar
28. **toenails** uñas (*de los pies*)
29. **wrist** muñeca
30. **waist** cintura

EXERCISE 3

Translate the following sentences and practice reading them.

1. The Germans will have to deliver it.
2. The Germans won't have to deliver it.
3. Will the Germans have to deliver it?
4. Won't the Germans have to deliver it?

100

5. When will the Germans have to deliver it?
6. The Germans would have to deliver it.
7. The Germans wouldn't have to deliver it.
8. Would the Germans have to deliver it?
9. Wouldn't the Germans have to deliver it?
10. When would the Germans have to deliver it?
11. It was going to be cold.
12. It wasn't going to be cold.
13. Was it going to be cold?
14. Wasn't it going to be cold?
15. When was it going to be cold?
16. He won, didn't you?
17. He didn't win, did you?
18. He lost, didn't she?
19. He didn't lose, did she?
20. He went out, did they?
21. Maybe they're going to deliver it.
22. Maybe they aren't going to deliver it.
23. Maybe they'll deliver it.
24. Maybe they won't deliver it.
25. Perhaps they'll deliver it.

EXERCISE 4

Translate the following sentences. Change them to the negative, inter-rogative, and interrogative negative.

1. I feel sorry for Joan.
2. We felt sorry for the prisoners.
3. He will feel sorry for them.
4. She has been feeling sorry for herself.
5. They would feel sorry for the beggar.
6. He felt sorry for her.
7. The people should feel sorry for their neighbors.
8. The children are going to feel sorry for their friends.
9. That woman was feeling sorry for the sick child.
10. The students are going to feel sorry for us.

EXERCISE 5

Give the past tense and past participle of the following verbs.

insult	kill	laugh (at)	look (at)
introduce	kill yourself	learn	look (for)
jump	knit	like	look out (of)
join	knock (on)	listen (to)	love
joke	kick	live	last

EXERCISE 6

Give the past tense and past participle of the following verbs.

hide	know	lie down	make a living
hit	keep	lose	make a mistake
hang up	lay eggs	lend	make fun of
hold	leave	make	make money
have an accident	let	meet	mean

EXERCISE 7

Verb Practice *Expand the following verb practice, using different tenses.*

1. The Mexicans arranged everything.
2. The Mexicans didn't arrange everything.
3. Did the Mexicans arrange everything?
4. Didn't the Mexicans arrange everything?
5. Why didn't the Mexicans arrange everything?

EXERCISE 8

Verb Practice *Make short sentences with forms of the verbs* **sterilize, poison, commit suicide, kill yourself, heal, cure, mention, feel sorry for, blow your nose, get well, fill a prescription.** *Expand each verb practice to include different tenses, as in the exercise above. Use a different noun or pronoun with each verb. Use the interrogative words when it is possible.*

EXERCISE 9

Translate into Spanish.

1. If your hands are red, use lotion.
2. His hair is blond and his eyes are blue.

3. I feel sorry for people who have to beg for a living.
4. Her hair is long.
5. How can anyone make a living on a farm?
6. You made a big mistake when you bought that house.
7. You should never make fun of a tourist's Spanish.
8. Did you make a lot of money in the United States?
9. I hope the doctor makes you stop smoking.
10. I wish the doctor would make you stop smoking.
11. Make Johnny blow his nose.
12. He hasn't been able to get a haircut yet.
13. If I were you, I wouldn't take charge of the meeting.
14. If I had time, I'd take a walk.
15. When will the meeting take place?

EXERCISE 10

Translate into English.

1. Yo estaba tan ronco que apenas podía hablar.
2. Se cayó mi abuelita y se rompió la cadera.
3. Use su pañuelo para sonarse.
4. ¿Cree Ud. que el farmacéutico podrá surtir la receta antes de que cierre la botica?
5. ¡Que te alivies pronto!
6. ¿No le molesta a Ud. esperarme unos minutos?
7. Si tiene dolor de cabeza, tome una aspirina.
8. Asegúrese de esterilizar las botellas antes de alimentar al bebé.
9. No tengo ni la menor (least) idea de por qué se suicidó.
10. ¿Ya lo atienden?

EXERCISE 11

Answer the following questions.

1. Would you mind taking me home?
2. Would you mind leaving early?
3. Would you mind if I came later?
4. Would she mind if we left early?
5. Do you pay attention to the teacher?
6. Will you pay attention to the movie?
7. Are you going to pay attention to him?

8. Are you paying attention?
9. Were you paying attention?
10. How long has it been since you were in Acapulco?
11. How long has it been since you paid the rent?
12. How long has it been since you talked to him?
13. How long has it been since you bought your car?
14. How long has it been since you had a vacation?
15. How long has it been since you got a raise?
16. How long has it been since you got married?

Answer the following questions in the affirmative and in the negative.

17. Do you ever feel sorry for John?
18. Did he feel sorry for that woman?
19. Did he get well soon?
20. Did the druggist fill the prescription?
21. Did you get the prescription filled?
22. Do you have any aspirins in stock?
23. Can you change a five-dollar bill for me, please?
24. Did he blow his nose?
25. Did he get well?

Lección 14

Vocabulary

1. **to print, printed, printed** imprimir
2. **to scratch, scratched, scratched** rascar, rasguñar
3. **to waste, wasted, wasted** desperdiciar; perder (*tiempo*)
4. **to thank, thanked, thanked** dar las gracias
5. **to imagine, imagined, imagined** imaginar (se); explicarse
6. **to envy, envied, envied** envidiar **envious** envidioso
7. **soda fountain** fuente de sodas
8. **ice cream** helado **ice cream cone** barquillo **ice cream soda** helado con soda **sundae** sundae
9. **malted milk (shake)** leche malteada
10. **Coke** Coca, Coca-Cola
11. **straw** popote
12. **lemonade** limonada
13. **vanilla** vainilla
14. **juke box** sinfonola
15. **penny** centavo **nickel** quinto **dime** moneda de 10 centavos **quarter** moneda de 25 centavos **half a dollar** moneda de 50 centavos
16. **flavor** sabor
17. **janitor** portero
18. **private** particular, privado
19. **gentleman** caballero
20. **lady** dama
21. **flag** bandera
22. **rainbow** arco iris
23. **supply** provisión, abastecimiento
24. **upstairs** arriba (*en una casa o edificio*)
25. **downstairs** abajo (*en una casa o edificio*)
26. **check** cuenta (*de restaurante*)

105

IDIOMS

1. **to feel like (present participle)** tener ganas de (infinitivo)
   I feel like eating. Tengo ganas de comer.
2. **to sit (down) at a table** sentarse a una mesa
   to sit at the counter sentarse en la barra
3. **to get paid** cobrar (*salario*)
   I'll get paid tomorrow. Cobro mañana.
4. **to play the piano, etc.** tocar el piano, etc.
5. **can afford** darse el lujo de, poder costear, tener con que; convenir
   I can't afford that car. No tengo con que comprar ese coche.
   I can't afford to waste so much time. No me conviene perder tanto tiempo.
6. **We don't carry that.** No tenemos (trabajamos) eso.
7. **I can't (couldn't) imagine why.** No me explico (explicaba) por qué.
8. **Can (May) I have a glass of water?** ¿Quiere Ud. darme un vaso de agua?
9. **What are you going to have?** ¿Qué vas a pedir (tomar, comer)?

EXERCISE 1

Practice the following dialogue.

AT THE SODA FOUNTAIN

Tom: Do you want to sit at the counter or at a table?
Betty: Oh, it doesn't make any difference. Let's sit at a table.
Waiter: What are you going to have?
Betty: I want an ice cream soda.
Waiter: What kind of ice cream do you want?
Betty: Strawberry.
Tom: I want a chocolate sundae with vanilla ice cream and a Coke. And bring me some nickels, please. I want to play the juke box.
Betty: May I have a straw, please?
Waiter: They're on the table.
Tom: Can I have a quart of ice cream to take out?
Waiter: Of course. What flavor would you like? We carry quart packages in all flavors.
Tom: Do you have coffee and pistachio?
Waiter: No, we don't have that combination in packages, but we can make it up for you.

Tom:	Fine—and I'd also like four Cokes to take out.
Betty:	Don't forget the bacon and egg (sandwich) for Dorothy.
Tom:	Oh, yes. Just before you bring us the check, will you make a bacon and egg (sandwich) on toast—tomatoes, but no butter or mayonnaise.
Waiter:	Sure. Just call me when you want the check.
Tom:	All right. Thank you.

EXERCISE 2

Learn these words.

ARTICLES OF CLOTHING

1. **bathrobe** bata
2. **belt buckle** hebilla para cinturón
3. **blouse** blusa
4. **blue jeans** pantalones vaqueros
   a pair of blue jeans pantalones vaqueros
5. **cane** bastón
6. **evening gown** vestido de noche
7. **fur coat** abrigo de piel
8. **garters** ligas
   a pair of garters un par de ligas
9. **girdle** faja
10. **house coat** bata de mujer
11. **house slippers** pantuflas
    a pair of house slippers un par de pantuflas
12. **jacket** chaqueta, chamarra
13. **lingerie** lencería, ropa interior (*de mujer*)
14. **negligee** camisón transparente
15. **nightgown** camisón
16. **overalls** overol
    a pair of overalls un overol
17. **pants** pantalones
    a pair of pants unos pantalones
18. **trousers** pantalones

   a pair of trousers unos pantalones
19. **pajamas** pijama
    a pair of pajamas una pijama
20. **scarf** bufanda
21. **shorts** shorts; calzoncillos
    a pair of shorts unos calzoncillos
22. **slacks** pantalón sport
    a pair of slacks unos pantalones sport
23. **sleeveless sweater** sweater sin mangas, chaleco
24. **slip** fondo
25. **sport coat** saco sport
26. **sport shirt** camisa sport
27. **stole** rebozo
28. **supporters** ligas (*para hombre*)
    a pair of supporters un par de ligas
29. **suspenders** tirantes
    a pair of suspenders unos tirantes

107

30. **T-shirt** camiseta (*de manga corta*)
31. **tuxedo** smoking
32. **umbrella** sombrilla, paraguas
33. **undershirt** camiseta
34. **underwear** ropa interior
35. **vest** chaleco (*de traje*)
36. **wardrobe** guardarropa
37. **button** botón
38. **buttonhole** ojal
39. **collar** cuello
40. **French cuff** puño doblado
41. **full skirt** falda amplia
42. **hem** bastilla, dobladillo
43. **pleat** pliegue
44. **shoelaces** agujetas
45. **sleeve** manga
46. **snap** broche de presión

EXERCISE 3

Translate the following sentences and practice reading them.

1. He's had to borrow money.
2. He hasn't had to borrow money.
3. Has he had to borrow money?
4. Hasn't he had to borrow money?
5. Why has he had to borrow money?
6. They're going to be afraid.
7. They aren't going to be afraid.
8. Are they going to be afraid?
9. Aren't they going to be afraid?
10. When are they going to be afraid?
11. He studies, and they do too.
12. He doesn't study, and they don't either.
13. They worked, and he did too.
14. They didn't work, and he didn't either.
15. I have to wait, and you do too.
16. I don't have to wait, and you don't either.
17. We've gone, and she has too.
18. We haven't gone, and she hasn't either.
19. She'll sell fruit, and you will too.
20. She won't sell fruit, and you won't either.
21. You're going swimming, and they are too.
22. You aren't going swimming, and they aren't either.
23. You were going to play, and we were too.
24. You weren't going to play, and we weren't either.
25. He'd win, and I would too.
26. He wouldn't win, and I wouldn't either.

27. They might sleep.
28. They might not sleep.
29. They may sleep.
30. They may not sleep.

EXERCISE 4

Translate the following sentences and practice reading them.

1. I feel like going for a walk.
2. He said he felt like sleeping for a while.
3. We'll feel like eating after the game.
4. She is going to feel like dancing tonight.
5. They have felt like getting rid of their maid many times.
6. I like that dress, but I can't afford it.
7. He can't afford to get married yet.
8. He can't afford to get drunk because he has to get up early.
9. In a few years I'll be able to afford a new car.
10. I can't afford to spend all my time reading silly novels.

EXERCISE 5

Give the past tense and past participle of the following verbs.

lift	melt	match	open a business
look alike	miss a person	mention	own
lock	miss a train,	need	owe
move	bus, etc.	name	operate on
measure	mix	notice	pass
			print

EXERCISE 6

Give the past tense and past participle of the following verbs.

oversleep	put on	run around	rise
put	make-up	run out of	ring
put on	read	run a busines,	say
pay	run	etc.	see
pay atten-	ride	run after	sell
tion (to)	run away	run over	make a trip

109

EXERCISE 7

Verb Practice *Expand the following verb practice, using different tenses.*

1. That newspaper would have been printed.
2. That newspaper wouldn't have been printed.
3. Would that newspaper have been printed?
4. Wouldn't that newspaper have been printed?
5. Why wouldn't that newspaper have been printed?

EXERCISE 8

Verb Practice *Make short sentences with forms of the verbs* **waste, envy, thank, imagine, scratch, feel like, sit at a table, sit at the counter, play the piano, get paid, can afford.** *Expand each verb practice to include different tenses, as in the exercise above. Use a different noun or pronoun with each verb. Use the interrogative words when it is possible.*

EXERCISE 9

Translate into Spanish.

1. Her hair is long and curly.
2. I can't afford to waste so much time.
3. Don't feel sorry for me.
4. Do you part your hair on the left side?
5. Would you mind taking care of my baby for a few minutes?
6. I want to thank you for the nice birthday present.
7. Can you afford a maid?
8. We ran out of money before we could pay the rent.
9. The boys ran around until three o'clock in the morning.
10. He didn't commit suicide. He was run over by a truck.
11. I ran a boardinghouse for ten years, but I certainly didn't get rich.
12. You're going to get hurt if you don't stop playing with that dog.
13. How often do you pluck your eyebrows?
14. We'll have to sit at the counter. There aren't any tables for two.
15. Since I hurt my hand, I haven't been able to play the piano.

EXERCISE 10

Transalate into English.

1. Quedémonos en casa. No tengo ganas de ir.

2. No podemos costear un carro nuevo este año.
3. No me explico por qué se mató. Parecía estar bastante feliz.
4. ¿Tocas el piano? No, no toco nada, ¿y tú?
5. No he tenido ocasión para darle las gracias por lo que ha hecho por mis niños.
6. Estoy seguro de que se habría matado (would have been killed) si el carro se hubiese volteado.
7. Estará lista tan pronto como se maquille.
8. ¿Cuándo cobras? No cobro hasta mañana.
9. Un coche atropelló a ese perro que estaba persiguiendo a tu gato.
10. No me conviene acostarme tan tarde, porque mañana tengo que levantarme temprano.

EXERCISE 11

Answer the following questions.

1. Do you feel like dancing?
2. Do you feel like studying?
3. Do you feel like working?
4. Do you feel like sleeping?
5. Have you been working for two hours?
6. Have you been waiting for fifteen minutes?
7. Have you been studying for twenty minutes?
8. Do you make fun of Hollywood movies?
9. Did you make fun of his English?
10. Have you been making fun of my Spanish?
11. Will you make fun of her new hat?
12. How far is it from here to the beauty parlor?
13. How far is it from here to the barber shop?
14. How far is it from here to the drugstore?
15. How far is it from here to Laredo?
16. When do you get paid?
17. Do you get paid every week?
18. Have you already been paid?
19. Did the workers get paid?
20. Does he get paid on Saturday?

Vocabulary

1. **to cheat, cheated, cheated** hacer trampa, ser tramposo; engañar
2. **to tarnish, tarnished, tarnished** opacarse (*metal*)
3. **to quit, quit, quit** dejar (*el empleo*); renunciar (a); dejar de
4. **to apologize (to), apologized (to), apologized (to)** disculparse (con)
5. **to faint, fainted, fainted** desmayar (se)
6. **shift** turno (*de trabajo*)
7. **jewelry store** joyería
   jewelry shop joyería
8. **jeweler** joyero
9. **costume jewelry** joyería de fantasía
10. **synthetic** sintético
11. **karat** quilate
12. **precious stones** piedras preciosas
    semiprecious stones piedras semipreciosas
13. **ring** anillo
    wedding ring anillo de matrimonio
    wedding band argolla de matrimonio
14. **bracelet** pulsera
15. **necklace** collar
16. **earring** arete
17. **buckle** hebilla
18. **rhinestones** piedras falsas
19. **set** juego
20. **string** cordón
21. **bead** cuenta (de collar), abalorio
22. **brooch** broche, prendedor
23. **cameo** camafeo
24. **cuff link** mancuerna
25. **tie pin** fistol; pisacorbata
26. **setting** montadura
27. **plain** sencillo; sin dibujo
28. **silverware** (*sing.*) cubiertos

112

IDIOMS

1. **to break out** brotar; estallar; salirle a uno
2. **to set your watch (clock)** poner su reloj
   to set the alarm poner el despertador
3. **to wind, wound, wound your watch (clock)** darle cuerda al reloj
4. **have got** tener; tener que
   I've got two cars. Tengo dos coches.
   I haven't got two cars. No tengo dos coches.
   He's got to go now. El tiene que irse ahora.
   Has he got to go now? ¿Tiene que ir ahora?
5. **a string of pearls, beads** un hilo de perlas, cuentas
6. **What's it like?** ¿Cómo es?
   What are they like? ¿Cómo son?
7. **My watch (clock) is slow.** Mi reloj está atrasado.
   My watch (clock) is fast. Mi reloj está adelantado.
   My watch (clock) stopped. Se me paró el reloj.
   My watch (clock) doesn't run. Mi reloj no camina.
   My watch (clock) isn't running. Mi reloj no está caminando.

EXERCISE 1

Practice the following dialogue.

AT THE JEWELRY STORE

Helen: Ruth, have you seen Joan's engagement ring?
Ruth: No, what's it like?
Helen: It's beautiful. It's a one karat diamond in a platinum setting. The wedding band will be plain. She and Bob will get married in June.
Ruth: Have you seen the bracelet her father gave her?
Helen: No, I haven't.
Ruth: The stones are amethysts, I believe.
Helen: Did you see her at the dance last night? She looked so pretty.
Ruth: What was she wearing?
Helen: She had on a pink evening dress with a rhinestone necklace, bracelet, and earrings to match. She looks good in pink because she's small and blonde.
Ruth: You know, you've also got a beautiful engagement ring.

113

Helen: Thanks. I'll be wearing the wedding ring this time next year. Jim and I plan to get married in June.

EXERCISE 2

Learn these words.

NAMES OF METALS AND STONES

1. **alexandrine** alejandrina
2. **aluminum** aluminio
3. **amethyst** amatista
4. **brass** latón
5. **copper** cobre
6. **diamond** brillante, diamante
7. **emerald** esmeralda
8. **gold** oro
9. **garnet** granate
10. **granite** granito
11. **iron** hierro, fierro
12. **ivory** marfil
13. **jade** jade
14. **lead** plomo
15. **marble** mármol
16. **opal** ópalo
17. **pearl** perla
18. **platinum** platino
19. **quartz** cuarzo
20. **ruby** rubí
21. **sapphire** zafiro
22. **silver** plata
23. **steel** acero
24. **tile** azulejo
25. **topaz** topacio
26. **turquoise** turquesa

EXERCISE 3

Translate the following sentences and practice reading them.

1. He was going to be sleepy.
2. He wasn't going to be sleepy.
3. Was he going to be sleepy?
4. Wasn't he going to be sleepy?
5. Why was he going to be sleepy?
6. There's a diamond, isn't there?
7. There isn't a diamond, is there?
8. Is there a diamond?
9. Isn't there a diamond?
10. How many diamonds are there?
11. There were two rings, weren't there?
12. There weren't two rings, were there?
13. Were there two rings?

14. Weren't there two rings?
15. How many rings were there?
16. There'll be a jewelry store here, won't there?
17. There won't be a jewelry store here, will there?
18. Will there be a jewelry store here?
19. Won't there be a jewelry store here?
20. How many jewelry stores will there be here?
21. There have been many storms, haven't there?
22. There haven't been many storms, have there?
23. Have there been many storms?
24. Haven't there been many storms?
25. Why have there been so many storms?

EXERCISE 4

Translate the following sentences. Change them to the negative, interrogative, and interrogative negative.

1. A war broke out in Europe.
2. Polio will break out among the children.
3. He always breaks out in a rash when he eats candy.
4. Her face broke out in pimples.
5. Disease can break out suddenly.
6. He's got to be there by five.
7. I've got to study tonight.
8. They've got millions of dollars.
9. She's got two brothers and one sister.
10. I've got a beautiful house in Acapulco.

EXERCISE 5

Give the past tense and past participle of the following verbs.

pick out	paint	punish	pull a tooth
pick up	play	push	pluck your
place	prefer	part your	eyebrows
practice	prepare	hair	polish
pronounce	pull	promise	poison
		pick (a per-	print
		son) up	

115

EXERCISE 6

Give the past tense and past participle of the following verbs.

set	stand up	shine	swim
set the table	send	shoot	sink
sit	shake	sing	strike a match
sleep	shake hands	spend	spread
speak	with	stand in line	sit at a table
			sit at the counter

EXERCISE 7

Verb Practice *Expand the following verb practice, using different tenses.*

1. The students will be able to cheat.
2. The students won't be able to cheat.
3. Will the students be able to cheat?
4. Won't the students be able to cheat?
5. How will the students be able to cheat?

EXERCISE 8

Verb Practice *Make short sentences with forms of the verbs* **tarnish, quit, apologize (to), faint, break out, set your watch (clock), set the alarm, wind your watch (clock).** *Expand each verb practice to include different tenses, as in the exercise above. Use a different noun or pronoun with each verb. Use the interrogative words when it is possible.*

EXERCISE 9

Translate into Spanish.

1. Polio broke out in the United States.
2. I've got to take the children to the zoo in the morning.
3. My watch has stopped. I'll have to set it again.
4. There used to be a jewelry store on this block.
5. My watch is fast. That's why I'm so early.
6. I feel like having a drink.
7. I plan to quit working in the bank.
8. He works on the night shift and his brother works on the morning shift.

9. Does this bus go down Wilson Avenue?
10. Will you have time to give me a shine before the train leaves?
11. What did the barber cut your hair so short for?
12. My sleeves are too long.
13. This dress is too big for me.
14. Stand still while I take your pulse.
15. Where did you find those pants? I've looked all over town for a pair just like (igual a) them.

EXERCISE 10

Translate into English.

1. Tengo que ir al mercado antes de que cierre.
2. Acabo de renunciar a mi empleo.
3. No creí que me daría sueño esta tarde.
4. Quiero disculparme con el profesor por llegar tarde.
5. Que no te hagan trampa cuando estés en el mercado.
6. Pienso dejar mi trabajo el año entrante.
7. Se rascó la mano hasta que se la sangró.
8. Estoy seguro que es más tarde de (than) las cuatro. Se me debe haber parado el reloj.
9. Todos estos cubiertos están deslustrados. Ud. tendrá que sacarles brillo.
10. Creí que se iba a desmayar mi hermano cuando le dije que me había casado.

EXERCISE 11

Answer the following questions.

1. Did polio break out?
2. Did the disease break out in the whole city?
3. Did John's father break out in a rash?
4. Will you miss me when I'm in the United States?
5. Did you miss your husband when he was in the war?
6. Did you miss the fresh eggs you had on the farm?
7. Did you miss the bus this morning?
8. How many diamonds are missing?
9. How many earrings are missing?
10. Do you have to go now?

117

Answer the following questions, using **have got** *in the affirmative.*

11. Does she have to sleep in that room?
12. Do they have to come before supper?
13. Who has got ten dollars to lend me?
14. Does she have any brothers?
15. Does he have a good memory?

Lección 16

Vocabulary

1. **to resign, resigned, resigned**
   renunciar
2. **to wonder, wondered, wondered**
   preguntarse
3. **to trust, trusted, trusted**
   confiar en; fiarse de
4. **to give out, gave out, given out**
   repartir
5. **to vomit, vomited, vomited**
   vomitar (se)
6. **to tip, tipped, tipped**
   dar propina
   tip propina
7. **to order, ordered, ordered**
   pedir, ordenar
   order pedido, orden
8. **waiter** mesero
   waitress mesera
9. **napkin** servilleta
10. **tablecloth** mantel

11. **sugar bowl** azucarera
12. **cream pitcher** cremera
13. **salt shaker** salero
    pepper shaker pimentero
14. **cereal** cereal
15. **oatmeal** avena
16. **menu** menú
17. **waffles** waffles
18. **syrup** jarabe
    maple syrup miel de maple (arce)
19. **toast** pan tostado
20. **per cent** por ciento
21. **cashier** cajero (a)
22. **honey** miel
23. **picnic** día de campo
24. **spoonful** cucharada
    teaspoonful cucharadita
25. **handful** manojo, puñado

IDIOMS

1. **to take advantage of** aprovecharse de
2. **to take your order** tomar su orden
3. **to go on a picnic** ir de día de campo
4. **Can (May) I take your order?** ¿Quiere que tome su orden?
5. **I haven't had breakfast yet.** Todavía no he desayunado, Todavía no desayuno.
6. **Do you want to order now?** ¿Quiere dar su orden ahora?
   Have you ordered yet? ¿Ya pidió?
7. **Will you please bring me____?** ¿Me trae____por favor?
   Will you please bring me a glass of water? ¿Me trae un vaso de agua por favor?
8. **I wonder what time it is (was).** ¿Qué hora será (sería)?
   I wonder why. ¿Por qué será, sería?
   I wonder who it is (was). ¿Quién será (sería)?
   I wonder what he's doing. ¿Qué estará haciendo?
   I wonder where he is. ¿Dónde estará?

EXERCISE 1

Practice the following dialogue.

ORDERING BREAKFAST

Waitress:	May I take your order?
First Customer:	Are you still serving breakfast?
Waitress:	Yes, we serve breakfast until twelve o'clock. Would you like to see a breakfast menu instead of a lunch menu?
First Customer:	Yes, please give us the breakfast menu. We haven't had breakfast yet.
Waitress:	Do you want to order now?
Second Customer:	Scrambled eggs—with ham instead of bacon. And I want coffee with cream and sugar.
Waitress:	Do you want your coffee now or later?
Second Customer:	Later, please—when you bring my eggs.
First Customer:	I want number five with tomato juice, fried eggs with sausage and black coffee.
Waitress:	Do you want your coffee now?
First Customer:	Yes, please.

120

First Customer: Will you bring me some more butter, please?
Waitress: Of course. And would you like more coffee?
First Customer: I believe I would.
Waitress: Will there be anything else?
First Customer: No, thank you.
Second Customer: No, thank you.
Waitress: Here's your check. Please pay the cashier.

EXERCISE 2

Learn these words.

NAMES OF ANIMALS

1. **alligator** caimán
2. **bat** murciélago
3. **bear** oso
4. **beaver** castor
5. **bull** toro
6. **buzzard** buitre
7. **calf** becerro
8. **colt** potro
9. **coyote** coyote
10. **duck** pato
11. **eagle** águila
12. **frog** rana
13. **giraffe** jirafa
14. **goat** chivo (a), cabra
15. **hawk** gavilán
16. **hen** gallina
17. **hippopotamus** hipopótamo
18. **leopard** leopardo
19. **mare** yegua
20. **mink** visón

21. **monkey** chango, mono
22. **moose** alce
23. **owl** lechuza
24. **ox** buey
25. **peacok** pavo real
26. **pigeon** pichón, paloma
27. **rat** rata
28. **rattlesnake** serpiente de cascabel
29. **reindeer** reno
30. **rhinoceros** rinoceronte
31. **rooster** gallo
32. **shark** tiburón
33. **sheep** oveja, ovejas
34. **skunk** zorrillo
35. **squirrel** ardilla
36. **swan** cisne
37. **tiger** tigre
38. **turkey** pavo
39. **whale** ballena

EXERCISE 3

Translate the following sentences and practice reading them.

1. There'd be a duck.

2. There wouldn't be a duck.
3. Would there be a duck?
4. Wouldn't there be a duck?
5. How many ducks would there be?
6. There ought to be some napkins.
7. There shouldn't be any napkins.
8. Should there be napkins on the table?
9. Shouldn't there be napkins on the table?
10. How many napkins should there be?
11. It's always hot.
12. It isn't always hot.
13. Is it always hot?
14. Isn't it always hot?
15. Why is it always hot?
16. It was never cold.
17. It wasn't ever cold.
18. Was it ever cold?
19. Wasn't it ever cold?
20. Why wasn't it ever cold?
21. It'll be warm.
22. It won't be warm.
23. Will it be warm?
24. Won't it be warm?
25. When will it be warm?

EXERCISE 4

Translate the following sentences. Change them to the negative, interrogative, and interrogative negative.

1. You should take advantage of this opportunity.
2. We took advantage of the time.
3. They'll take advantage of you.
4. He has taken advantage of every day of school.
5. She's taking advantage of her good luck.
6. I'm going to take advantage of these few days of good weather.
7. He was taking advantage of me.
8. They'll be able to take advantage of their vacation.
9. He wants her to take advantage of her free time.
10. They've been able to take advantage of every minute.

122

EXERCISE 5

Give the past tense and past participle of the following verbs.

play the piano	remember	rot	rinse
reach	rent	raise	resign
reply	repeat	recommend	show
rain	rest	remove	start
realize	return	rub	stop

EXERCISE 6

Give the past tense and past participle of the following verbs.

take	take away	throw	take your
teach	take a bath	throw away	tonsils out
tell	take a shower	take a walk	take your
think	take care of	take place	pulse
think of	take off	take charge	take your
think about		(of)	blood pressure
			take a trip
			take a ride

EXERCISE 7

Verb Practice *Expand the following verb practice, ussing different tenses.*

1. The boss would have resigned.
2. The boss wouldn't have resigned.
3. Would the boss have resigned?
4. Wouldn't the boss have resigned?
5. Why would the boss have resigned?

EXERCISE 8

Verb Practice *Make short sentences with forms of the verbs* **tip, wonder, trust, give out, vomit, take advantage of, order, take your order, go on a picnic.** *Expand each verb practice to include different tenses, as in the exercise above. Use a different noun or pronoun with each verb. Use the interrogative words when it is possible.*

123

EXERCISE 9

Translate into Spanish.

1. Has the waiter taken your order yet?
2. I would have eaten breakfast if I had had time.
3. You should have ordered scrambled eggs.
4. I feel like having breakfast in bed.
5. We invited him to sit at the table with us.
6. A fire started in the woods where we went on a picnic.
7. You must learn to take advantage of every opportunity.
8. When was the last time you went on a picnic?
9. You should set your watch every morning before you leave home.
10. His feet and hands are very big.
11. Have you been waited on?
12. We ran out of gas about five miles out of town.
13. Will you bring me a napkin, please?
14. How much sugar is left?
15. I've got a terrible headache.

EXERCISE 10

Translate into English.

1. ¿Me ayuda Ud. a repartir los papeles?
2. No confío en ese hombre, ¿y tú?
3. ¿Es suficiente una propina del diez por ciento?
4. Ud. no debería renunciar antes de fin de mes.
5. Ella no confía en mí. ¿Por qué será?
6. ¿Para qué le estás poniendo miel a tu cereal?
7. ¿Con qué va Ud. a comer sus waffles?
8. Por favor páguele a la cajera.
9. ¿Por qué no renunciaría?
10. Cuente esos boletos antes de repartirlos.

EXERCISE 11

Answer the following questions.

1. Did you take advantage of the time?
2. Will you take advantage of your vacation?
3. Are you going to take advantage of this opportunity?

124

4. Did the waiter take your order?
5. Has the waitress taken your order?
6. Is the waiter going to take your order?
7. When will the meeting take place?
8. Where did the meeting take place?
9. What time is the meeting going to take place?
10. Who is going to take charge of the meeting?

Answer the following questions, using **have got** *in the affirmative.*

11. Do you have lots of free time?
12. Do they have any daughters?
13. Do you have any more bread in the kitchen?
14. Do you have to leave very soon?
15. Does John have to go with you?

Lección 1

Vocabulary

1. **to plant, planted, planted** plantar; sembrar
2. **to mash, mashed, mashed** machacar
3. **to propose (to), proposed (to), proposed (to)** proponer; proponer matrimonio
4. **to attend, attended, attended** asistir (a)
5. **to marry, married, married** casarse con
6. **to congratulate, congratulated, congratulated** felicitar
   congratulations felicitaciones
7. **dessert** postre
8. **desert** desierto
9. **vinegar** vinagre
10. **catsup** salsa dulce de jitomate
11. **pie** pay
    pie crust pasta (*del pay*)
12. **filling** relleno
13. **custard** flan
14. **pudding** pudín

15. **choice** selección
16. **gravy** salsa, jugo (*de carne*)
17. **cinnamon** canela
18. **salad** ensalada
    fruit salad ensalada de frutas
    tuna salad ensalada de atún
    potato salad ensalada de papas
19. **mustard** mostaza
20. **mayonnaise** mayonesa
21. **bowl** tazón (*para sopa*)
22. **platter** platón
23. **mashed potatoes** puré de papas
    French fried potatoes papas fritas (*al estilo francés*)
    French fries papas fritas (*al estilo francés*)
    baked potatoes papas al horno
    potato chips hojuelas de papa

126

24. **day off** día libre, día de descanso	**rudeness** mala educación, falta de educación
25. **rude** mal educado, grosero	

IDIOMS

1. **to be supposed (infinitive)** deber (infinitivo)
   He's supposed to come at five. Debe venir a las cinco.
   He was supposed to come at five. Debió (Debía) venir a las cinco.
2. **to beat, beat, beaten someone** ganar a alguien
   He beat me playing tennis. Me ganó jugando tenis.
   to beat, beat, beaten batir
3. **to get beat** ser derrotado por alguien
   He got beat. Lo derrotaron.
4. **to get a divorce** divorciarse
   He got a divorce. Él se divorció.
   to divorce someone divorciarse de alguien
   He divorced his wife. Se divorció de su mujer.
5. **by the way** a propósito
6. **ahead** adelante
7. **tomorrow night** mañana por la noche
8. **apple pie a la mode** tarta de manzana con helado encima

EXERCISE 1

Practice the following dialogue.

ORDERING LUNCH

Waitress:	May I take your order?
First Customer:	What kind of soup do you have?
Waitress:	We have vegetable, tomato, and potato.
First Customer:	A bowl of tomato soup and a hamburger, please. I don't want onions or mustard on the hamburger.
Waitress:	What do you want to drink? We have coffee, tea, and milk.
First Customer:	Milk, please.
Second Customer:	I want the dinner—vegetable soup and pork chops.
Waitress:	You can have a choice of two of the three vegetables.

127

Second Customer:	Then give me peas and carrots, please.
Waitress:	What do you want do drink? You can have tea, coffee, or milk.
Second Customer:	Hot tea, please—lemon, no cream.
Waitress:	What do you want for dessert—ice cream, pie, or fruit?
Second Customer:	What kind of pie do you have?
Waitress:	Apple, lemon, pineapple, cherry, coconut, banana, custard, pecan, and chocolate.
Second Customer:	Cherry.
Waitress:	Would you like your coffee with the meal or after?
Second Customer:	I've already ordered hot tea.
Third Customer:	I want a vegetable salad, an order of French fries, and a piece of pie.
Waitress:	What kind of pie do you want?
Third Customer:	Apple a la mode—with strawberry ice cream.
Waitress:	Do you want anything to drink?
Third Customer:	Milk, please.

First Customer:	Will you bring me some catsup, please?
Second Customer:	And may I have some more bread?
Waitress:	Certainly. And would you like some more coffee?
Second Customer:	Yes, please, and a little more cream.
Waitress:	Do you want anything else?
Third Customer:	No, Thank you.

EXERCISE 2

Learn these words.

WORDS CONNECTED WITH WEDDINGS

1. **anniversary** aniversario
2. **best man** padrino (*en la boda*)
3. **boyfriend** novio
4. **bride** novia (*en la boda*)
5. **bridesmaid** dama de honor
6. **girlfriend** novia
7. **groom** novio (*en la boda*)
8. **honeymoon** luna de miel, viaje de bodas
9. **maid of honor** madrina (*en la boda*)
10. **proposal (of marriage)** petición matrimonial
11. **veil** velo

128

12. **wedding** boda, casamiento
13. **wedding anniversary** aniversario de boda
14. **wedding cake** pastel de bodas
15. **wedding day** día de la boda
16. **wedding dress (gown)** vestido de novia
17. **wedding march** marcha nupcial
18. **wedding present** regalo de bodas
19. **wedding ring** anillo de boda
20. **to elope** fugarse

EXERCISE 3

Translate the following sentences and practice reading them.

1. It'd been cold.
2. It hadn't been cold.
3. Had it been cold?
4. Hadn't it been cold?
5. When had it been cold?
6. It should be cold.
7. It shouldn't be cold.
8. Should it be cold?
9. Shouldn't it be cold?
10. When should it be cold?
11. It's going to be hot.
12. It isn't going to be hot.
13. Is it going to be hot?
14. Isn't it going to be hot?
15. When is it going to be hot?
16. It was going to be cold.
17. It wasn't going to be cold.
18. Was it going to be cold?
19. Wasn't it going to be cold?
20. When was it going to be cold?
21. We're usually hungry.
22. We aren't usually hungry.
23. Are we usually hungry?
24. Aren't we usually hungry?
25. Why are we usually hungry?

EXERCISE 4

Translate the following sentences. Change them to the negative, interrogative, and interrogative negative.

1. You're supposed to be there at three o'clock.
2. He was supposed to work yesterday.
3. They're supposed to pay me on Friday.
4. She's supposed to let us know.
5. I'm supposed to wait for them.
6. You were supposed to introduce us.
7. We were supposed to have met them here.
8. Mr. Nelson is supposed to take charge.
9. My watch is supposed to be fast.
10. That waiter is supposed to take your order.

EXERCISE 5

Give the past tense and past participle of the following verbs.

study	shout (at)	sound	slice
satisfy	smell	spill	serve
save	smile (at)	stay	shave
seem	smoke	suffer	step (on)
sew	snow	surprise	swallow

EXERCISE 6

Give the past tense and past participle of the following verb.

take a sun bath	understand	wake up	become
take advan- tage of	wear	wet	bet
take your order	win	beat	be worth
	write	be	bleed
	wear out	be over	blow
	weave	be supposed	

EXERCISE 7

Verb Practice *Expand the following verb practice, using different tenses.*

1. The farmers should have planted the corn.

130

2. The farmers shouldn't have planted the corn.
3. Should the farmers have planted the corn?
4. Shouldn't the farmers have planted the corn?
5. Where should the farmers have planted the corn?

EXERCISE 8

Verb Practice *Make short sentences with forms of the verbs* **mash**, **propose (to)**, **get a divorce**, **divorce someone**, **elope**, **attend**, **marry**, **congratulate**, **beat**, **get beat**. *Expand each verb practice to include different tenses, as in the exercise above. Use a different noun or pronoun with each verb. Use the interrogative words when it is possible.*

EXERCISE 9

Translate into Spanish.

1. Aren't you supposed to keep the children from playing in the street?
2. Did you say the Yankees got beat yesterday? Yes, the Giants beat them.
3. By the way, what do you plan to do tomorrow night?
4. If they're in a hurry, let them go ahead. We'll come later.
5. How long did it take you to get a divorce?
6. My mother just told me that you're going to marry Jenny. Congratulations to both of you.
7. Don't tell anyone what I said. I wasn't supposed to say anything about it.
8. You should have got a haircut on your day off.
9. Tony has just left. He wanted to go to the bank to see if he could borrow some money.
10. Henry must have forgotten that this is his wedding aniversary.
11. I won't be able to attend Jane's wedding. Will you?
12. Joan forgot to congratulate Dick, and I did too.
13. We haven't had breakfast yet, and they haven't either.
14. You shouldn't have taken advantage of that old man.
15. We plan to spend our honeymoon in Acapulco, and so do they.

EXERCISE 10

Translate into English.

1. ¿A dónde te gustaría ir de viaje de bodas?

2. Él no se disculpó por su falta de educación.
3. Creo que me casaré con Tomás. Me propuso matrimonio anoche.
4. Ud. tendrá que batir los huevos y hacer el puré de papas.
5. No me gustan las papas al estilo francés, ¿y a ti?
6. De todos modos, lo veremos mañana.
7. El mesero debió haberle servido café con la comida.
8. Ella se quemó mientras estaba tomando un baño de sol.
9. ¿Quién ganó el juego? Mi hermana le ganó a ella.
10. No he podido averiguar cuándo se verificará la boda, ni ella tampoco.

EXERCISE 11

Answer the following questions.

1. Are you supposed to be there tomorrow?
2. Was he supposed to pick you up?
3. Were they supposed to help you?
4. Did you take a trip last August?
5. Do you take a trip every summer?
6. Will you take a trip when you get your vacation?
7. Would you take a trip if you had enough money?
8. Would you like to take a trip to Mexico?
9. Whose house is that?
10. Do you know whose house that is?
11. Whose baby is that?
12. Do you know whose baby that is?
13. Whose car is that?
14. Do you know whose car that is?
15. Whose book is this?

Lección 18

Vocabulary

1. **to offer, offered, offered** ofrecer
2. **to suggest, suggested, suggested** sugerir
3. **to pour, poured, poured** servir o vaciar (*líquido*)
4. **to pour (something) out, poured (something) out, poured (something) out** tirar (*líquido*)
5. **to plan, planned, planned** planear; pensar
6. **to enjoy, enjoyed, enjoyed** gozar de, disfrutar de
7. **to belch, belched, belched** eructar
8. **head waiter** jefe de meseros, capitán
9. **host** anfitrión **hostess** anfitriona; encargada (*de un restaurant*)
10. **guest** invitado
11. **cocktail** cocktail
12. **manager** gerente
13. **crowded** concurrido
14. **whipped cream** crema batida
15. **fireplace** chimenea (*del cuarto*)
16. **banquet** banquete
17. **well-known** (*adj.*) bien conocido
18. **salary** sueldo
19. **witch** bruja
20. **ghost** fantasma
21. **hall** pasillo; corredor
22. **tiresome** aburrido, fastidioso
23. **moss** musgo
24. **battle** batalla
25. **expensive** caro; costoso
26. **mouthful** bocado; bocanada; buche
27. **appetite** apetito
28. **mold** moho **moldy** mohoso

133

IDIOMS

1. **to have a dress, suit, pair of shoes, etc. made** mandar hacerse un vestido, traje, par de zapatos, etc.
2. **to get behind** atrasarse
   I got behind in my work. Me atrasé en mi trabajo.
   I'm behind in my work. Estoy atrasado en mi trabajo.
3. **to take (something) back** devolver o regresar (algo)
   He bought a hat, but then he took it back. Compró un sombrero, pero después lo devolvió.
4. **to give (something) back** devolver o regresar (algo)
   If you don't want my present, give it back to me. Si no quieres mi regalo, devuélvemelo.
5. **Is anything wrong?** ¿Pasa algo malo? ¿Qué pasa?
6. **You can't miss it.** No se puede equivocar, No se puede perder.
7. **How can you tell them apart?** ¿Cómo puede distinguirlos?
8. **well done** bien cocido
   medium medio cocido
   rare casi crudo, poco cocido, rojo, a la inglesa

EXERCISE 1

Practice the following dialogue.

ORDERING DINNER

Hostess:	How many, please?
First Customer:	A table for two, please.
Hostess:	This way, please. Would you like a drink before you have dinner?
First Customer:	No, thank you.
Hostess:	Here's a menu. A waiter will take your order right away.
First Customer:	Thank you.
Waiter:	Would you like to order now?
First Customer:	Yes, please. I want an oyster cocktail and a T-bone steak.
Waiter:	How do you want your steak?
First Customer:	Well done.
Waiter:	What would you like to drink?

First Customer:	Coffee, please. And could I have it now?
Waiter:	Certainly. Do you want any dessert?
First Customer:	Yes, ice cream and cake, please.
Second Customer:	I want fruit cocktail and fried chicken.
Waiter:	What would you like to drink?
Second Customer:	Tea, please, with lemon; and for dessert I want strawberries with whipped cream.

———

Waiter:	Is anything wrong?
First Customer:	Yes, I ordered my steak well done, and you brought it rare. Will you please take it back to the kitchen and cook it a little more?
Waiter:	Of course. I'm very sorry, sir.
Second Customer:	May I have a little more water, please?
Waiter:	Yes, certainly.

———

Hostess:	I hope you enjoyed your dinner. Please come back again soon.
First Customer:	Thank you, we will.
Second Customer:	Thank you.

EXERCISE 2

Learn these words.

WORDS CONNECTED WITH THE BULLFIGHTS

1. **bull** toro
2. **bullfight** corrida de toros
3. **bullfighter** torero
4. **bullring** arena
5. **cape** capa
6. **pass** pase
7. **sword** estoque; espada
8. **to go to the bullfights** ir a los toros
9. **to gore** empitonar, cornear, coger
10. **to get gored** ser empitonado, ser corneado, ser cogido

EXERCISE 3

Translate the following sentences and practice reading them.

1. He was rarely sleepy.

2. He wasn't ever sleepy.
3. Was he sometimes sleepy?
4. Wasn't he often sleepy?
5. Why was he always sleepy?
6. They'll be hungry.
7. They won't be hungry.
8. Will they be hungry?
9. Won't they be hungry?
10. When will they be hungry?
11. She'll be thirsty.
12. She won't be thirsty.
13. Will she be thirsty?
14. Won't she be thirsty?
15. Why will she be thirsty?
16. They'd be hungry.
17. They wouldn't be hungry.
18. Would they be hungry?
19. Wouldn't they be hungry?
20. Why would they be hungry?
21. You ought to be thirsty.
22. You shouldn't be thirsty.
23. Should you be thirsty?
24. Shouldn't you be thirsty?
25. Why should you be thirsty?

EXERCISE 4

Translate the following sentences. Change them to the negative, interrogative, and interrogative negative.

1. I'm going to have a suit made.
2. He has all his shoes made.
3. They had their dresses made.
4. You've had two suits made this month.
5. We'll have our hats made.
6. She wants me to have a coat made.
7. We told her to have a hat made.
8. Walter should have a suit made.
9. Marge is having a skirt and blouse made.
10. Judith said she could have a pair of slacks made.

136

EXERCISE 5

Give the past tense and past participle of the following verbs.

sign	scratch	turn on	turn
suggest	talk	test	turn over
soak	translate	tie	trim your
smear	try	touch	moustache,
sterilize	turn off	travel	beard
		try hard	taste

EXERCISE 6

Give the past tense and past participle of the following verbs.

build	bring	be operated	beat
be	buy	on	come
become	bite	blow your	come back
begin	be missing	nose	cut a tooth
break	be out of	break out	catch
		be supposed	go dancing

EXERCISE 7

Verb Practice *Expand the following verb practice, using different tenses.*

1. The cook should have offered you coffee.
2. The cook shouldn't have offered you coffee.
3. Should the cook have offered you coffee?
4. Shouldn't the cook have offered you coffee?
5. How much coffee should the cook have offered you?

EXERCISE 8

Verb Practice *Make short sentences with forms of the verbs* suggest, pour, pour (something) out, plan, enjoy, belch, have (something) made, get behind, take (something) back, go to the bullfights, gore, get gored. *Expand each verb practice to include different tenses, as in the exercise above. Use a different noun or pronoun with each verb. Use the interrogative words when it is possible.*

137

EXERCISE 9

Translate into Spanish.

1. Where did you have your dress made?
2. If you don't come to class every day, you'll get behind.
3. Please take this book back to the library for me.
4. How can you tell the twins apart?
5. The book store is two blocks down the street. You can't miss it.
6. If anything is wrong. I'll let you know.
7. He got so far behind that he couldn't go on with the class.
8. I have to have my shoes made. The ones I buy in the stores don't fit me very well.
9. If the jacket you bought doesn't fit, return it and get your money back.
10. My husband didn't order his steak well done, and I didn't either.
11. Maybe we should complain to the manager about this terrible service.
12. I can't tell those boys apart, can you?
13. He got a small raise, and so did I.
14. Don't tell me that you got beat again.
15. Will you bring me some catsup?

EXERCISE 10

Translate into English.

1. Tal vez el jefe de meseros nos pueda conseguir una mesa.
2. Ud. debió haberle dicho al mesero que le trajera más café.
3. Me hubiera mandado hacer un traje si hubiera tenido dinero.
4. ¿No me quiere servir otra taza de café? Tenga cuidado de no derramarlo.
5. Tire esa agua sucia.
6. ¿Quieres tu bistec bien cocido, medio o poco?
7. Se deben plantar estas semillas en musgo.
8. Conocí al Sr. Beltrán, un autor bien conocido, en Europa.
9. Estaba tan concurrida la tienda que no pudimos entrar.
10. Tu trabajo ha de ser muy aburrido.

EXERCISE 11

Answer the following questions.

138

1. Where did you have your dress made?
2. When did you have your shoes made?
3. Why do you have your hats made?
4. Do you have all your clothes made?
5. Whose glass is this?
6. Do you know whose glass this is?
7. Whose hat is this?
8. Do you know whose hat this is?
9. Whose coat is this?
10. Do you know whose coat this is?
11. Who runs that beauty shop?
12. Who runs that café?
13. Who runs that drugstore?
14. Who runs that restaurant?
15. Is the bread moldy?

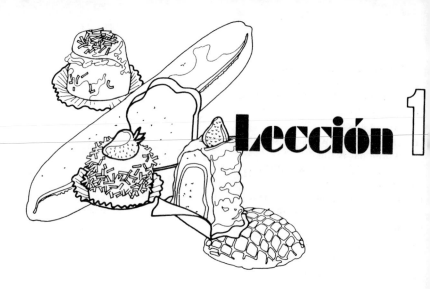

Lección 1

Vocabulary

1. **to gather (up), gathered (up), gathered (up)**
   juntar y recoger
2. **to beg, begged, begged**
   rogar, suplicar; pedir limosna
3. **to float, floated, floated** flotar
4. **to reduce, reduced, reduced**
   reducir; bajar de peso, adelgazar
5. **to crush, crushed, crushed**
   aplastar, machucar; machacar
6. **to admit, admitted, admitted**
   admitir
7. **bakery** panadería
8. **baker** panadero
9. **dough** masa
10. **cracker** galleta (*salada*)
11. **cooky** galleta (*dulce*)
12. **cup cake** panqué
13. **doughnut** dona
14. **whole wheat bread** pan de trigo entero

a sliced rye un pan de centeno rebanado
slice rebanada
15. **corn bread** pan de maíz
16. **flour** harina
17. **corn meal** harina de maíz
18. **baking powder** polvo de hornear
19. **yeast** levadura
20. **eggwhite** clara
21. **eggyolk** yema
22. **frosting** betún
   icing betún
23. **roll** bolillo
24. **biscuit** bisquet
25. **oven** horno
26. **layer** piso (*de pastel*)
27. **fresh bread** pan caliente; pan del día
28. **stale (*bread, cake*)** duro, seco, viejo

140

IDIOMS

1. **had better** sería mejor, más vale
   You'd better go. Sería mejor que te fueras.
   You'd better not lose it. Vale más que no lo pierdas.
2. **to itch** tener comezón
   My nose itches. Tengo comezón en la nariz.
3. **to gain weight** aumentar de peso
4. **to lose weight** perder peso
5. **to go on a diet** ponerse a dieta
   to be on a diet estar a dieta
6. **might as well** es mejor que, de una vez
   You might as well come, since you have nothing to do. Es mejor que vengas, puesto que no tienes nada que hacer.
   I might as well not go on a diet; I won't lose any weight. Mejor no me pongo a dieta; No bajaré de peso.
   Since I have the money, I might as well pay you. Puesto que tengo el dinero, de una vez le pago.
7. **It'll (they'll) do.** Servirá (n).
8. **How can you tell it (them) from _____?** ¿Cómo puede distinguirlo (los) de _____?
9. **That's it.** Eso es.
10. **God bless you.** Salud. (*al estornudar*)

EXERCISE 1

Practice the following dialogue.

AT THE BAKERY

Baker: Have you been waited on?
Customer: Do you have any fresh rolls?
Baker: No, we're out of fresh rolls right now. There'll be some out of the oven in about thirty minutes. If you'll leave your address, the boy can deliver them to you then.
Customer: All right. And since he's going to deliver the rolls, he might as well deliver the whole order.
Baker: Of course. What else would you like?
Customer: I want a chocolate cake with white frosting.
Baker: The cake on the end with white frosting is chocolate.

141

Customer:	That one seems a little too big. They dry out so fast if they aren't eaten right away. Do you have a smaller one like it?
Baker:	No, all our cakes are the same size, except the wedding cakes, which are much bigger.
Customer:	Well, I guess it'll do.
Baker:	We have some fresh doughnuts now. Would you like some of them?
Customer:	Yes, give me about a dozen with chocolate icing.
Baker:	Will there be anything else?
Customer:	I want two loaves of white bread, a loaf of whole wheat bread, and a sliced rye.
Baker:	Is that all?
Customer:	Yes, that's all. When can you deliver these things?
Baker:	They'll be there in an hour.
Customer:	All right. But wrap the cake carefully and be sure not to crush the frosting.
Baker:	I'll take care of it. Don't worry.
Customer:	How much do I owe you?
Baker:	That'll be $ 4.00. Thank you and come back again.

EXERCISE 2

Learn these words.

WORDS CONNECTED WITH RELIGION

1. **altar** altar
2. **archbishop** arzobispo
3. **baptism** bautismo; bautizo
4. **Bible** Biblia
5. **bishop** obispo
6. **cardinal** cardenal
7. **Catholic** católico
8. **choir** coro
9. **Christian** cristiano
10. **communion** comunión
11. **confession** confesión
12. **confessional booth** confesionario
13. **convent** convento
14. **cross** cruz
15. **devil** diablo
16. **holy** sagrado
17. **holy water** agua bendita
18. **hymn** himno
19. **heaven** cielo
20. **hell** infierno
21. **Jesus Christ** Jesucristo
22. **Jewish** (*adj.*) judío
23. **Lent** cuaresma
24. **minister** ministro
25. **monastery** monasterio
26. **monk** monje
27. **nun** monja

142

28. **orthodox** ortodoxo
29. **pastor** pastor
30. **penance** penitencia
31. **pew** banco de iglesia
32. **pilgrim** peregrino
33. **pope** papa
34. **prayer** oración
35. **prayer book** devocionario
36. **preacher** predicador
37. **priest** sacerdote
38. **Protestant** protestante
39. **psalm** salmo
40. **pulpit** púlpito
41. **purgatory** purgatorio
42. **rabbi** rabí
43. **religion** religión
44. **religious** religioso
45. **saint** santo (a)
46. **sermon** sermón
47. **shrine** santuario, lugar sagrado

48. **sin** pecado
49. **sinner** pecador (a)
50. **synagogue** sinagoga
51. **Testament** Testamento
52. **virgin** virgen
53. **to baptize** bautizar
54. **to bless** bendecir
55. **to cross yourself** persignarse; santiguarse
56. **to kneel** arrodillarse
57. **to pray** rezar
58. **to repent** arrepentirse
59. **to sacrifice** sacrificar
60. **to say your prayers** decir las oraciones, rezar
61. **to sin** pecar
62. **to take communion** comulgar
63. **to worship** adorar

EXERCISE 3

Translate the following sentences and practice reading them.

1. You should be warm.
2. You shouldn't be warm.
3. Should you be warm?
4. Shouldn't you be warm?
5. Why should you be warm?
6. I'm going to be thirsty.
7. I'm not going to be thirsty.
8. Am I going to be thirsty?
9. Am I not going to be thirsty?
10. When am I going to be thirsty?
11. Plant the seeds.
12. Don't plant the seeds.
13. Let me plant the seeds.
14. Don't let me plant the seeds.
15. Let her plant the seeds.

143

16. Don't let her plant the seeds.
17. Let them plant the seeds.
18. Don't let them plant the seeds.
19. Let's plant the seeds.
20. Let's not plant the seeds.
21. Let him plant the seeds.
22. Don't let him plant the seeds.

THE AUXILIARY *HAD BETTER*

Had better (sería mejor, más vale) is followed by the infinitive without **to**. It can indicate time in the present or in the future. Notice the examples.

> We had (we'd) better go early.
> We'd better not go early.
> Had we better go early?
> Hadn't we better go early?

EXERCISE 4

Translate the following sentences. Change them to the negative, interrogative, and interrogative negative.

1. He'd better come on Tuesday.
2. She'd better finish before two o'clock.
3. We'd better eat before we go.
4. They'd better stop working.
5. You'd better study your lesson.
6. Marjorie had better marry Louis.
7. Charley had better practice his English.
8. The children had better go to bed early.
9. Ben had better have a new suit made.
10. Virginia had better hurry.

EXERCISE 5

Give the past tense and past participle of the following verbs.

| thank | visit | wash | wrap |
| tarnish | wait (for) | work | weigh |

tip	vomit	watch	wait on
trust	walk	wish	whistle
use	want	worry	brush your teeth

EXERCISE 6

Give the past tense and past participle of the following verbs.

choose	draw	forget	fight
cost	draw interest	fall (down)	find out
do	drive	fall in love	fly
drink	eat	(with)	freeze
dig	find	feed	feel sorry for
			feel like

EXERCISE 7

Verb Practice *Expand the following verb practice, using different tenses.*

1. Those books should be gathered up.
2. Those books shouldn't be gathered up.
3. Should those books be gathered up?
4. Shouldn't those books be gathered up?
5. When should those books be gathered up?

EXERCISE 8

Verb Practice *Make short sentences with forms of the verbs* beg, float, reduce, crush, admit, itch, gain weight, lose weight, go on a diet, be on a diet, baptize, bless, cross yourself, knell, pray, repent, sacrifice, say your prayers, take communion, worship, sin. *Expand each verb practice to include different tenses, as in the exercise above. Use a different noun or pronoun with each verb. Use the interrogative words when it is possible.*

EXERCISE 9

Translate into Spanish.

1. I'd like to lose about ten pounds.
2. How can you tell a Ford from a Buick?

3. How can you tell the first and second books apart?
4. I can't eat potatoes because I'm on a diet.
5. If you want to lose weight, why don't you go on a diet?
6. He lost about ten pounds when he was sick.
7. We might as well go home. I don't think the teacher is going to come.
8. You'd better not eat bread if you don't want to gain weight.
9. These shoes are a little too big for me, but I guess they'll do.
10. I won't be able to have lunch with you. I'm supposed to be on a diet.
11. I think I'll have a cake made for my husband's birthday.
12. He told her she was too fat and that she'd better reduce.
13. I don't think he'll break out in a rash.
14. Since you've got to do it, you might as well start now.
15. My wife has been running this business for ten years.

EXERCISE 10

Translate into English.

1. Algunos indios acostumbraban adorar al sol.
2. Debes hacer que los niños digan sus oraciones antes de acostarse.
3. Tengo comezón en la espalda.
4. Hemos sido invitados a un bautismo, ¿y tú?
5. Parece que has perdido peso.
6. ¿Sabe Ud. de quién es este reloj?
7. Sería mejor que no dejaras tu bicicleta afuera.
8. ¿Cómo puede Ud. distinguir sus calcetines de los de él?
9. ¿Crees que este vestido oscuro servirá para la boda?
10. Me dan lástima las personas que tienen que estar a dieta todo el tiempo.

EXERCISE 11

Answer the following questions.

1. Do you know who runs that bakery?
2. Do you know who runs that hotel?
3. Do you know who runs that café?
4. Did you run out of gas?
5. Will you run out of water?
6. Have you run out of food?
7. Has he run out of milk?

8. Have they run out of potatoes?
9. Did you gain weight?
10. Did you lose weight?
11. Hadn't you better go now?
12. Hadn't they better go before it rains?
13. Hadn't he better work on Saturday?
14. Hadn't she better save her money?
15. Hadn't you better start studying?

Vocabulary

1. **to analyze, analyzed, analyzed** analizar
2. **to fire, fired, fired** despedir (*del empleo*)
3. **to forgive, forgave, forgiven** perdonar
4. **to suppose, supposed, supposed** suponer
5. **to iron, ironed, ironed** planchar
6. **to discuss, discussed, discussed** discutir, hablar de
7. **bar** bar, cantina
8. **bartender** cantinero
9. **floor show** variedad (*de un club de noche*)
10. **whiskey** whiskey
    straight whiskey whiskey solo
11. **beer** cerveza
12. **wine** vino
13. **rum** ron
14. **gin** ginebra
15. **row** hilera
16. **tourist** turista
17. **success** éxito
18. **stool** taburete
19. **stingy** avaro, tacaño
20. **sample** muestra
21. **bottle opener** destapador
    corkscrew sacacorcho
22. **alcoholic** alcohólico
23. **hail** granizo
24. **fog** niebla
25. **mist** neblina

IDIOMS

1. **to apply for** hacer una solicitud para, solicitar
2. **to have a hangover** estar crudo

148

3. **to get fired** ser despedido de un empleo
   She got fired. La despidieron.
4. **to be successful** tener éxito
5. **to run the risk** correr el riesgo, arriesgar
   I can't run the risk. No puedo correr el riesgo.
6. **a shot of whiskey** una copa de whiskey
7. **Forgive me.** Perdóneme Ud.
8. **I'm single.** Soy soltera (o).
9. **the night before last** anteanoche
10. **cover charge** derecho de mesa
11. **beer on tap** cerveza de barril

EXERCISE 1

Practice the following dialogue.

AT A BAR

Waiter:	Would you like to sit at a table or at the bar?
First Customer:	We'll sit at the bar.
Bartender:	What would you like?
First Customer:	I want a whiskey and soda—without ice.
Bartender:	Scotch or bourbon?
First Customer:	Scotch.
Second Customer:	Give me a shot of whiskey with water on the side.
Third Customer:	I'll have a bottle of beer.
First Customer:	Will you put a little more soda in my drink, please.
Bartender:	Certainly.
Second Customer:	Do you have a floor show here?
Bartender:	Yes, there's a floor show at ten-thirty, twelve-thirty, and two.
Third Customer:	Give me another beer, please.
Bartender:	The same kind?
Third Customer:	Yes.
Bartender:	Do you want another drink?
First Customer:	Yes, please.
Bartender:	What were you drinking?
First Customer:	Scotch and soda.
Bartender:	Would you like another drink too?
Second Customer:	No, thank you. Not yet. Will you give me all three checks, please.

149

Bartender:	There'll be a floor show in half an hour if you'd like to wait.
Second Customer:	I'm sorry. I can't stay. I have another engagement.
Bartender:	Please pay the cashier. Come back again.

EXERCISE 2

Learn these words.

SUPPLEMENTARY VOCABULARY

1. **apology** disculpa
2. **arrangement** arreglo
3. **attendance** asistencia
4. **beggar** mendigo
5. **braid** trenza
6. **brush** brocha, cepillo
7. **congratulations** felicitaciones
8. **dye** tinte
9. **imagination** imaginación
10. **offer** oferta
11. **plant** planta
12. **polish** grasa
13. **printer** impresor
14. **press** prensa
15. **recommendation** recomendación
16. **resignation** renuncia
17. **suggestion** sugerencia
18. **sterilization** esterilización
19. **tip** propina

EXERCISE 3

Translate the following sentences and practice reading them.

1. What were you dreaming about?
2. What did you dream about?
3. What will you dream about?
4. What would you like to dream about?
5. What's he complaining about?
6. What was he complaining about?
7. What did he complain about?
8. What has he complained about?
9. Who are they talking to?
10. Who were they talking to?
11. Who did they talk to?
12. Who have they talked to?
13. Who did she go with?
14. Who did she come with?
15. What's the book about?

16. What was the book about?
17. What's the movie about?
18. What was the movie about?
19. What's the lesson about?
20. What was the lesson about?
21. What are you doing that for?
22. What were you doing that for?
23. What did you do that for?
24. What will you do that for?
25. What would you do that for?
26. Before going on a diet, you should see the doctor.
27. After going on a diet, you should see the doctor.
28. Instead of going on a diet, you should see the doctor.
29. In spite of going on a diet, he gained weight.
30. Without going on a diet, he lost weight.

EXERCISE 4

Translate the following sentences. Change them to the negative, interrogative, and interrogative negative.

1. He applies for work.
2. They applied for a loan.
3. You should apply for that job.
4. We were going to apply for work in an office.
5. She'll apply for a job teaching school.
6. Joan applied for work in the factory.
7. The boys have applied for work everywhere.
8. Edward's boss applied for a better job.
9. The girls should apply for work in the country.
10. Many people are applying for this job.

EXERCISE 5

Give the past tense and past participle of the following verbs.

wash your	answer	agree	analyze
mouth out	arrive	appear	arrange
wonder	ask	attack	apologize
worship	add	avoid	attend
x-ray	admire	arrest	believe
			telephone

EXERCISE 6

Give the past tense and past participle of the following verbs.

get angry (at)	get here	go	get better
get mad (at)	(there)	go back	get worse
get rich	get thirsty	go out	get dark
get sleepy	get up	go to bed late	get drunk
get to	give	go to sleep	get hurt
	give up	get away	get up early

EXERCISE 7

Verb Practice *Expand the following verb practice, using different tenses.*

1. Your thoughts should be analyzed.
2. Your thoughts shouldn't be analyzed.
3. Should your thoughts be analyzed?
4. Shouldn't your thoughts be analyzed?
5. Why should your thoughts be analyzed?

EXERCISE 8

Verb Practice *Make short sentences with forms of the verbs* **fire, forgive, suppose, iron, discuss, apply for, have a hangover, be successful, get fired, run the risk.** *Expand each verb practice to include different tenses, as in the exercise above. Use a different noun or pronoun with each verb. Use the interrogative words when it is possible.*

EXERCISE 9

Translate into Spanish.

1. If you're late to work again, the boss is going to fire you.
2. I had such a hangover after the party that I couldn't work the next day.
3. He's very successful in whatever he does.
4. I suppose they'll be early. At least I hope they will.
5. They don't like to drink, and he doesn't either.
6. If you don't stop drinking, you're going to get drunk.
7. He was fired because he came to work drunk.

152

8. What's their new house like?
9. She had an appointment with Mr. Graves the day before yesterday.
10. Sweet drinks will make you gain weight.
11. Before I went on a diet. I weighed almost 200 pounds.
12. If you come to class every day, you won't get behind.
13. I feel sorry for alcoholics.
14. My watch stopped last night.
15. We went on a picnic last Thursday.

EXERCISE 10

Translate into English.

1. Este ron debería mezclarse con Coca-Cola.
2. ¿Por qué te despidieron?
3. Quisiera que me plancharas esta blusa.
4. Debimos haber tenido una fiesta el día de tu cumpleaños.
5. ¿Vio Ud. a esa mujer que estaba pidiendo limosna en la calle?
6. Voy a hacer una solicitud para un trabajo en la compañía General Motors.
7. Tomé mucho en la fiesta anoche, y ahora estoy crudo.
8. Voy a ponerme los shorts y tomar un baño de sol.
9. ¿Cómo prefiere su whiskey—con soda, agua o solo?
10. ¿Es casada o soltera?

EXERCISE 11

Answer the following questions.

1. What's her new dress like?
2. What's his new car like?
3. What's his wife like?
4. What's her boy friend like?
5. What's Mexico City like?
6. Did you run around with George?
7. Did you run around much at night?
8. Did you run around town?
9. Did you run around much after work?
10. Did he run over the dog?
11. Did he run over the children?

12. Did he run over the cat?
13. Was he successful?
14. Was the business successful?
15. Will he be successful?
16. Did you apply for the job?
17. Will you apply for work?
18. Have you applied for work?
19. Did you get fired or did you quit?
20. Are they going to fire him?
21. Do you have a hangover?
22. Won't you have a hangover if you drink straight whiskey?

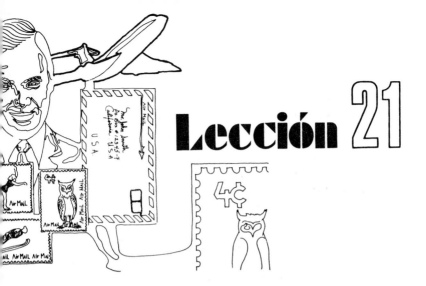

Lección 21

Vocabulary

1. **to mail, mailed, mailed** mandar por correo
2. **to register, registered, registered** certificar; inscribir (se)
3. **to seal, sealed, sealed** cerrar (*carta*)
4. **to address, addressed, addressed** poner nombre y dirección; rotular
5. **to recognize, recognized, recognized** reconocer
6. **stamp** estampilla, timbre
7. **post card** tarjeta postal
8. **parcel post** servicio de paquetes postales
9. **air**-mail (*adj.*) correo aéreo
10. **alive** vivo
11. **postmaster** administrador de correos
    post-office clerk empleado postal
12. **mailbox** buzón

13. **post office** oficina de correos
14. **night letter** carta nocturna
15. **telegram** telegrama
16. **money order** giro postal
17. **envelope** sobre
    stamped envelope sobre timbrado
18. **stationery** papel y sobre
    stationery store papelería
19. **return address** remite; remitente
20. **special delivery** entrega inmediata
21. **nearly** casi
22. **string** cordón
23. **matter** asunto
24. **factory** fábrica
25. **glue** cola, pegamento, goma líquida
26. **paste** engrudo

IDIOMS

1. **to be well off** ser acomodado, tener buena posición
2. **to give (something) back** devolver (algo)
3. **to insure a package** certificar un paquete
4. **to stick, stuck, stuck** pegar
   to stick something on pegar algo
   Stick the stamp on the envelope. Pégale el timbre al sobre.
5. **to fall asleep** dormirse (*conseguir dormirse*)
   I went to bed very early, but I didn't fall asleep until very late.
   Me acosté muy temprano, pero no me dormí hasta muy tarde.
6. **registered letter** carta certificada
7. **a three-cent stamp** un timbre de tres centavos
   a five-room apartment un departamento de cinco piezas
   a two-story building una casa de dos pisos
8. **Shut up.** Cállese.
   Shut your mouth. Cállese la boca.

EXERCISE 1

Practice the following dialogue.

AT THE POST OFFICE

Post-office clerk: What can I do for you?

Customer: How much are air-mail stamps?

Post-office clerk: Six cents each.

Customer: Will this letter go for six cents?

Post-office clerk: Let me weigh it, and I can tell you. Yes, it'll go for six cents.

Customer: How much will it cost me to mail these Christmas cards?

Post-office clerk: You can send them for two cents each if the envelopes aren't sealed. If you seal them, it'll cost you three cents apiece.

Customer: They aren't sealed.

Post-office clerk: How many do you have?

Customer: I'll need twenty two-cent stamps, four three-cent stamps, and one air-mail stamp.

156

Post-office clerk:	Is that all?
Customer:	Do you have any stamped envelopes?
Post-office clerk:	**Yes, they're four cents each.**
Customer:	Give me half a dozen and half a dozen post cards. How much is that?
Post-office clerk:	That'll be eighty-eight cents. I notice that the air-mail stamp didn't stick on your letter very well. I'll put some more glue on it.
Customer:	Thank you. Oh, I forgot to put the return address on it. Will you give it back to me for a minute, please.
Post-office clerk:	Is everything all right now?
Customer:	Yes. Thank you very much. Oh, by the way, I have to mail a package later. How late do you stay open?
Post-office clerk:	We're open until six. Be sure and tie your package well before bringing it in.
Customer:	I will. Thank you.

EXERCISE 2

Learn these words.

GOVERNMENTAL TERMS

1. **bill** decreto
2. **Communism** comunismo
3. **communist** comunista
   Communist (*partido*) comunista
4. **Congress** Congreso
5. **congressman** diputado
6. **count** conde
   countess condesa
7. **democracy** democracia
8. **democrat** demócrata
9. **Democrat** (*partido*) demócrata
10. **dictator** dictador
11. **duchess** duquesa
    duke duque
12. **government** gobierno
13. **governor** gobernador
14. **king** rey
15. **queen** reina
16. **political party** partido político
17. **prince** príncipe
    princess princesa
18. **representative** diputado
19. **republic** república
20. **republican** republicano
    Republican (*partido*) republicano
21. **Senate** Senado
    senator senador
22. **Supreme Court** Suprema Corte

157

EXERCISE 3

Translate the following sentences and practice reading them.

1. I apologize, but he doesn't.
2. I don't apologize, but he does.
3. They apologized, but we didn't.
4. They didn't apologize, but we did.
5. You've apologized, but she hasn't.
6. You haven't apologized, but she has.
7. You would apologize, but I wouldn't.
8. You wouldn't apologize, but I would.
9. He ought to apologize, but she shouldn't.
10. He shouldn't apologize, but she ought to.
11. We should have apologized, but they shouldn't have.
12. We shouldn't have apologized, but they should have.
13. You're going to apologize, but he isn't.
14. You aren't going to apologize, but he is.
15. She wanted to apologize, but I didn't.
16. She didn't want to apologize, but I did.
17. I told them to apologize, but she didn't.
18. I didn't tell them to apologize, but she did.
19. He was going to tell you to apologize, but I wasn't.
20. He wasn't going to tell you to apologize, but I was.
21. I apologized. Didn't you?
22. I didn't apologize. Did you?
23. He'll apologize. Won't she?
24. He won't apologize. Will she?
25. We want to apologize. Don't they?
26. We don't want to apologize. Do they?
27. You'll be able to apologize. Won't they?
28. You won't be able to apologize. Will they?
29. They would have apologized. Wouldn't he?
30. They wouldn't have apologized. Would he?

EXERCISE 4

Translate the following sentences. Change them to the negative, interrogative, and interrogative negative.

1. My grandfather was well off.
2. His family is well off.

158

3. They'll be well off someday.
4. The Dixon family used to be well off.
5. She's supposed to be well off.
6. Many of their relatives have been well off.
7. Your father should have been well off.
8. His uncle would have been well off.
9. He wants to be well off like his friends.
10. We used to be well off.

EXERCISE 5

Give the past tense and past participle of the following verbs.

boil	belong	braid	call
bother	bore	belch	change
burn	borrow	beg	clean
bury	brush	baptize	close
bake	bleach	bless	complete

EXERCISE 6

Give the past tense and past participle of the following verbs.

get in	get old	get scared	go on
get light	get on	get sick	go shopping
get lost	get out	get tired	go with
get off	get ready	get wet	grow
get married	get rid of	get worse	grind

EXERCISE 7

Verb Practice *Expand the following verb practice, using different tenses.*

1. This package was mailed.
2. This package wasn't mailed.
3. Was this package mailed?
4. Wasn't this package mailed?
5. When was this package mailed?

EXERCISE 8

Verb Practice *Make short sentences with forms of the verbs* **register, seal, address, stick, stick something on, recognize, be well off, give (something)**

back, insure a package, fall asleep. *Expand each verb practice to include different tenses, as in the exercise above. Use a different noun or pronoun with each verb. Use the interrogative words when it is possible.*

EXERCISE 9

Translate into Spanish.

1. You should marry a man who is well off.
2. What's Helen's wedding gown like?
3. You'll have to give that money back.
4. You'd better take that letter back to the post office.
5. Did you apply for a job as a post-office clerk?
6. How much weight did you lose while you were on a diet?
7. You'll have to have a box made to send your books in.
8. How can you tell real diamonds from synthetic ones?
9. My wife can't tell a last year's Ford from this year's, but I can.
10. He doesn't take advantage of the opportunities that his father gives him, and his brother doesn't either.
11. I hope you have a good time on your vacation.
12. Do you know how to play the piano?
13. The bus had an accident in front of my house.
14. He hung up before I could say good-bye.
15. I couldn't finish my new dress because I ran out of thread.

EXERCISE 10

Translate into English.

1. ¿Hará juego esta bolsa con tus zapatos?
2. Tenía mucho sueño pero no me pude dormir hasta la una de la mañana.
3. Ud. no debe discutir este asunto delante de los niños.
4. Quiero que certifique Ud. este paquete y esta carta.
5. ¿Cuándo te inscribiste para tomar clases de inglés?
6. ¿Cuántas tarjetas postales le quedan a Ud?
7. ¿Llegará este paquete a Chicago para el miércoles si lo mando hoy?
8. Se me olvidó poner el remitente en todas las cartas.
9. Vamos a ponerle un telegrama el día de su cumpleaños.
10. No importa lo que diga el administrador de correos.
11. No deberías mandar esta carta entrega inmediata.

EXERCISE 11

Answer the following questions.

1. Are you well off?
2. Are your parents well off?
3. Is your father-in-law well off?
4. Do you feel sorry for beggars?
5. Did you feel sorry for those children?
6. Do you feel sorry for the maid?
7. Did you feel sorry for Robert?
8. Would you mind helping me?
9. Would you mind going with me?
10. Would you mind coming an hour earlier?
11. Would you mind working late?
12. Would you mind lending me some money?
13. Did the child blow his nose?
14. Will the child blow his nose?
15. Has the child blown his nose?
16. At what time did you finally fall asleep?
17. Do you fall asleep easily?
18. Did he fall asleep as soon as he went to bed?

Lección 2

Vocabulary

1. **to wrinkle, wrinkled, wrinkled** arrugar
2. **to fit, fit, fit** quedar; ajustar; caber
3. **to ruin, ruined, ruined** arruinar; echar a perder
4. **to damage, damaged, damaged** dañar; maltratar
5. **to bark, barked, barked** ladrar
6. **to snore, snored, snored** roncar
7. **style** estilo; moda
8. **charge account** cuenta de crédito
9. **down payment** enganche
10. **solid color** color liso
11. **English cut** corte inglés
12. **single-breasted** abierto, recto
    double-breasted cruzado
13. **light weight material** tela ligera
    heavy weight material tela gruesa
14. **tailor** sastre
15. **fly** bragueta
16. **crease** raya (*del pantalón*)
17. **padding** guata
18. **design** dibujo, diseño
19. **conservative** serio
20. **cuff** valenciana; puño
21. **adventure** aventura
22. **announcement** aviso
23. **anxious** ansioso
24. **channel** canal (*natural*)
    canal canal (*construido*)
25. **uneven** disparejo
26. **harbor** puerto
27. **ever since** desde que

IDIOMS

1. **to bawl (someone) out** regañar (a alguien)

162

He bawled me out. Me regañó.
2. **to try (something) on** probarse (algo)
   Try it on. Pruébeselo.
3. **to look around** curiosear
4. **to hold a crease** conservar la raya (*del pantalón*)
5. **It's too big.** Me queda grande.
   It's too little. Me queda chico.
   It's too loud. Es demasiado chillante.
6. **What did you have in mind?** ¿Qué quería exactamente?
7. **What size do you wear?** ¿Qué talla es Ud?
8. **on sale** en barata
9. **on the installment plan** a plazos
10. **fifteen dollars down** quince dólares de enganche
11. **made to order** hecho a la medida
12. **a good buy** una ganga
13. **I'll take the coat in a little.** Le meteré al saco un poco.
    I'll let the coat out a little. Le sacaré al saco un poco.
14. **Anything else?** ¿Otra cosa?

EXERCISE 1

Practice the following dialogue.

BUYING A SUIT

Salesman: Is anybody taking care of you, sir?
Customer: No, I was just looking around.
Salesman: Is there anything in particular you had in mind?
Customer: Well, I was looking at these summer suits you have on sale.
           They aren't damaged, are they?
Salesman: No, sir. They're on sale because it's the end of the season.
           They're a very good buy. Look. They've been reduced for-
           ty per cent.
Customer: I'd like something light that holds a crease well. Do you have
           anything like that in a single-breasted?
Salesman: Well, here's one in a solid color that's wool and nylon. It's
           been very popular. The only trouble is that we only have
           blue left.
Customer: That's all right. I'd like to try one on, please. I wear size 38.
Salesman: You can use one of the booths over there at the end of the
           store.

163

Customer: It doesn't fit me at all. I look terrible in it.

Salesman: It's much too big for you. Why don't you try on one of these suits. They're light weight; and though they aren't on sale, they're still a good buy. Only $59.50.

Customer: Can I buy it on the installment plan?

Salesman: Yes, if you want to. It's $15.00 down and the rest in monthly payments. Why don't you try on this gray checked one?

Customer: I don't like the design. It's too loud. I'm looking for something more conservative.

Salesman: How about this blue pin-striped suit? It comes in your size.

Customer: It wrinkles in the back, and the trousers are too tight.

Salesman: You need a larger size. This gray flannel is nice and has an English cut. It's very popular. Here. Try it on.

Customer: That fits all right. I like the cut. The sleeves are a bit too long though, aren't they?

Salesman: Yes, but our tailor will fix that in a minute, and he'll also take the coat in a little. It hangs on you a little too much. You're very slim, you know. Do you want him to put more padding in the shoulders?

Customer: No, that would ruin the style.

Salesman: You're right. I don't use much padding myself.

Customer: When will the suit be ready?

Salesman: It'll be ready by next Tuesday.

Customer: That's fine. Then I'll pick it up sometime next week. Thank you.

EXERCISE 2

Learn these words.

NAMES OF MATERIALS

1. **canvas** lona
2. **corduroy** pana
3. **cotton** algodón
4. **felt** fieltro
5. **flannel** franela
6. **gabardine** gabardina
7. **jersey** jersey
8. **lace** encaje
9. **linen** lino
10. **bleached muslin** bramante blanqueado
    unbleached muslin bramante crudo
11. **nylon** nylon

12. **organdy** organdí
13. **rayon** rayón
14. **satin** satín
15. **silk** seda

16. **taffeta** tafeta
17. **velvet** terciopelo
18. **voile** espumilla
19. **wool** lana

EXERCISE 3

Translate the following sentences and practice reading them.

1. He always cheats, and I do too.
2. He doesn't ever cheat, and I don't either.
3. They sometimes cheated, and we did too.
4. They didn't usually cheat, and we didn't either.
5. We'll cheat, and you will too.
6. We won't cheat, and you won't either.
7. You'd cheat, and he would too.
8. You wouldn't cheat, and he wouldn't either.
9. She should cheat, and we should too.
10. She should never cheat, and we shouldn't either.
11. I'll always be able to cheat, and you will too.
12. I won't ever be able to cheat, and you won't either.
13. You've usually been able to cheat, and they have too.
14. You haven't usually been able to cheat, and they haven't either.
15. They're going to cheat, and he is too.
16. They aren't going to cheat, and he isn't either.
17. We're cheating, and she is too.
18. We aren't cheating, and she isn't either.
19. You were cheating, and he was too.
20. You weren't cheating, and he wasn't either.
21. I'll have to congratulate her.
22. I won't have to congratulate her.
23. Will I have to congratulate her?
24. Won't I have to congratulate her?
25. I'd have to congratulate her.
26. I wouldn't have to congratulate her.
27. Would I have to congratulate her?
28. Wouldn't I have to congratulate her?
29. I've had to congratulate her.
30. I haven't had to congratulate her.

EXERCISE 4

Translate the following sentences. Change them to the negative, interrogative, and interrogative negative.

1. She always bawls them out for being late.
2. I bawled them out last night.
3. He'll bawl him out for not finishing the work.
4. We should bawl the children out every day.
5. You felt like bawling us out.
6. They're bawling her out for not working.
7. The boss is going to bawl her out for losing the letter.
8. The teacher has bawled John out for not studying.
9. Her parents would like to bawl her out.
10. The principal had to bawl them out.

EXERCISE 5

Give the past tense and past participle of the following verbs.

capture	cover	comb your hair	cause
change your mind	commit suicide	cross	cough
clap	can	complain	cry
cook	climb	(about)	chew
count	chase	charge	cure
			cheat

EXERCISE 6

Give the past tense and past participle of the following verbs.

give (some-thing)	get a shave	go riding	be over
away	get a shine	go on a trip	be about
go up	get burned	go for a walk,	go out
go down	get excited	ride	go out of
get a haircut	go swimming	get a trim	get up early
	go dancing	get a permanent	

EXERCISE 7

Verb Practice *Expand the following verb practice, using different tenses.*

1. The speaker's clothes were wrinkled.

2. The speaker's clothes weren't wrinkled.
3. Were the speaker's clothes wrinkled?
4. Weren't the speaker's clothes wrinkled?
5. Why were the speaker's clothes wrinkled?

EXERCISE 8

Verb Practice *Make short sentences with forms of the verbs* **fit, ruin, damage, bark, snore, bawl (someone) out, try (something) on, look around, hold a crease.** *Expand verb practice to include different tenses, as in the exercise above. Use a different noun or pronoun with each verb. Use the interrogative words when it is possible.*

EXERCISE 9

Translate into Spanish.

1. What did he bawl you out for?
2. I would never buy a pair of shoes without trying them on.
3. May I help you? No, thank you. We're just looking around.
4. This suit isn't wool. That's why it doesn't hold a crease very well.
5. If he buys anything else on the installment plan, he won't be able. to make the payments.
6. You should have been making payments on the refrigerator instead of spending your money on that car.
7. How often do you have to wind your watch?
8. What's your new jacket like?
9. He has been well off ever since they found oil near his farm.
10. We went on a picnic on the Fourth of July.
11. You had better learn these verbs before you go to class tomorrow.
12. We're supposed to take advantage of every minute of this trip.
13. How long has it been since I met you?
14. The doctor told me I had better have my tonsils taken out.
15. Would you rahter make a dress than a skirt?

EXERCISE 10

Translate into English.

1. Iría de compras si tuviera cuenta de crédito.
2. ¿Cuánto fue el enganche del coche?

3. Porque está maltratado este abrigo, se lo vendo barato.
4. Mi compañero de cuarto ronca tan fuerte que no puedo dormir de noche.
5. ¿Sabe Ud. de lo que trata el aviso?
6. Me probé el traje azul, y como me quedó grande, le tuvieron que meter un poco.
7. Echarás a perder tu vestido si lo lavas en agua caliente.
8. Él no ha podido encontrar un traje que le quede, ni yo tampoco.
9. Acabo de rotular todos estos sobres.
10. Ellos deben decirle a él que no discuta este asunto con nadie.

EXERCISE 11

Answer the following questions.

1. Did you bawl him out?
2. Will you bawl him out?
3. Have you bawled him out?
4. Do you feel like sleeping?
5. Did you feel like eating?
6. Have you felt like going to the movies?
7. Will you feel like working tomorrow?
8. Can you keep them from stealing?
9. Will he keep them from staying?
10. Has he kept them from finishing?
11. Can you make them study?
12. Will he make them leave you alone?
13. Has he made them come on time?
14. Did he make them pay attention?
15. Shouldn't he make them get up early?
16. Do you want to try this suit on?
17. Has she tried the dress on yet?
18. Do you want to look around the store for a while?
19. Do your trousers hold a crease well?
20. Don't you think his suit is too loud?

168

Lección 23

Vocabulary

1. **to load, loaded, loaded** cargar
2. **to unload, unloaded, unloaded** descargar
3. **to increase, increased, increased** aumentar
4. **to roll, rolled, rolled** rodar
5. **to rescue, rescued, rescued** rescatar
6. **to protect, protected, protected** proteger
7. **to blush, blushed, blushed** ruborizarse
8. **dots** puntos
9. **dressing room** vestidor
10. **alteration** compostura
11. **discount** descuento
12. **lining** forro
13. **subject** materia; asunto
14. **honest** honrado

dishonest no honrado
15. **industry** industria
16. **insurance** seguros
17. **tournament** torneo
18. **loyal** leal
19. **paragraph** párrafo
20. **pleasure** gusto, placer
21. **secret** secreto
22. **silent** callado
23. **bashful** vergonzoso, cohibido, tímido
24. **souvenir** recuerdo
25. **port** puerto
26. **saleslady** dependienta, vendedora
 salesman dependiente, vendedor
27. **cool** fresco
28. **mesh** tejido, malla

IDIOMS

1. **to move** cambiarse (*de casa*), mudarse (*de casa*)

169

2. **to change clothes** cambiarse de ropa
3. **to give a discount** hacer un descuento
4. **at the top of my (your, his, etc.) voice** a grito abierto
5. **Come this way, please.** Por aquí, por favor.
6. **It's too short.** Me queda corto.
   It's too long. Me queda largo.
   It's too tight. Me queda apretado, Me aprieta.
   It's too loose. Me queda ancho.
7. **awful** terrible, horrible, pésimo
   awfully terriblemente, muy
   The movie was awful. La película estuvo pésima.
   I'm awfully tired. Estoy cansadísimo.
8. **The + comp. + sub. + verb, the + comp. + sub. + verb** mientras
   + suj. + verbo, mientras + comp. + suj. + verbo.
   The more I study, the less I learn. Mientras más estudio, menos
   aprendo.
   The more I rest, the better I feel. Mientras más descanso, mejor me
   siento.
   The + comparative, the + comparative. Mientras + comparativo,
   comparativo.
   The colder, the better. Mientras más frío, mejor.
9. **How come?** ¿Cómo?
   How come you're late? ¿Cómo que llegó tarde?
   How come he went? ¿Cómo que se fue?
   (*Note that the word order in English is in the affirmative.*)
10. **Roll up the carpet.** Enrolla la alfombra.

EXERCISE 1

Practice the following dialogue.

BUYING A DRESS AND A PAIR OF SHOES

Saleslady:	May I help you?
Customer:	Yes, I'd like to see a dress.
Saleslady:	A sport dress or an afternoon dress?
Customer:	An afternoon dress—something in blue.
Saleslady:	What size?
Customer:	Size twelve.
Saleslady:	Here are three—a light blue, a dark blue, and a navy blue. Which do you prefer?

Customer:	I'd like to try on the navy blue one. It looks cool with the collar and white dots.
Saleslady:	Come this way, please. The dressing room is over here.
Customer:	Size twelve is too large. Do you have a smaller size?
Saleslady:	Not in this model. We could make a few alterations, and it would fit. The hem has to be shortened about an inch. We could have it ready for you in a couple of days.
Customer:	How much is it?
Saleslady:	It's twenty dollars.
Customer:	I'll take it. Can I pick it up on Wednesday—about noon?
Saleslady:	Yes, it'll be ready by then.

Customer:	I'd like a pair of black low-heeled slippers.
Saleslady:	What size, please?
Customer:	Size five and a half, double A.
Saleslady:	I'll measure your foot just to be sure. Here's a pair of black and white nylon mesh shoes. You only have to wash them to get them clean.
Customer:	They look very nice.
Saleslady:	How do they feel?
Customer:	They feel very comfortable. Are all of them open-toed?
Saleslady:	Yes, they are. That's the style. Here's another pair of black kid.
Customer:	The black ones are better for summer. I think I'll take those. How much are they?
Saleslady:	They're six dollars. Do you want to take them with you, or do you want me to deliver them?
Customer:	I'll take them with me, thank you.
Saleslady:	Thank you. And come back again.

EXERCISE 2

Learn these words.

WORDS CONNECTED WITH SHOES

1. **high heels** tacón alto
2. **high-heeled** de tacón alto
3. **(house) slippers** pantuflas, chancletas
4. **kid** cabritilla
5. **low heels** tacón bajo
6. **low-heeled** de tacón bajo
7. **open-toed** de punta descubierta

171

8. **oxfords** choclos
9. **patent leather** charol
10. **platform shoes** zapatos con plataforma
11. **pumps** zapatillas
12. **rubbers** zapatos de hule (*para la lluvia*)
13. **sandals** sandalias
14. **suede** gamuza, ante

EXERCISE 3

Translate the following sentences and practice reading them.

1. Maybe there's one left.
2. Maybe there isn't one left.
3. Perhaps there's one left.
4. Perhaps there isn't one left.
5. There might be one left.
6. There might not be one left.
7. There may be one left.
8. There may not be one left.
9. There's a dressing room.
10. There isn't a dressing room.
11. Is there a dressing room?
12. Isn't there a dressing room?
13. Where's there a dressing room?
14. There were two bartenders.
15. There weren't two bartenders.
16. Were there two bartenders?
17. Weren't there two bartenders?
18. How many bartenders were there?
19. There'll be a bullfight.
20. There won't be a bullfight.
21. Will there be a bullfight?
22. Won't there be a bullfight?
23. Why won't there be a bullfight?
24. There have always been a lot of weddings.
25. There haven't always been a lot of weddings.
26. Have there always been a lot of weddings?
27. Haven't there always been a lot of weddings?
28. There'd been some factories there before.
29. There hadn't been any factories here before.
30. Had there been any factories here before?

172

EXERCISE 4

Translate the following sentences. Change them to the negative, interrogative, and interrogative negative.

1. He moves every year.
2. They moved on the first of the month.
3. My brother will move when they paint the house.
4. We've moved twice this year.
5. She'd move if she found a cheaper apartment.
6. He should move downtown.
7. They had to move last week.
8. We'll be able to move before Thursday.
9. You're going to move next year.
10. She's moving to a house in the next block.

EXERCISE 5

Give the past tense and past participle of the following verbs.

congratulate	decide	dress	direct
crush	die	drown	dry up
dictate	die down	describe	destroy
drop	disappear	dial	develop
dance	discover	dream (about)	drill

EXERCISE 6

Give the past tense and past participle of the following verbs.

get a manicure	get hurt	get sick	go swimming
get a tan	give out	get fired	have
get sunburned	go on a diet	give (something) back	hear
get run over	get beat	go dancing	hang
get well	get a divorce	go riding	have a good time
	get behind		

EXERCISE 7

Verb Practice *Expand the following verb practice, using different tenses.*

1. Henry should have loaded the train.

2. Henry shouldn't have loaded the train.
3. Should Henry have loaded the train?
4. Shouldn't Henry have loaded the train?
5. Why shouldn't Henry have loaded the train?

EXERCISE 8

Verb Practice *Make short sentences with forms of the verbs* **unload, increase, roll, rescue, protect, blush, move, change clothes, give a discount.** *Expand each verb practice to include different tenses, as in the exercise above. Use a different noun or pronoun with each verb. Use the interrogative words when it is possible.*

EXERCISE 9

Translate into Spanish.

1. This is a cheap suit. That's why it won't hold a crease very well.
2. Lana Turner changed dresses fifteen times in that movie.
3. The children were talking at the top of their voices, but the noise died down as soon as their mother came into the house.
4. Come this way, please, if you want to look at ladies' dresses.
5. This dress is too long. Can you put a hem in it for me (me puede subir la bastilla)?
6. I felt like bawling them out.
7. She plans to lose a little weight this summer because she's awfully fat.
8. How long has it been since you lived in Paris?
9. He must have moved. There isn't anyone here.
10. I had my shoes made, and he did too.
11. She shot (le dio un tiro) her husband because he was running around with another woman.
12. How come there are seven pairs of shoes missing?
13. Would you mind waiting while the druggist fills your prescription?
14. Would you rather sit at a table or at the counter?
15. He ran out of paper before he finished the letters. How come?

EXERCISE 10

Translate into English.

1. ¿Regaló Ud. algunos de los recuerdos que trajo de México?

2. Se me rompió el forro del abrigo cuando me lo puse.
3. Le digo un secreto si promete no decírselo a nadie.
4. Siempre hablaba él a voz en cuello.
5. En esa tienda les hacen a los alumnos un descuento del diez por ciento.
6. Más vale que aprendas a cuidarte.
7. Estos zapatos me aprietan mucho. Por favor me da un tamaño más grande.
8. El niño tiene los ojos azules, y su mamá también.
9. Él debería haber estado estudiando en vez de jugar.
10. Hubiera ido con Ud. si me hubiera llamado más temprano.
11. Mientras menos vea a Juan, tanto mejor.

EXERCISE 11

Answer the following questions.

1. How come you moved last week?
2. Will you move next week?
3. Are you going to move next week?
4. Do you have your suits made to order?
5. Did you have your dress made to order?
6. Are you going to have your hat made to order?
7. Have you ever had a pair of shoes made to order?
8. How come you've never had a pair of shoes made?
9. Did you ever have a coat made?
10. Does he take advantage of every opportunity?
11. Did she take advantage of every minute?
12. Will they take advantage of every day?
13. Should I take advantage of the time?
14. Will we be able to take advantage of every class?
15. Is he taking advantage of his vacation?
16. Do you think these pants are too short on me?
17. Isn't your dress a little too long?
18. Isn't that dress too tight for you?
19. Is the jacket too loose?
20. Wasn't that an awful thing to say?
21. Was the picture awful?
22. Isn't that an awful dress?
23. Isn't that suit awfully tight?
24. Was it awfully hot in Acapulco?
25. Did they give you a discount?

Vocabulary

1. **to memorize, memorized, memorized** memorizar
2. **to decorate, decorated, decorated** decorar, adornar; condecorar
3. **to handle, handled, handled** manejar (*personas, negocios*)
4. **to yell (at), yelled (at), yelled (at)** gritar
5. **to wink (at), winked (at), winked (at)** guiñar el ojo
6. **to disappoint, disappointed, disappointed** desilusionar, decepcionar
   disappointment desilusión
7. **serious** serio
8. **tax** impuesto, contribución
   duty derecho aduanal; deber
9. **shoehorn** calzador
10. **genius** genio
11. **expert** experto, perito
12. **equipment** equipo
13. **callus** callo
14. **corn** callo (*del pie*)
15. **dust** polvo
    dusty polvoso
16. **dull** aburrido (*ser*)
17. **effort** esfuerzo
18. **surface** superficie
19. **sea level** nivel del mar
20. **warehouse** almacén, depósito
21. **overtime** tiempo extra
22. **tower** torre
23. **shape** figura, horma; forma
24. **sincere** sincero
25. **employer** patrón
26. **employee** empleado
    employment empleo

IDIOMS

1. **to say good-bye (to)** despedirse (de)

176

2. **to wrap (something) up** envolver (algo)
3. **to get wrinkled** arrugarse
4. **Never mind.** No le hace, No importa.
5. **handmade** hecho a mano
6. **spare time** tiempo libre
7. **It was a mess.** Era un lío.
8. **no matter how much...** por mucho...
   No matter how much I work,... Por mucho que trabajo,...
   No matter how many... Por muchos...
   No matter how many he has,... Por muchos que tenga,...
   No matter how rich he is,... Por muy rico que sea,...
9. **pretty** muy, bastante
   pretty good muy bueno (bien), bastante bueno (bien)
   He's pretty intelligent. Es muy (bastante) inteligente.
   (**Pretty** *is not used in the negative.*)
   How are you? Pretty good. ¿Cómo estás? Muy bien.
   He's a pretty good swimmer. Nada bastante bien, Es muy buen nadador.

EXERCISE 1

Practice the following dialogue.

AT THE SHOE STORE

Salesman: May I help you?
Customer: I'd like to look at some shoes, please.
Salesman: All right. What did you have in mind?
Customer: A pair of oxfords. Let me see the model you have in the window.
Salesman: All right. We have this model in black and brown. Which do you want?
Customer: Brown, I think.
Salesman: What size do you wear?
Customer: I take an eight and a half C or a nine B.
Salesman: Let me measure your foot to be sure. I think an eight and a half will be all right. Try this one on. Is it all right?
Customer: It's a little too tight, and it hurts my toe.
Salesman: I'll bring you a size bigger. How's this?
Customer: It's too big. It isn't too-wide, but it's too long.

Salesman: A half size smaller should be all right then. Does this one fit?

Customer: Yes, this one seems to fit all right.

Salesman: Do you want to try the other one on?

Customer: Yes, please.

Salesman: Do you want me to wrap them up, or are you going to wear them?

Customer: Wrap them up, please.

Salesman: That'll be $14.95 with the tax.

EXERCISE 2

Learn these words.

WORDS CONNECTED WITH SHOES

1. **boots** botas
2. **cowboy boots** botas vaqueras
3. **field shoes** zapatos mineros
4. **rubber boots** botas de hule
5. **tennis shoes** zapatos tenis
6. **track shoes** spikes
7. **sole** suela
8. **rubber sole** suela de hule
9. **leather sole** suela de cuero
10. **rubber heel** tacón de hule
11. **leather heel** tacón de cuero
12. **tongue** (*of shoe*) lengüeta

EXERCISE 3

Translate the following sentences and practice reading them.

1. There'd be a tax.
2. There wouldn't be a tax.
3. Would there be a tax?
4. Wouldn't there be a tax?
5. Why wouldn't there be a tax?
6. There should be a warehouse here.
7. There shouldn't be a warehouse here.
8. Should there be a warehouse here?
9. Shouldn't there be a warehouse here?
10. How many warehouses should there be?
11. It's always cold here.
12. It isn't always cold here.
13. Was it ever cold here?
14. Wasn't it ever cold here?

178

15. Why was it cold here?
16. It'll be cold.
17. It won't be cold.
18. Will it be cold?
19. Won't it be cold?
20. When will it be cold?
21. It's been hot.
22. It hasn't been hot.
23. Has it been hot?
24. Hasn't it been hot?
25. Why has it been hot?
26. It'd be cold.
27. It wouldn't be cold.
28. Would it be cold?
29. Wouldn't it be cold?
30. When would it be cold?

EXERCISE 4

Translate the following sentences. Change them to the negative, interrogative, and interrogative negative.

1. He said good-bye to me.
2. She came to say good-bye.
3. We'll say good-bye tomorrow.
4. You have said good-bye to your guests.
5. They're going to say good-bye to us.
6. I should say good-bye to him.
7. She wants to say good-bye to her husband.
8. We can say good-bye to them tomorrow.
9. He's saying good-bye to the boys.
10. They'll have to say good-bye.

EXERCISE 5

Give the past tense and past participle of the following verbs.

deliver	escape	end	form
dye	examine	envy	fail
discuss	expect	fill	follow
damage	explain	finish	fry
disappoint	express	fix	fine

179

EXERCISE 6

Give the past tense and past participle of the following verbs.

have fun	hold	hold a crease	leave
have a good time	have an ac- cident	know	let
		keep	lie down
hide	have (some- thing) made	kneel	lose
hit		lay	lend
hang up	have a hangover	lay eggs	

EXERCISE 7

Verb Practice *Expand the following verb practice, using different tenses.*

1. Those idioms should be memorized.
2. Those idioms shouldn't be memorized.
3. Should those idioms be memorized?
4. Shouldn't those idioms be memorized?
5. When should those idioms be memorized?

EXERCISE 8

Verb Practice *Make short sentences with forms of the verbs* **decorate, handle, yell (at), wink (at), disappoint, say good-bye (to), wrap (something) up, get wrinkled.** *Expand each verb practice to include different tenses, as in the exercise above. Use a different noun or pronoun with each verb. Use the interrogative words when it is possible.*

EXERCISE 9

Translate into Spanish.

1. Let's wrap these presents up and put them under the bed.
2. Can you tell me how I can keep my clothes from getting wrinkled when I travel?
3. I forgot to say good-bye to the hostess.
4. The party was a mess. Two of the guests got drunk and began to fight.
5. He painted handmade furniture in his spare time.
6. Do you get paid for working overtime?
7. The boss bawled him out because he was late.

8. His relatives aren't rich, but they're well off.
9. How long has it been since you took charge of the office?
10. You're supposed to be able to answer all the questions in English.
11. Why don't you take the car out of the garage before it's time to go?
12. I can see the place where I work when I look out of the window.
13. We spent a great deal of time looking for a telephone that wasn't out of order.
14. I often get sleepy about noon.
15. We didn't go out of the house yesterday because it rained all day.
16. No matter how early I get up, I'm always late.

EXERCISE 10

Translate into English.

1. Le dije a ella que no adornara el árbol de Navidad.
2. Esos niños deben ser fáciles de manejar.
3. Marta no memorizó los verbos, ni tampoco Carlos.
4. Él estaba gritando tan fuerte que no pude entender lo que estaba diciendo, ¿y tú?
5. Debiste haber estado estudiando en lugar de jugar fútbol.
6. Habría comprado ese carro si hubiera sido un modelo 1955.
7. Si él fuera rico no tendría que trabajar.
8. No queremos desilusionarlo, pero creemos que no podremos hacer el viaje la semana próxima.
9. He estado pensando pasar mis vacaciones en las montañas.
10. Por más dinero que él tiene, no es feliz.
11. Por mucho que estudio, no puedo aprender español.

EXERCISE 11

Answer the following questions.

1. Did you say good-bye to your mother?
2. Will you say good-bye to your friends?
3. Have you said good-bye to Mr. Blake?
4. Do you feel like working?
5. Did you feel like going?
6. Will you feel like singing?
7. Have you felt like swimming?
8. Would you feel like reading?

9. Did he take advantage of the time?
10. Will she take advantage of her vacation?
11. How come they haven't taken advantage of this opportunity?
12. Are you supposed to be in school?
13. Were they supposed to be here?
14. Is he supposed to work late?
15. Was she supposed to help us?
16. Did the clerk wrap up the package for you?
17. Who wrapped it up?
18. Did your suit get wrinkled?
19. How did her dress get so wrinkled?
20. Is that dining room table handmade?
21. You're pretty tired, aren't you?
22. Are you awfully tired?
23. She sings pretty well. Do you?
24. Those students are pretty intelligent. Are the others?
25. Aren't those students awfully intelligent?

Lección 25

Vocabulary

1. **to leak, leaked, leaked**
   gotear, salirse (*refiriéndose al objeto de donde sale*)
2. **to drip, dripped, dripped**
   chorrear; gotear (*refiriéndose al líquido*)
3. **to collide, collided, collided**
   chocar
4. **to tighten, tightened, tightened**
   apretar
5. **to patch, patched, patched**
   parchar
6. **to grease, greased, greased**
   engrasar
7. **tire** llanta
8. **radiator** radiador
9. **windshield** parabrisas
10. **windshield wipers** limpiadores
11. **spare (tire)** llanta de refacción

12. **wheel** rueda, rin
13. **hydraulic** hidráulico
14. **hobby** pasatiempo
15. **parade** desfile
16. **statue** estatua
    monument monumento
17. **housewife** ama de casa
    housekeeper ama de llaves
18. **flood** inundación
19. **riot** motín, tumulto
20. **firecracker** cohete
21. **fireworks** fuegos artificiales
22. **material** tela; casimir
23. **clever** listo
24. **union** sindicato
25. **fisherman** pescador
26. **(gas) attendant** despachador (*de una gasolinera*)
27. **estimate** presupuesto

183

IDIOMS

1. **to check the oil, gas, tires, etc.** revisar el aceite, gasolina, llantas, etc.
2. **to step on the brake** frenar
3. **to shift (gears)** cambiar velocidades
4. **to blow your horn** tocar el claxon
5. **to fix a flat** reparar una ponchadura
6. **to charge a battery** cargar una batería
7. **to shoot off firecrackers** echar cohetes
8. **Fill it up.** Llénelo. (*tanque de gasolina*)
9. **There's no hurry.** No hay prisa.
10. **There was a collision.** Hubo un choque.
    There was a wreck. Hubo un choque muy fuerte.
11. **I heard the water drip (dripping).** Oí el agua gotear, Oí que el agua estaba goteando.
    The faucet is leaking. La llave está goteando.
    Do you smell the bacon frying? ¿Huele el tocino que se está friendo?
    Did you see John come in? ¿Viste a Juan entrar?
    (*After* **hear, see, feel** *we use the infinitive without* **to** *or the gerund. After* **smell** *we use only the present participle.*)
12. **Put it in first.** Meta primera.

EXERCISE 1

Practice the following dialogue.

AT THE GAS STATION

Attendant:	What can I do for you?
Customer:	I need some gas.
Attendant:	How much?
Customer:	Fill it up.
Attendant:	How about the oil? Do you want me to check it?
Customer:	Yes, please. And check the tires, too.
Attendant:	The oil is a little low. You'll need about a quart. What weight do you use?
Customer:	Medium weight.
Attendant:	The tires are O. K. Do you need anything else?
Customer:	See if I need some water in the radiator.

184

Attendant:	Yes, you do, and your windshield needs cleaning. Do your windshield wipers work all right?
Customer:	Yes, they're all right. Do you fix flats?
Attendant:	Yes, we do.
Customer:	My spare tire has a leak. How long will it take you to patch it?
Attendant:	Do you need it right away?
Customer:	There's no hurry.
Attendant:	Then why don't you leave it and pick it up tomorrow? It'll be ready in the morning.
Customer:	All right. Then I'll pay the whole bill tomorrow when I pick the tire up.
Attendant:	O. K.
Customer:	Good-bye.
Attendant:	Good-bye.

EXERCISE 2

Learn these words.

TYPES OF VEHICLES

1. **delivery truck** camión de entrega
2. **jeep** jeep
3. **taxi** libre
   taxi cab libre
4. **tow car** remolcador, grúa
5. **truck** camión de carga
6. **station wagon** camioneta
7. **wrecker** demoledora
8. **trailer** remolque

EXERCISE 3

Translate the following sentences and practice reading them.

1. It'd be cold, wouldn't it?
2. It wouldn't be cold, would it?
3. Would it be cold?
4. Wouldn't it be cold?
5. Why wouldn't it be cold?
6. It should be cold, shouldn't it?
7. It shouldn't be cold, should it?
8. Should it be cold?
9. Shouldn't it be cold?

10. Why should it be cold?
11. It's going to be cold, isn't it?
12. It isn't going to be cold, is it?
13. Is it going to be cold?
14. Isn't it going to be cold?
15. When is it going to be cold?
16. It was going to be cold, wasn't it?
17. It wasn't going to be cold, was it?
18. Was it going to be cold?
19. Wasn't it going to be cold?
20. Why was it going to be cold?
21. They're usually afraid, aren't they?
22. They aren't usually afraid, are they?
23. Are they ever afraid?
24. Aren't they ever afraid?
25. Why aren't they ever afraid?
26. We were hungry, weren't we?
27. We weren't hungry, were we?
28. Were we hungry?
29. Weren't we hungry?
30. Why were we hungry?

EXERCISE 4

Translate the following sentences. Change them to the negative, interrogative, and interrogative negative.

1. He checks the oil.
2. You checked the gas.
3. They'll check the tires.
4. We've checked the water.
5. He should check the oil.
6. You should check the gas.
7. They'll be able to check the tires.
8. We've been able to check the water.
9. He's been checking the oil.
10. I was checking the gas.

EXERCISE 5

Give the past tense and past participle of the following verbs.

fill a tooth
fill a pre-
    scription
file your
    (finger)nails
faint

float
fire
gather (up)
gain weight
guess
grease

help
hurry
hope
hunt
hate

heal
handle
invite
insist (on)
insult

EXERCISE 6

Give the past tense and past participle of the following verbs.

lose weight
make
make a living
make a mis-
        take
make fun of

make a trip
meet
mean
put
put on
pay

pay attention
            (to)
put on make-
            up
quit
read

run
run away
run around
run out of
strike
fall asleep

EXERCISE 7

Verb Practice *Expand the following verb practice, using different tenses.*

1. The radiator is leaking.
2. The radiator isn't leaking.
3. Is the radiator leaking?
4. Isn't the radiator leaking?
5. Why is the radiator leaking?

EXERCISE 8

Verb Practice *Make short sentences with forms of the verbs* **drip, collide, tighten, patch, grease, check the oil, step on the brake, shift gears, blow your horn, fix a flat, charge a battery, shoot off firecrackers.** *Expand each verb practice to include different tenses, as in the exercise above. Use a different noun or pronoun with each verb. Use the interrogative when it is possible.*

EXERCISE 9

Translate into Spanish.

1. It's against the law (es infracción) to blow your horn.

187

2. I told you not to check the oil, didn't I?
3. How long will it take you to fix this flat?
4. Does your battery need charging?
5. Don't run over anybody.
6. You shouldn't get so far behind with your school work.
7. Do you think the Yankees can beat the Giants?
8. If I were in your place, I wouldn't get a divorce.
9. I haven't had breakfast yet. Have you?
10. I'm going to take a sun bath before taking a steam bath.
11. Let's give this money back to the boy who lost it.
12. We ran out of books and couldn't get any more.
13. Did you tell the barber to trim your mustache?
14. I feel sorry for people who have to work for a living.
15. Here's a handkerchief. Blow your nose.
16. Did you hear him talking in the next room?

EXERCISE 10

Translate into English.

1. Yo hubiera tomado un libre si hubiera estado lloviendo.
2. ¿Le gustaría ver los fuegos artificiales el 16 de septiembre?
3. No eches cohetes a las muchachas. Las vas a asustar.
4. No debe hacer frío en Chicago en abril, ¿verdad?
5. No toques el claxon en el centro.
6. ¿Oyes el agua gotear?
7. Debió haber engrasado las ruedas y ajustado los limpiadores.
8. Todos deberían tener un pasatiempo.
9. ¿De qué clase de tela está hecho su traje?
10. ¿Para qué está tocando el claxon ese ruletero?

EXERCISE 11

Answer the following questions.

1. Did he check the oil?
2. Is he checking the gas?
3. Is he going to check the tires?
4. Who blew the horn?
5. Why didn't you step on the brake?
6. Did he charge the battery?

188

7. Did you gain weight?
8. How much weight did you lose?
9. Are you on a diet?
10. Were you on a diet?
11. Have you been on a diet?
12. Are you going to go on a diet?
13. Were you going to go on a diet?
14. Whose house is that over there?
15. Whose car were you riding in?
16. Is the roof leaking?
17. Does this bucket leak?
18. Can't you hear the water dripping?
19. Is there blood dripping down his leg?
20. Was there blood dripping from his nose?
21. Don't you hear it raining?
22. Have you heard him speak Spanish?
23. Didn't you see the car coming?
24. Do you feel the plane moving?
25. Do you smell anything cooking?

Lección 2

Vocabulary

1. **to flatter, flattered, flattered** halagar, lisonjear
2. **to issue, issued, issued** expedir
3. **to advance, advanced, advanced** adelantar, avanzar
4. **to criticize, criticized, criticized** criticar
5. **to shock, shocked, shocked** escandalizar
6. **to lie, lied, lied** mentir
   liar mentiroso
7. **to speed, speeded, speeded** llevar mucha velocidad (*manejando*)
   speed velocidad
8. **license** licencia
   driver's license licencia para manejar
   license plates placas
9. **mechanic** mecánico
10. **traffic** tránsito
    traffic light semáforo
11. **fire hydrant** toma de agua para incendios
12. **shock** toque (*eléctrico*); golpe (*mental*)
13. **speedometer** velocímetro
14. **detour** desviación
15. **(police) officer** policía
16. **go** adelante, siga, continúe
    stop alto
17. **slow down** despacio
18. **red light** luz roja
    green light luz verde
19. **tame** manso
20. **magic** mágico
21. **magician** mago
22. **male** varón, macho
23. **female** hembra
24. **lavatory** baño, sanitario
25. **rest room** baño, sanitario
26. **ownership papers** documentos de propiedad
27. **violation** infracción
28. **police station** delegación
29. **traffic violators** infractores

IDIOMS

1. **to be all gone** (*subject must be a thing*) acabarse
   The cake is all gone. Ya se acabó el pastel.
   The cake was all gone. El pastel se había acabado.
2. **to be shocked (at)** escandalizarse (de)
   I was shocked at her. Me escandalicé de ella.
3. **to get a shock** darle a uno toques
4. **to start your motor** arrancar el motor
5. **to dim your lights** bajar o disminuir las luces
6. **to be polite** tener buena educación
7. **to slow down** disminuir la velocidad
8. **Pull over to the curb.** Arrímese a la banqueta.
9. **no right turn** prohibido dar vuelta a la derecha
   no left turn prohibido dar vuelta a la izquierda
10. **Keep to the right, left.** Conserve su derecha, izquierda.
11. **double parking** doble fila
12. **Don't change lanes.** No cambie de carril.
13. **no parking** prohibido estacionarse
14. **as long as** con tal que
15. **The light is green (red).** Está el siga (alto).

EXERCISE 1

Practice the following dialogue.

A TRAFFIC VIOLATION

Policeman: Pull over to the curb.
Driver: What for, officer? What have I done?
Policeman: You were going about sixty miles an hour in a school zone. Don't you know that the speed limit is twenty? You almost ran over a little boy.
Driver: I'm sorry, officer, but I didn't realize I was driving so fast. And the boy ran in front of my car.
Policeman: Let's see your driver's license.
Driver: Here it is. It wasn't issued here, but it's good in the United States too.
Policeman: The judge will decide that. Be at court tomorrow morning at ten o'clock. Here's your ticket.
Driver: How much do you think he'll fine me?

Policeman: I don't know, but the judge is hard on traffic violators. You can start your motor now, but don't make any left turns on this street and don't park near a fire hydrant.

Driver: O. K. I hope I don't pass a red light.

Policeman: As long as you drive carefully, you won't have anything to worry about.

EXERCISE 2

Learn these words.

PARTS OF A CAR

1. **accelerator** acelerador
2. **bumper** defensa
3. **carburetor** carburador
4. **clutch** cluch, embrague
5. **grill** parrilla
6. **hood** cofre
7. **fender** salpicadera
8. **hub cap** tapón
9. **(gas) tank** tanque
10. **gear shift** palanca de cambio de marcha
11. **(steering) wheel** volante

EXERCISE 3

Translate the following sentences and practice reading them.

1. We'll be hungry.
2. We won't be hungry.
3. Will we be hungry?
4. Won't we be hungry?
5. When will we be hungry?
6. They've been cold.
7. They haven't been cold.
8. Have they been cold?
9. Haven't they been cold?
10. Why have they been cold?
11. You were sometimes warm.
12. You weren't ever warm.
13. Were you ever warm?
14. Weren't you ever warm?
15. Why weren't you ever warm?
16. I'd be sleepy.

17. I wouldn't be sleepy.
18. Would I be sleepy?
19. Wouldn't I be sleepy?
20. When would I be sleepy?
21. You should be thirsty.
22. You shouldn't be thirsty.
23. Should you be thirsty?
24. Shouldn't you be thirsty?
25. Why should you be thirsty?
26. She's going to be afraid.
27. She isn't going to be afraid.
28. Is she going to be afraid?
29. Isn't she going to be afraid?
30. Why isn't she going to be afraid?

EXERCISE 4

Translate the following sentences. Change them to the negative, interrogative, and interrogative negative.

1. It's all gone.
2. The food was all gone when we got there.
3. The money will be all gone before fall.
4. The books should be all gone by this time.
5. The sandwiches are all gone.
6. The tickets were all gone by nine o'clock.
7. The magazines will be all gone before tomorrow.
8. He said the candy would be all gone.
9. They're going to be all gone soon.
10. My money is all gone.

EXERCISE 5

Give the past tense and past participle of the following verbs.

introduce	issue	joke	kick
imagine	insure a	kill	kill yourself
itch	package	kiss	lie
iron	jump	knit	laugh (at)
increase	join	knock (on)	learn

EXERCISE 6

Give the past tense and past participle of the following verbs.

rise	say	stand up	shine
ring	see	send	shoot
run a business,	sit (down)	shake	sing
etc.	set	shake hands	spend
run after	sleep	with	stand in line
run over	speak		

EXERCISE 7

Verb Practice *Expand the following verb practice, using different tenses.*

1. They'd have had to flatter me.
2. They wouldn't have had to flatter me.
3. Would they have had to flatter me?
4. Wouldn't they have had to flatter me?
5. Who would have had to flatter me?

EXERCISE 8

Verb Practice *Make short sentences with forms of the verbs* issue, advance, criticize, shock, lie (mentir), speed, be all gone, be shocked (at), get a shock, start your motor, dim your lights, be polite, slow down. *Expand each verb practice to include different tenses, as in the exercise above. Use a different noun or pronoun with each verb. Use the interrogative words when it is possible.*

EXERCISE 9

Translate into Spanish.

1. That driver coming toward me wouldn't (no quiso) dim his lights.
2. The policeman told him to pull over to the curb.
3. Who wouldn't be afraid to drive in all this traffic?
4. I can't mail your letter today because the stamps are all gone.
5. How many stamps do you have left?
6. You shouldn't give up so soon.

7. As far as I know, he got rich in the oil business.
8. I can't stop and talk to you now because I'm in a hurry.
9. What did he tell you he was going out of town for?
10. After a while the children got sleepy.
11. We hurried to the store where they were having a sale, but we got there too late.
12. It really doesn't make any difference what kind of lipstick you use.
13. He was issued a driver's license.
14. You should lie down and rest for about an hour after dinner.
15. I'd like to ask a question about the use of *any* and *some*.

EXERCISE 10

Translate into English.

1. ¿Quién me expedirá una licencia para manejar?
2. No es necesario halagarla.
3. Todos nos escandalizábamos de la mala educación del guía.
4. No debió haberlo criticado tanto. Todos nos equivocamos.
5. Podrá Ud. adelantar mucho más rápido con este grupo.
6. Si Ud. tuviera buena educación, no mentiría tanto.
7. Disminuya la velocidad. El límite aquí es treinta millas por hora.
8. ¿Es su perro macho o hembra?
9. Permítame su licencia para manejar.
10. Si le hubiera mentido, me hubiera despedido.

EXERCISE 11

Answer the following questions.

1. Is the beer all gone?
2. Is the food all gone?
3. How come the water is all gone?
4. Was the money all gone?
5. Was the time all gone?
6. Hadn't you better go now?
7. Hadn't you better work tomorrow?
8. Hadn't you better pay this bill?
9. Hadn't we better leave early?
10. Hadn't he better take his raincoat?
11. Did the truck run over him?

12. Did the streetcar run over him?
13. How come he didn't get run over?
14. Will they get run over?
15. Would they get run over?
16. Why were you speeding?
17. How come he's always speeding?
18. Did the truck driver dim his lights?
19. Can't you start your motor?
20. Don't you think you'd better slow down?

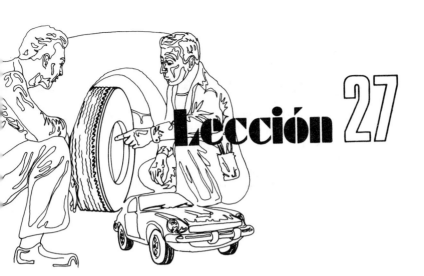

Lección 27

Vocabulary

1. **to park, parked, parked**
   estacionar (se)
2. **to dent, dented, dented** abollar
   dent abolladura
3. **to trade in, traded in, traded in**
   cambiar (*el coche*)
   trade in cambalache, trueque
4. **to skid, skidded, skidded**
   derraparse (*coche*); resbalarse
   (*personas*)
5. **to embarrass, embarrassed,**
   embarrassed apenar
6. **to adjust, adjusted, adjusted**
   ajustar
7. **to discourage, discouraged,**
   discouraged desanimar,
   desalentar
8. **to screw something in, screwed**
   something in, screwed
   something in atornillar algo
   screwdriver desarmador
9. **(inner) tube** cámara
10. **tube** cámara

   tubeless tire llanta sin
   cámara
11. **jack** gato
12. **trunk** cajuela
13. **slight** leve
14. **uphill** cuesta arriba
    downhill cuesta abajo
15. **pale** pálido
16. **scenery** paisaje
17. **scene** escena
18. **kid** chamaco
19. **view** panorama, vista
20. **fur** piel (*para abrigo*)
21. **nickname** apodo
22. **awkward** desgarbado, torpe
23. **disgrace** deshonra,
    desprestigio
    disgraced deshonrado,
    desprestigiado, avergonzado
24. **scarce** escaso
25. **mud** lodo
26. **manner** modo, manera

197

IDIOMS

1. **to get acquainted with** llegar a conocer; conocer; ambientarse en relacionarse con
2. **to give (someone) a ring** llamar (a alguien) por teléfono
3. **to be in mourning** estar de luto
4. **to tow (a car) in** remolcar (un coche)
5. **to get stuck** atascarse
6. **to get back** estar de vuelta (regreso), regresar (*de allá para acá*)
   When do you plan to get back? ¿Para cuándo piensas regresar (estar de regreso)?
7. **to be embarrassed** apenarse, darle pena
8. **to start back** emprender el regreso, salir de regreso
   Let's start back now. Vamos a regresar ahora.
9. **to have a flat** poncharse una llanta
   to have a blowout poncharse una llanta, tener un reventón
10. **Your motor knocks.** Su motor golpea.
11. **What's wrong with it (you, him, her, etc.)?** ¿Qué tiene (Ud., él, ella, etc.)?
12. **The spark plugs are missing.** Las bujías están fallando.
13. **car trouble** avería o desperfecto de un coche
14. **a four-door sedan** un sedán de cuatro puertas
    a two-door convertible un convertible de dos puertas

EXERCISE 1

Practice the following dialogue.

CAR TROUBLE

Customer: Pardon me. I've had some trouble with my car. Can you send someone to pick it up?

Mechanic: Sure. We're not too busy now. Where is it?

Customer: It's about a quarter of a mile down the road.

Mechanic: I'll get the jeep—no, I think I'd better get the tow car in case we have to tow it in.

Customer: There's the car over there.

Mechanic: Let's see. What happened?

Customer: I don't know. The car skidded and got stuck in the mud. It won't (no quiere) start now.

Mechanic: Let's push it to one side of the road.

198

Customer: Yes, I think we'd better. It's dangerous here in the middle of the road.

Mechanic: Look. You've got a blowout (flat), too. I'd better get the jack and change the tire before I tow you in. If we don't, it'll ruin the tire.

Customer: My spare tire is in the trunk.

Mechanic: O. K. It'll only take a minute, and then we can start back. When we get back to the garage, I can check the car carefully.

Customer: Well, what was wrong with it?

Mechanic: A couple of your spark plugs are missing.

Customer: Is that all that's wrong with it?

Mechanic: No, your radiator has a slight leak, and your motor knocks.

Customer: Yes, I know. And why does my motor heat up going uphill?

Mechanic: I won't be able to tell until I check it.

Customer: How long will it take you to fix all that?

Mechanic: I'll need, at least, a couple of days to work on the motor. You'd better give me until Saturday morning.

Customer: Do you want me to lock the car?

Mechanic: No, that's not necessary. Just leave the keys with me.

Customer: How can I get back to town?

Mechanic: One of the mechanics will take you.

Customer: O. K. Thanks. Then I'll give you a ring on Saturday before I come for the car. I don't want to make a trip for nothing, if the car isn't ready.

Mechanic: All right. If you want to. But it'll probably be ready.

EXERCISE 2

Learn these words.

PARTS OF A CAR

1. **dashboard** tablero
2. **dashboard light** luz del tablero
3. **back seat** asiento trasero
4. **door handle** manija
5. **front seat** asiento delantero
6. **glove compartment** cajuela interior
7. **headlights** faros
8. **horsepower** caballo (*de fuerza*)
9. **seat cover** cubreasiento
10. **shock absorber** amortiguador
11. **spring** muelle; resorte
12. **taillight** calavera
13. **rear view mirror** espejo retrovisor

EXERCISE 3

Translate the following sentences and practice reading them.

1. She was going to be hungry.
2. She wasn't going to be hungry.
3. Was she going to be hungry?
4. Wasn't she going to be hungry?
5. Why wasn't she going to be hungry?
6. Criticize.
7. Don't criticize.
8. Let me criticize.
9. Don't let me criticize.
10. Let him criticize.
11. Don't let him criticize.
12. Let her criticize.
13. Don't let her criticize.
14. Let's criticize.
15. Let's not criticize.
16. Let us criticize.
17. Don't let us criticize.
18. Let them criticize.
19. Don't let them criticize.

EXERCISE 4

Translate the following sentences. Change them to the negative, interrogative, and interrogative negative.

1. You ought to get acquainted with your teacher.
2. He'll get acquainted with some girls at college.
3. She got acquainted with the girls in the office.
4. We'll be able to get acquainted with our new job.
5. They've been getting acquainted with the children.
6. He's getting acquainted with his stepmother.
7. She's going to get acquainted with her husband's family.
8. We've got acquainted with many people in Mexico.
9. They want me to get acquainted with the manager.
10. I'd like to get acquainted with him.

EXERCISE 5

Give the past tense and past participle of the following verbs.

like	love	lock	move
listen (to)	last	look around	measure
live	lift	load	melt
look (at)	look alike	leak	miss a person
look (for)	lean back	lie	miss a bus
			(plane, etc.)

EXERCISE 6

Give the past tense and past participle of the following verbs.

swim	sit at the	take	take a bath
sink	counter	teach	take a shower
strike a	set your	tell	take off
match	watch, clock	think	throw
spread	stick	think of	throw away
sit at a table	say good-bye	take away	
	(to)		

EXERCISE 7

Verb Practice *Expand the following verb practice, using different tenses.*

1. The mechanic should have parked near the curb.
2. The mechanic shouldn't have parked near the curb.
3. Should the mechanic have parked near the curb?
4. Shouldn't the mechanic have parked near the curb?
5. When should the mechanic have parked near the curb?

EXERCISE 8

Verb Practice *Make short sentences with forms of the verbs* skid, dent, trade in, embarrass, adjust, discourage, screw something in, get acquainted with, give (someone) a ring, be in morning, tow (a car) in, get stuck, get back, start back, have a flat, have a blowout, be embarrassed. *Expand each verb practice to include different tenses, as in the exercise above. Use a different noun or pronoun with each verb. Use the interrogative words when it is possible.*

201

EXERCISE 9

Translate into Spanish.

1. Where are you supposed to be at ten o'clock?
2. What's wrong with your motor? It knocks.
3. I'll give you a ring some Sunday when I know you're not out of town.
4. We started back around eleven-thirty.
5. We're late because we had a flat about a mile down the road.
6. You'll get stuck if you try to drive through that sand.
7. The policeman is trying to keep the cars from parking on the left side of the street.
8. I wish you would find out what's wrong with my car.
9. I hope you get acquainted with your new neighbors soon.
10. How many screwdrivers do you have left?
11. If you have car trouble between here and San Diego, call a mechanic.
12. I don't want you to ask any more questions.
13. This coat is too loose. Please bring me a smaller size.
14. You should dim your lights when you see a car coming toward you.
15. Can you tell me how I can get back to town from here?
16. Why don't you trade in your old car and buy a two-door Cadillac convertible?

EXERCISE 10

Translate into English.

1. ¿Por qué se está estacionando enfrente de una toma de agua para incendios?
2. Ud. no debe estar apenado, ni él tampoco.
3. No quiero desanimarte; más vale que no hagas tu solicitud por ahora.
4. Las llantas estuvieron muy escasas durante la guerra, ¿verdad?
5. Tendrás que cambiar de velocidad cuando vayas cuesta arriba.
6. Me hubiera apenado si él hubiera oído lo que dije.
7. ¿Todavía no ha encontrado un apodo para los niños?
8. Parece que ha estado enfermo. Está tan pálido.
9. De joven era muy tímido y desgarbado.
10. Qué lastima que tu trabajo sea tan fastidioso.
11. Voy a llevar mi coche con (to) el mecánico para ver si le pueden sacar todas las abolladuras.

EXERCISE 11

Answer the following questions.

1. Did you get acquainted with him?
2. Will you get acquainted with him?
3. Have you got acquainted with him?
4. Did you run after the child?
5. Will you run after the child?
6. Have you run after the child?
7. What's your new suit like?
8. What are your new dresses like?
9. What was your old car like?
10. What were the houses like?
11. Are you well off?
12. Was he well off?
13. Do you bawl them out?
14. Has he bawled you out?
15. How come he bawled you out?
16. Did the car get stuck in the mud?
17. How did you get back after the accident?
18. Does your motor knock?
19. What's wrong with you?
20. Can you give me a ring about ten?
21. Is there a "no parking" sign across the street?
22. Are you having car trouble?
23. Are your spark plugs missing?
24. When did you have a flat?
25. What's wrong with her?

Lección 2

1. **to type, typed, typed** escribir en máquina
2. **to file, filed, filed** archivar **file** archivo, expediente
3. **to copy, copied, copied** copiar
4. **to staple, stapled, stapled** engrapar **staple** grapa **stapler** engrapadora
5. **to disturb, disturbed, disturbed** molestar
6. **to train, trained, trained** enseñar, instruir, adiestrar; entrenar **training** instrucción, enseñanza, adiestramiento; entrenamiento
7. **to erase, erased, erased** borrar **eraser** borrador; goma
8. **secretary** secretario (a) **private secretary** secretario (a) particular
9. **executive** ejecutivo
10. **office boy** muchacho mandadero, mozo
11. **typewriter** máquina de escribir
12. **adding machine** sumadora
13. **blotter** secante
14. **carbon paper** papel carbón **carbon copy** copia (*al carbón*)
15. **original** original
16. **(paper) clip** clip
17. **accounting** contabilidad **accountant** contador
18. **desk** escritorio
19. **desk drawer** cajón de escritorio
20. **memorandum** memorándum
21. **district** distrito
22. **paragraph** párrafo
23. **typist** mecanógrafo (a) **typing** mecanografía
24. **stenographer** taquígrafo (a)

stenography taquigrafía	27. **block** block
25. **shorthand** taquigrafía	28. **letterhead** membrete
26. **stenotypist** taquimecanógrafo (a)	29. **onion skin paper** papel cebolla
stenotyping taquimecanografía	30. **steno pad** block de taquigrafía

IDIOMS

1. **to finish + (present participle)** terminar de + (infinitivo)
   I finished eating. Terminé de comer.
2. **to remind someone (of)** recordarle a uno
   You remind me of my brother. Me recuerda a mi hermano.
   Don't remind me of that. No me recuerdes eso.
   Remind me to buy some stamps. Recuérdame comprar unos timbres.
   Who does he remind you of? ¿A quién te recuerda él?
3. **to cut a stencil** sacar un estencil
4. **absolutely not** desde luego que no, de ninguna manera
5. **Please send him in.** Que pase él, por favor.
6. **by means of** por medio de
7. **by heart** de memoria
8. **I can't stand him (her).** No lo (la) soporto.
   I can't stand the pain. No soporto el dolor.
9. **quite** muy, bastante
   She's quite pretty. Es muy (bastante) bonita.
   The movie was quite good. La película estaba muy (bastante) buena.

EXERCISE 1

Practice the following dialogue.

AT THE OFFICE

Executive: Will you come in for dictation, Miss Young?
Miss Young: Yes, sir.
Executive: And please bring me the file on the Lombard Company.
Miss Young: Yes, sir.

Executive:	Will you find the copy of the letter that was written to the manager of the Lombard Company on March 21?
Miss Young:	Here it is, sir.
Executive:	We're going to make up a memorandum to be sent to all executives of the company in this district. Use the second and third paragraphs of this letter as the opening paragraphs of the memorandum, and I'll dictate the rest of the memorandum.
Miss Young:	Yes, sir. When do you want this?
Executive:	As soon as possible. When can you have it ready?
Miss Young:	It'll be ready in two hours, sir.
Executive:	Fine. Are you ready to take dictation?
Miss Young:	Excuse me, sir. You have an appointment now with Mr. Longstreet. Shall I tell him to wait, or shall I come back for dictation after you finish speaking to him?
Executive:	Maybe it would be better if you took dictation later. This appointment with Mr. Longstreet is very important. Please send him in.
Miss Young:	Do you want to receive any telephone calls during the conference (entrevista)?
Executive:	Absolutely not. I don't want to be disturbed for any reason for the next half hour.
Miss Young.	Yes, sir.

EXERCISE 2

Learn these words.

NAMES OF INSECTS

1. **ant** hormiga
2. **bee** abeja
3. **beehive** colmena
4. **beetle** escarabajo
5. **bedbug** chinche
6. **bug** insecto, bicho
7. **butterfly** mariposa
8. **caterpillar** oruga
9. **centipede** cienpiés
10. **chigger** nigua
11. **cockroach** cucaracha
12. **cricket** grillo
13. **earthworm** lombriz de tierra
14. **flea** pulga
15. **fly** mosca
16. **grasshopper** saltamontes, chapulín
17. **insect** insecto, bicho
18. **locust** langosta
19. **louse** piojo

20. **lice** piojos
21. **mosquito** mosquito, mosco
22. **moth** polilla
23. **scorpion** alacrán, escorpión
24. **snail** caracol

25. **spider** araña
   black widow spider viuda negra, araña capulina
26. **tick** garrapata
27. **wasp** avispa
28. **worm** gusano

EXERCISE 3

Translate the following sentences and practice reading them.

1. What's the dog barking at?
2. What was the dog barking at?
3. What did the dog bark at?
4. What are you ironing for?
5. What were you ironing for?
6. What did you iron for?
7. Who are you living with?
8. Who were you living with?
9. Who did you live with?
10. Where is the package from?
11. Where was the package from?
12. Where did the package come from?
13. What are you listening to?
14. Did you use to live there?
15. Did you use to work there?
16. Did you use to go there?
17. Did you use to smoke?
18. Did you use to eat a lot?
19. Did you use to help them?
20. Did she use to cook?
21. Did she use to study English?
22. Did she use to start at eight o'clock?
23. What has the dog been barking at?
24. What have you been ironing for?
25. Who have you been living with?
26. What have you been listening to?
27. What have you been laughing at?
28. What have you been looking for?
29. What have you been looking at?
30. What have you been thinking about?

207

EXERCISE 4

Translate the following sentences. Change them to the negative, interrogative, and interrogative negative.

1. He finishes opening the mail before ten o'clock every day.
2. They finished painting the house about twelve-thirty.
3. We'll finish paying the men early.
4. You should finish counting the money.
5. They've finished washing the dishes.
6. He's going to finish dressing now.
7. She was going to finish putting on her make-up.
8. We want him to finish making the chairs.
9. They've told her to finish reading the lesson.
10. They told me to finish getting ready.

EXERCISE 5

Give the past tense and past participle of the following verbs.

blush	marry	need	offer
mix	mail	name	order
match	move (resi-	notice	owe
mention	dence)	neglect	operate on
mash	memorize	open	pass
		own	pick out

EXERCISE 6

Give the past tense and past participle of the following verbs.

take place	take your	take advan-	wear
take charge	blood pressure	tage of	win
(of)	take a trip	take your	write
take your	take a walk,	order	wear out
tonsils out	ride	take (some-	weave
take your	take a sun	thing) back	wet
pulse	bath	understand	wind a watch,
		wake up	clock

EXERCISE 7

Verb Practice *Expand the following verb practice, using different tenses.*

1. He has told her to type a letter.
2. He hasn't told her to type a letter.
3. Has he told her to type a letter?
4. Hasn't he told her to type a letter?
5. How many letters has he told her to type?

EXERCISE 8

Verb Practice *Make short sentences with forms of the verbs* **file, copy, staple, disturb, train, remind someone (of), erase, finish + gerund, cut a stencil.** *Expand each verb practice to include different tenses, as in the exercise above. Use a different noun or pronoun with each verb. Use the interrogative words when it is possible.*

EXERCISE 9

Translate into Spanish.

1. What are you going to finish cutting this stencil for?
2. Can you type and take shorthand?
3. I can't stand that class. I'll be glad when it's over.
4. You should learn all these verbs by heart.
5. When Mr. Green comes, please send him in.
6. If you don't finish typing that letter, the boss is going to get mad.
7. It must be a mosquito. It's too little for a fly.
8. What did you shake hands with all those people for?
9. I didn't know the Coca-Colas were all gone, did you?
10. We plan to run this business ourselves.
11. That speech isn't worth listening to.
12. He said it wouldn't take long to get there.
13. How far is it to the nearest filling station?
14. How often do you make a trip to Denver?
15. Would you rather have red wine or white wine?
16. She sings quite well, but her sister is an awful singer.

EXERCISE 10

Translate into English.

1. Le dijimos a él que no nos molestara.

2. Esa mujer me recuerda a mi primera profesora.
3. Por favor recuérdame hablar por teléfono.
4. Le he dicho al portero que borre el pizarrón todos los días.
5. Por favor escriba esta carta en máquina y haga cinco copias.
6. Le diré a ella que archive todas las cartas que están sobre su escritorio.
7. Después de que termine Ud. de escribir esta carta en máquina, archive una copia y deje el original sobre mi escritorio.
8. ¿Cuánto tiempo hace que estudió taquigrafía?
9. Él dijo que no podría escribir este memorándum en máquina hasta mañana.
10. ¿Qué te recuerda este lugar?

EXERCISE 11

Answer the following questions.

1. Did you finish eating?
2. Have you finished typing the letters?
3. Will you finish counting the copies?
4. Did he wrap the books up?
5. Has he wrapped the presents up?
6. Will you wrap this gift up?
7. Did your jacket get wrinkled?
8. Will your ties get wrinkled?
9. Did he check the tires?
10. Have they checked the water?
11. Will you check the oil?
12. Did he step on the brake?
13. Did he shift gears?
14. Did he blow the horn?
15. Did he fix the flat?
16. Did the secretary send Mr. Brown in?
17. Didn't she send him in?
18. Doesn't he remind you of Jim?
19. Do I remind you of anyone?
20. Didn't he remind you to phone?

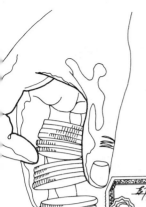

Lección 29

Vocabulary

1. **to bloom, bloomed, bloomed** florecer, abrir (*una flor*)
2. **to stretch, stretched, stretched** estirar (se); extender (se)
3. **to consist of, consisted of, consisted of** consistir en, constar de
4. **to mortgage, mortgaged, mortgaged** hipotecar
   mortgage hipoteca
5. **to perspire, perspired, perspired** sudar
6. **to sweat, sweat, sweat** sudar
7. **to deposit, deposited, deposited** depositar
   deposit depósito
   deposit slip esqueleto para depositar dinero
8. **to withdraw, withdrew, withdrawn** sacar, retirar
   withdrawal retiro
   withdrawal slip esqueleto para retirar dinero

9. **to loan, loaned, loaned** prestar
   loan préstamo
10. **check** cheque
11. **cash** efectivo; en efectivo; al contado
12. **bank account** cuenta de banco
    savings account cuenta de ahorros
    joint account cuenta mancomunada
    joint checking account cuenta mancomunada de cheques
13. **teller** pagador, cajero
14. **bank statement** estado de cuenta
15. **burglar** ladrón (*que se mete en casa ajena*)
16. **security** seguridad
17. **share** acción (*de la bolsa*)
18. **stock** acciones (*de la bolsa*)
    stock market bolsa
    stock exchange bolsa

211

19. **dividend** dividendo	25. **thumb tack** chinche
20. **profit** ganancia	26. **overdrawn** sobregirado
21. **stockholder** accionista	27. **deed** escritura
22. **branch** sucursal	28. **collateral** garantía (*para*
23. **stub** talón	*préstamo bancario*)
24. **calendar** calendario	29. **bank draft** giro (*bancario*)

IDIOMS

1. **to lose your temper** perder la paciencia
2. **to get nervous** ponerse nervioso
3. **to cash a check** cambiar (cobrar) un cheque
4. **to fill out a form** llenar un esqueleto (formulario)
5. **to endorse a check** endosar un cheque
6. **lack of funds** falta de fondos, insuficientes fondos
   insufficient funds falta de fondos, insuficientes fondos
7. **in duplicate** en duplicado
8. **It's up to you.** Depende de Ud.; Allá Ud.
9. **It's free (of charge).** Es gratis.
10. **sunup** salida de sol
    sundown puesta de sol
    from sunup to sundown de sol a sol
11. **in order to + (infinitive without to)** para + (infinitivo)
    I'm hurrying in order to finish early. Me estoy apresurando para aca
    temprano.

EXERCISE 1

Practice the following dialogue.

AT THE BANK

Teller: Good morning. What can I do for you?
Customer: I want to make a deposit.
Teller: Do you have an account here with us, or do you want to
           open an account?
Customer: My husband and I have a joint checking account here; but
           since he always takes care of our banking business, you'll
           have to tell me what forms to fill out in order to make a
           deposit.

Teller:	How much do you want to deposit?
Customer:	I have $200.00 in cash and $100.00 in checks. That's $300.00 altogether.
Teller:	Endorse the checks and make out a deposit slip in duplicate. You'll find the deposit slips over there on the table.
Customer:	Will you please let me know how much money we'll have in our account after I make this deposit. I lost the last bank statement I received and can't remember what the amount was.
Teller:	Whose name is your account in?
Customer:	Our account is in the names of Mr. and Mrs. Henry C. Wilson.
Teller:	Just a minute, please. This deposit will bring your account up to $1,600.00 Would you and your husband be interested in opening a savings account? Your money will draw two per cent interest.
Customer:	I'll tell my husband to talk to you about it the next time he's in the bank.
Teller:	Thank you very much, Mrs. Wilson.
Customer:	You're welcome. Good-bye.

EXERCISE 2

Learn these words.

NAMES OF FLOWERS

1. **blossom** flor de árbol frutal
2. **bud** capullo, botón
3. **carnation** clavel
4. **corsage** corsage
5. **daisy** margarita
6. **gardenia** gardenia
7. **gladiola** gladiola
8. **lilac** lila
9. **lily** lirio
10. **orchid** orquídea
11. **rose** rosa
12. **rose bush** rosal
13. **wreath** corona (*de flores*)

EXERCISE 3

Translate the following sentences and practice reading them.

1. before copying
2. after copying

3. instead of copying
4. in spite of copying
5. without copying
6. besides copying
7. on copying
8. He snores, but I don't.
9. He doesn't snore, but I do.
10. He snored, but I didn't.
11. He didn't snore, but I did.
12. She'll cheat, but they won't.
13. She won't cheat, but they will.
14. She's cheated, but they haven't.
15. She hasn't cheated, but they have.
16. I can iron, but you can't.
17. I can't iron, but you can.
18. I like to iron, but you don't.
19. I don't like to iron, but you do.
20. We wanted to resign, but he didn't.
21. We didn't want to resign, but he did.
22. We're going to resign, but he isn't.
23. We aren't going to resign, but he is.
24. He got married, did you?
25. He's going to get married. Are you?
26. They've eaten. Has she?
27. They've been eating, has she?
28. I can swim, can they?
29. I like to swim, do they?
30. You were working, was he?

EXERCISE 4

Translate the following sentences. Change them to the negative, interrogative, and interrogative negative.

1. He loses his temper every morning.
2. I lost my temper yesterday.
3. She'll lose her temper.
4. They've lost their temper many times.
5. You should lose your temper.
6. We're going to lose our temper.
7. She was going to lose her temper.

214

8. He likes to lose his temper.
9. They had to lose their temper.
10. You're losing your temper.

EXERCISE 5

Give the past tense and past participle of the following verbs.

pick up	paint	punish	pluck your
place	play	push	eyebrows
practice	prefer	promise	polish
pronounce	prepare	pick (a per-	poison
perspire	pull	son) up	print
		pull a tooth	play the piano

EXERCISE 6

Give the past tense and past participle of the following verbs.

be in mourn-	begin	be over	bite
ing	break	be worth	be missing
be shocked	bring	bet	be out of
(at)	buy	bleed	be operated on
become	be born	blow	blow your nose
		build	break out

EXERCISE 7

Verb Practice *Expand the following verb practice, using different tenses.*

1. That bush used to bloom.
2. That bush didn't use to bloom.
3. Did that bush use to bloom?
4. Didn't that bush use to bloom?

EXERCISE 8

Verb Practice *Make short sentences with forms of the verbs* **stretch, consist of, mortgage, perspire, sweat, deposit, withdraw, loan, lose your temper, get nervous, fill out a form, cash a check, endorse a check.** *Expand each verb practice to include different tenses, as in the exercise above. Use a different noun or pronoun with each verb. Use the interrogative words when it is possible.*

215

EXERCISE 9

Translate into Spanish.

1. You shouldn't lose your temper in front of the children.
2. I got so nervous during the examination that I could hardly write
3. If you buy this purse, we'll put your name on it free of charge
4. I don't care where we go on our vacation. It's up to you.
5. The parade began at sunup and didn't end until sundown.
6. Whether we go to the movies or go dancing is up to you. It doesn't matter to me.
7. You should get acquainted with your in-laws.
8. There was only a little gas left when we got home.
9. I used to spend a great deal of time at the movies, but I don't go any more.
10. Don't walk so fast. I'm not in a hurry, and he isn't either.
11. Don't take the presents out of the box while the children are here.
12. I've told him not to turn on the record player while you're trying to sleep.
13. There ought to be enough time to say good-bye to all the students before they have to leave.
14. That must be Mrs. Wilson's son. He looks just like her.
15. Maybe it would be better if we began earlier in the morning instead of working so late at night.
16. The bank won't give you a loan if you don't have any collateral.

EXERCISE 10

Translate into English.

1. ¿En qué dijo que consistiría su trabajo?
2. Él dijo que tendría que hipotecar su casa para pagar sus cuentas.
3. Si hubieras depositado todo tu dinero en el banco, no lo hubieras gastando tan pronto.
4. El señor Russell tenía una cuenta de ahorros aquí, pero ya no la tiene.
5. Le tendré que decir a ella que su cuenta está sobregirada.
6. Sería mejor que abriéramos una cuenta mancomunada de cheques.
7. Me fijé que sus claveles están abriendo.
8. Estos rosales tienen muchos botones que todavía no han florecido.
9. Me gustaría una casa con jardín, donde pudiera cultivar algunas flores.

10. ¿Quieres que te endose este cheque ahora?
11. El banco no quiso cambiarme este cheque.

EXERCISE 11

Answer the following questions.

1. Did you lose your temper?
2. Will you lose your temper?
3. Are you going to lose your temper?
4. Is the money all gone?
5. Was the food all gone?
6. Are the cigarettes all gone?
7. Did you get acquainted with him?
8. Will you get acquainted with him?
9. Are you getting acquainted with him?
10. Did you finish eating?
11. Will you finish eating soon?
12. Have you finished eating yet?
13. Does he remind you of anyone?
14. Who does he remind you of?
15. What does this remind you of?
16. Do you want to cash this check?
17. Can you cash a twenty-dollar check for me?
18. Did you withdraw any money from the bank?
19. Did the bank refuse to cash the check?
20. Is your account overdrawn?

Lección 3

1. **to pack, packed, packed** empacar
2. **to press, pressed, pressed** planchar
3. **to starch, starched, starched** almidonar
   starch almidón
4. **to fade, faded, faded** decolorar (se), desteñir (se)
5. **to stain, stained, stained** manchar
   stain mancha
6. **to shrink, shrank, shrunk** encoger (se)
7. **laundry** lavandería; ropa sucia
8. **(dry) cleaners** tintorería
9. **spot** mancha
10. **stiff** tieso

11. **suds** espuma de jabón
12. **bluing** azul (*añil*)
13. **rust** moho
    rusty oxidado; enmohecido
14. **sheet** sábana
15. **pillowcase** funda
16. **steep** empinado, pendiente
17. **shell** concha; carapacho
18. **cabin** cabaña
19. **greedy** codicioso
20. **ball** pelota
21. **partner** socio
22. **contract** contrato
23. **vacant** vacío, desocupado
24. **up-to-date** al corriente, al día; a la moda; a la fecha
25. **hut** choza
    shack choza
26. **frayed** luido, raído

IDIOMS

1. **I had my suit cleaned.** Mandé (Hice) limpiar mi traje.

218

I had the maid clean my suit. Mandé (Hice) que la criada limpiara mi traje.
When the person who performs the action is mentioned, we use the infinitive *without* to. *Otherwise we use the* past participle.

2. **I want the suit pressed.** Quiero que planchen el traje.
   I want the maid to press my suit. Quiero que la criada planche mi traje.
   I got my suit pressed. Mandé (Hice) planchar mi traje.
   I got the maid to press my suit. Mandé (Hice) que la criada planchara mi traje.
   When the person who performs the action is mentioned, we use the infinitive. *Otherwise we use the* past participle.

3. **to show off** presumir; lucir
   He's showing off in front of his friends. Está presumiendo con sus amigos.
   She wants to show off her new dress. Quiere lucir su nuevo vestido.

4. **to get infected** infectarse

5. **The colors won't run.** Los colores no se destiñen (no se corren, no se despintan).

6. **fast colored** colores firmes

7. **How about _____?** ¿Qué tal si _____?
   How about going to the movies? ¿Qué tal si vamos al cine?

8. **just pressed** nada más planchado

9. **laundry slip** nota de la lavandería

10. **(dry) cleaned** lavado en seco

11. **What do you want done to the suit?** ¿Qué quiere que le hagamos al traje?

EXERCISE 1

Practice the following dialogue.

AT THE LAUNDRY AND DRY CLEANERS

Employee: Good Morning. Can I help you?
Customer: I want this suit cleaned and pressed.
Employee: All right. And what do you want done to the dress?
Customer: I want the dress cleaned and pressed too if you are sure it won't fade or the colors won't run.
Employee: These colors are fast. They won't run.

Customer: Do you think you can take that stain out of the collar? don't know what it is.
Employee: It looks like rust. If it is, we can take it out.
Customer: There is a grease spot on the hem in the back. Will it come out?
Employee: Yes, we can take it out. Do you want this jacket cleaned and pressed?
Customer: No, just pressed. It isn't dirty. It got wrinkled in the closet. You'll be careful with the buttons, won't you?
Employee: Yes, we'll take the buttons off before pressing it. How about the shirts?
Customer: Starch the collars and cuffs, but not too stiff.
Employee: All right. How about the sheets and pillowcases? Do you want me to put any starch in them?
Customer: Don't starch the sheets, but please put a little in the pillow cases.
Employee: Is there anything else?
Customer: You deliver, don't you?
Employee: Yes, we do. We'll deliver these clothes on Wednesday afternoon. Here's your laundry slip.
Customer: That'll be fine. Good-bye.
Employee: Good-bye.

EXERCISE 2

Learn these words.

WORDS CONNECTED WITH MUSIC

1. **accordion** acordeón
2. **band** banda
3. **band leader** director de orquesta
4. **bass** bajo
5. **baton** batuta
6. **bow** arco de violín
7. **cello** violoncelo
8. **clarinet** clarinete
9. **composer** compositor
10. **conductor** director (*de orquesta*)
11. **cornet** corneta
12. **dance band** orquesta de baile
13. **drum** tambor
14. **drummer** el que toca el tambor; baterista
15. **duet** dueto
16. **flute** flauta
17. **guitar** guitarra
18. **harmonica** organillo
19. **harmony** armonía
20. **harp** arpa
21. **mandolin** mandolina
22. **notes** notas
23. **orchestra** orquesta

24. **orchestra leader** director de orquesta
25. **organ** órgano
26. **piano** piano
27. **pianist** pianista
28. **quartet** cuarteto
29. **record** disco
30. **rhythm** ritmo
31. **rhyme** rima
32. **saxophone** saxofón
33. **solo** solo
34. **soprano** soprano
35. **symphony orchestra** sinfónica
36. **tenor** tenor
37. **trombone** trombón
38. **trumpet** trompeta
39. **violin** violín
40. **violinist** violinista

EXERCISE 3

Translate the following sentences and practice reading them.

1. That man used to go too.
2. That man didn't use to go either.
3. Did that man use to go too?
4. Didn't that man use to go either?
5. He gets nervous, and she does too.
6. He doesn't get nervous, and she doesn't either.
7. They went on a diet, and we did too.
8. They didn't go on a diet, and we didn't either.
9. She'll lose weight, and you will too.
10. She won't lose weight, and you won't either.
11. You have gained weight, and I have too.
12. You haven't gained weight, and I haven't either.
13. We're going to get sunburned, and they are too.
14. We aren't going to get sunburned, and they aren't either.
15. I'll be able to take a trip, and she will too.
16. I won't be able to take a trip, and she won't either.
17. I'd like to go, and they would too.
18. I wouldn't like to go, and they wouldn't either.
19. You should brush your teeth, and I should too.
20. You shouldn't brush your teeth, and I shouldn't either.
21. Maybe he criticizes too much.
22. Maybe he doesn't criticize enough.
23. Perhaps he criticizes too much.
24. Perhaps he doesn't criticize enough.
25. He may criticize too much.
26. He may not criticize enough.

221

27. They might pack the trunk.
28. They might not pack the trunk.
29. Maybe they'll pack the trunk.
30. Maybe they won't pack the trunk.

EXERCISE 4

Translate the following sentences. Change them to the negative, interrogative, and interrogative negative.

1. I have my husband paint my kitchen every spring.
2. You had your car washed.
3. He had the dentist pull his tooth.
4. She'll have her hair washed.
5. We should have the record player fixed.
6. They'd like to get the grass cut.
7. I'm going to get that contractor to build my new house.
8. You were going to get your rugs cleaned.
9. You were going to get John to clean your rugs.
10. He's getting the maid to press his suit.
11. She was getting her hair dyed.

EXERCISE 5

Give the past tense and past participle of the following verbs.

propose (marriage)	pray	perspire	realize
pour	protect	press	remember
pour (something) out	patch	plant	rain
	phone	plan	rent
	park	reach	repeat
		reply	rest

EXERCISE 6

Give the past tense and past participle of the following verbs.

beat	catch	dig	find
be on a diet	choose	draw interest	forget
be well off	cost	draw	fall
come	do	drive	fall in love (with)
cut a tooth	drink	eat	feel

222

EXERCISE 7

Verb Practice *Expand the following verb practice, using different tenses.*

1. We'd like to pack.
2. We wouldn't like to pack.
3. Would we like to pack?
4. Wouldn't we like to pack?
5. How many would we like to pack?
6. How much would we like to parck?

EXERCISE 8

Verb Practice *Make short sentences with forms of the verbs* **press, starch, fade, stain, shrink, show off, get infected.** *Expand each verb practice to include different tenses, as in the exercise above. Use a different noun or pronoun with each verb. Use the interrogative words when it is possible.*

EXERCISE 9

Translate into Spanish.

1. What did you have that plant taken out of the house for?
2. Don't pay any attention to him. He's just showing off.
3. You'd better put some medicine on your finger to keep it from getting infected.
4. How about having dinner with me some evening?
5. Do you think that stain will come out of the tablecloth?
6. I had a new collar put on this shirt.
7. Haven't you finished painting the house yet?
8. He lost his temper, but I didn't.
9. That reminds me of a joke I heard last night.
10. She'll get nervous if she has to wait a long time.
11. You'd better not show off in front of your grandmother.
12. Let me give you my new address. I moved, you know.
13. He used to be well off.
14. Whose ring is this?
15. I wish they'd take these books off my desk.

EXERCISE 10

Translate into English.

1. ¿Cree Ud. que el sol (*will*) decolora la ropa?
2. Sus camisas se verían mejor si estuvieran almidonadas, ¿verdad?
3. Dijo que no se encogería esta chamarra.
4. Esa casa está desocupada. ¿Estará a la venta?
5. Dijo el dueño que tendrías que firmar un contrato por tres años.
6. Nació en una choza hace cuarenta y cinco años.
7. ¿Crees que este jugo de fruta (*will*) deje una mancha en mi corbata?
8. Está tan tieso el cuello de mi camisa que no lo puedo abrochar.
9. Se deberían remojar estas sábanas toda la noche antes de que se laven.
10. Más vale que no pierdas la nota de la lavandería.

EXERCISE 11

Answer the following questions.

1. Did you have your suit pressed?
2. Did you have your mother press your suit?
3. Will you have your coat cleaned?
4. Will you have the dry cleaners clean your coat?
5. Are you going to have your dress washed?
6. Are you going to have the maid wash your dress?
7. Do you always have your shirts starched?
8. Do you always have her starch your shirts?
9. Do you always have your shoes shined?
10. Do you always have him shine your shoes?
11. Will you get nervous?
12. How long does it take to press a suit?
13. How long does it take to get a permanent?
14. How long does it take to wash a shirt?
15. How long will it take to fix a flat?
16. How long will it take to charge the battery?
17. How long will it take to check the oil?
18. How long did it take to take his temperature?
19. How long did it take to pull his tooth?
20. How long did it take to make that dress?

Lección 31

Vocabulary

1. **to collect, collected, collected** cobrar (*una cuenta*) coleccionar; colectar
2. **to strain, strained, strained** colar
3. **to combine, combined, combined** combinar
4. **to guarantee, guaranteed, guaranteed** garantizar **guarantee** garantía
5. **to threaten, threatened, threatened** amenazar **threat** amenaza
6. **to lack, lacked, lacked** faltar
7. **butter knife** cuchillo mantequillero
8. **teaspoon** cucharita **teaspoonful** cucharadita
9. **tablespoon** cuchara **tablespoonful** cucharada
10. **(soup) ladle** cucharón (*para sopa*)
11. **handle** mango

plain-handled (*adj.*) de mango sin dibujo
12. **blade** hoja de un cuchillo
13. **can opener** abrelatas
14. **salad bowl** ensaladero
15. **salad spoon** cuchara para servir ensalada **salad fork** tenedor para servir ensalada
16. **glassware** cristalería
17. **pot holder** agarradera
18. **stainless steel** (*adj.*) de acero inoxidable
19. **old-fashioned** anticuado
20. **friendship** amistad
21. **paradise** paraíso
22. **dizzy** mareado
23. **width** anchura
24. **unusual** poco común, raro
25. **silverware** (*sing.*) cubiertos
26. **design** grabado, dibujo, diseño
27. **enamel** esmalte

IDIOMS

1. **to hear from** tener noticias de, saber de
   Have you heard from John? ¿Has sabido de Juan?
2. **to hear about** saber de, oír hablar de
   Have you heard about the accident? ¿Supiste del accidente?
3. **to get loose** soltarse, zafarse
   The dog got loose. El perro se soltó.
4. **to turn (someone or something) loose** soltar (a alguien o algo)
   We turned the dog loose. Soltamos al perro.
5. **to be crazy about** estar loco por, gustar muchísimo, encantarle
   a uno
   I'm crazy about her. Estoy loco por ella.
   He's crazy about football. Le encanta el fútbol.
6. **to have on hand** tener en existencia
7. **loose pieces** piezas sueltas
8. **a set of silver** un juego de cubiertos de plata
   a set of dishes una vajilla
   a set of glasses un juego de vasos
   a set of cups and saucers un juego de té
9. **the front of the house** la fachada de la casa

EXERCISE 1

Practice the following dialogue.

BUYING THINGS FOR THE KITCHEN

Clerk: Have you been waited on?
Customer: I wonder if you have any plain-handled, silver teaspoons to
           match a set of silverware I have.
Clerk: It's possible. Let's look at the loose pieces of silver that we
           have on hand and see if we can find what you want. Do you
           see any pieces here that are like your set?
Customer: I believe these will do. I think they're exactly like the ones I
           have.
Clerk: Would you be interested in some tablespoons?
Customer: No, I have plenty of tablespoons, but I'll take a butter knife
           and a soup ladle, if you have them.
Clerk: We don't have a butter knife or a soup ladle that will match
           your set. Would you be interested in a similar design?

226

Customer: No, I don't think so. But I need a butcher knife—one with a thick blade—and a can opener.

Clerk: Do you want a combination can opener, bottle opener, and corkscrew?

Customer: It doesn't make any difference.

Clerk: Is your set of salad forks complete? Do you need any glassware or cups and saucers? Let me show you an unusual set of dishes that we have on hand.

Customer: No, thank you. I won't have time. I don't need anything else this morning except a few pot holders.

Clerk: All right. Please pay the cashier—and come in again

EXERCISE 2

Learn these words.

THINGS FOR THE KITCHEN

1. **blender** licuadora
2. **buffet** aparador
3. **candleholder** palmatoria
   candlestickholder candelero
   candle vela
4. **china** vajilla de lujo
5. **china closet** vitrina
6. **cocktail shaker** coctelera
7. **coffeepot** cafetera
8. **cupboard** alacena
9. **deep freeze** congelador
10. **dishcloth** toalla de cocina
11. **dishpan** tina para lavar platos
12. **dishrag** trapo de cocina
13. **dishtowel** toalla de cocina
14. **double boiler** baño María
15. **dryer** secadora
16. **egg beater** batidor
17. **frying pan** sartén
18. **garbage can** bote de basura
19. **ice cube** cubo de hielo
20. **ice tray** charola de hielo
21. **ice water** agua helada
22. **kettle** caldera
23. **mixer** batidor eléctrico
24. **pan** charola para hornear
25. **percolator** cafetera de vapor
26. **pot** olla
27. **pressure cooker** olla express
28. **refrigerator** refrigerador
29. **roaster** asador
30. **sifter** cernedor
31. **sink** fregadero
32. **strainer** colador
33. **teapot** tetera
34. **toaster** tostador
35. **tray** charola
36. **waffle iron** waflera
37. **washing machine** lavadora

EXERCISE 3

Translate the following sentences and practice reading them.

227

1. He'll have to be successful.
2. He won't have to be successful.
3. Will he have to be successful?
4. Won't he have to be successful?
5. Why won't he have to be successful?
6. They'd have to be successful.
7. They wouldn't have to be successful.
8. Would they have to be successful?
9. Wouldn't they have to be successful?
10. Why wouldn't they have to be successful?
11. You've had to file your fingernails.
12. You haven't had to file your fingernails.
13. Have you had to file your fingernails?
14. Haven't you had to file your fingernails?
15. Why haven't you had to file your fingernails?
16. I used to phone.
17. I didn't use to phone.
18. Did I use to phone?
19. Didn't I use to phone?
20. Why didn't I use to phone?
21. She used to be able to type.
22. She didn't use to be able to type.
23. Did she use to be able to type?
24. Didn't she use to be able to type?
25. Why didn't she use to be able to type?
26. There is a frying pan.
27. There isn't a frying pan.
28. Is there a frying pan?
29. Isn't there a frying pan?
30. How many frying pans are there?

EXERCISE 4

Translate the following sentences. Change them to the negative, interrogative, and interrogative negative.

1. He hears from his wife every day.
2. They heard from Jim yesterday.
3. She's heard from him twice.
4. They'll hear from the President tomorrow.
5. We should hear from the boys soon.

6. He heard about your operation.
7. They've heard about the accident.
8. You'll hear about the football game.
9. We're going to hear about the storm.
10. She wanted to hear about our trip.

EXERCISE 5

Give the past tense and past participle of the following verbs.

return	rub	register	remind (some-
rot	rinse	recognize	one) of (some-
raise	resign	ruin	thing)
recommend	reduce	roll	show
remove	repent	rescue	start
			stop

EXERCISE 6

Give the past tense and past participle of the following verbs.

fall asleep	freeze	get	get thirsty
feed	feel sorry for	get mad (at)	get up early
feel at home	feel like	get rich	go to bed late
fight	fly	fit	get a shock
find out	forgive	get sleepy	give up

EXERCISE 7

Verb Practice *Expand the following verb practice, using different tenses.*

1. The lawyer will be able to collect the taxes.
2. The lawyer won't be able to collect the taxes.
3. Will the lawyer be able to collect the taxes?
4. Won't the lawyer be able to collect the taxes?
5. How will the lawyer be able to collect the taxes?
6. When will the lawyer be able to collect the taxes?

EXERCISE 8

Verb Practice *Make short sentences with forms of the verbs* strain, combine, guarantee, threaten, lack, hear from, hear about, get loose, turn

(something) loose, be crazy about, have on hand. *Expand each verb* *practice to include different tenses, as in the exercise above. Use a different noun or pronoun with each verb. Use the interrogative word when it is possible.*

EXERCISE 9

Translate into Spanish.

1. I haven't heard from him since last December.
2. Have you heard about the new law?
3. Tie that horse up so he can't get loose.
4. Hold this horse. Don't turn him loose.
5. Among her wedding presents were a set of silverware for eight and a complete set of dishes.
6. The front of the house will have to be painted before we move.
7. He's crazy about baseball.
8. She's crazy about chocolate cake.
9. Who turned that lion loose?
10. I wonder if this refrigerator is guaranteed.
11. Did you find a set of cups and saucers to match your dishes?
12. All children like to show off.
13. I had this shirt starched.
14. You'll have to be at home by sundown.
15. She reminds me of my first teacher.

EXERCISE 10

Translate into English.

1. Cuela la sopa antes de servirla.
2. ¿Sabes cómo se le quita (cure) esta enfermedad?
3. Amenazó con despedirla por llegar tarde.
4. Tengo dolor de cabeza y me siento mareado.
5. Tengo diez años de coleccionar estampillas.
6. ¿Tiene Ud. un cuchillo con mango largo?
7. ¿Has sabido de Enrique últimamente?
8. Su amistad vale mucho para mí.
9. ¿Prefiere Ud. los cubiertos de acero inoxidable?
10. El perro se soltó.

EXERCISE 11

Answer the following questions.

1. Did you hear from your family?
2. Will you hear from your wife?
3. Have you heard from Martha?
4. Did you hear about the storm?
5. Will you hear about the meeting?
6. Have you heard about the party?
7. Can you keep them from getting behind?
8. Could you keep them from getting behind?
9. Will you be able to keep them from getting behind?
10. Did they stop praying?
11. Will they stop looking around?
12. Did he stop snoring?
13. Did she take care of the silverware?
14. Will they take care of the piano?
15. Have you taken care of the passengers?
16. Are you going to have your shoes shined?
17. Are you going to have the boy shine your shoes?
18. Did she get her teeth fixed?
19. Did she get the dentist to fix her teeth?
20. Do you want to get your teeth fixed?

Lección 3

Vocabulary

1. **to heat, heated, heated** calentar
2. **to furnish, furnished, furnished** amueblar
3. **to fold, folded, folded** doblar (*tela, papel*)
4. **to bend, bent, bent** doblar (*metales, el cuerpo*)
5. **to argue (about), argued (about), argued (about)** discutir (de, por), argüir, alegar
   to argue with discutir con
   argument discusión
6. **to quarrel, quarreled, quarreled** reñir, pelear
   quarrel riña, pelea
7. **type** tipo, clase, estilo
8. **attractive** atractivo
9. **lamp** lámpara
   floor lamp lámpara de piso
10. **twin bed** cama gemela
    single bed cama individual

    double bed cama matrimonial
11. **bedroom set** juego de recámara
12. **chest of drawers** cómoda
13. **dressing table** tocador
    night table mesita de noche
14. **mattress** colchón
    innerspring mattress colchón con resortes interiores
15. **spring** tambor
    box spring box spring
16. **wholesale** mayoreo, por mayoreo
    retail menudeo, por menudeo
17. **bedspread** colcha
18. **lamp shade** pantalla para lámpara
19. **mahogany** caoba
20. **pine** pino
21. **cedar** cedro
22. **maple** maple, arce
23. **walnut** nogal

232

24. **delighted** encantado	**bathtub** tina de baño
25. **height** altura	**washtub** tina para lavar
26. **tub** tina	27. **alley** callejón

IDIOMS

1. **What makes _____?** ¿Qué hace _____?
   What makes the engine knock? ¿Qué hace que la máquina suene?
2. **to deal with, dealt with, dealt with** tratar con
3. **to have (something) re-covered** mandar retapizar (algo)
4. **upside down** al revés, lo de arriba abajo, volteado, invertido; patas arriba (*muebles*)
   This picture is upside down. Este cuadro está volteado.
5. **inside out** (*clothes*) al revés
   He has his socks on inside out. Tiene sus calcetines al revés.
6. **backwards** al revés; hacia atrás
   He does everything backwards. Hace todo al revés.
   He's walking backwards. Está caminando hacia atrás.
7. **Come this way.** Por aquí.
8. **one of these days** un día de estos
9. **Take your time.** Hágalo (Tómalo) con calma.
10. **furnished apartment** departamento amueblado
    unfurnished apartment departamento sin amueblar
11. **It's (That's) no fun.** No tiene chiste; No es divertido.

EXERCISE 1

Practice the following dialogue.

AT THE FURNITURE STORE

Clerk: What type of furniture are you interested in?

Customer: I'm furnishing a bedroom. I'd like to see some bedroom furniture.

Clerk: Come this way, please. This will furnish a bedroom very nicely. Six pieces—one of the most attractive we have—complete with twin beds, chest of drawers, dressing table, night table, and lamp for $265.00 It's on sale.

Customer: I'd prefer a double bed.

Clerk:	In that case let's look at these pieces in mahogany here. They come with double beds, and they're the same price as those with twin beds.
Customer:	What about the springs and the mattress?
Clerk:	The bed comes with a box spring and an innerspring mattress.
Customer:	When can you deliver this furniture?
Clerk:	We can deliver it this afternoon. Would you like to look at any other furniture while you're here?
Customer:	No, thank you. I bought a new floor lamp and a coffee table last month, and I'm having the sofa and chairs re-covered.
Clerk:	I see. Here's the bill for the pieces you bought.
Customer:	Will you take a check?
Clerk:	Yes, we will. Thank you and come back. I'll see that the furniture is delivered this afternoon.

EXERCISE 2

Learn these words.

THINGS FOR THE HOUSE AND YARD

1. **beach chair** silla para playa
2. **blinds** persianas
3. **broom** escoba
4. **coffee table** mesa para café
5. **cot** catre, cama de campaña
6. **curtain rod** armazón para cortinas, cortinero
7. **drapes** cortinas
8. **dust cloth** sacudidor
9. **feather duster** plumero
10. **folding chair** silla plegadiza
11. **footstool** taburete
12. **hanger** gancho para ropa
13. **hardwood floor** piso de madera
14. **lawn chair** silla para jardín
15. **medicine cabinet** botiquín (del baño)
16. **plaster** yeso
17. **rocking chair** silla mecedora
18. **shower** regadera
19. **shower curtain** cortina de baño
20. **varnish** barniz
21. **vacuum cleaner** aspiradora
22. **Venetian blinds** persianas
23. **tile floor** piso de azulejo
24. **wax** cera
25. **to dust** sacudir
26. **to plaster** enyesar
27. **to varnish** barnizar
28. **to wax** encerar

EXERCISE 3

Translate the following sentences and practice reading them.

1. There were two mosquitos.
2. There weren't two mosquitos.
3. Were there two mosquitos?
4. Weren't there two mosquitos?
5. How many mosquitos were there?
6. It was hot.
7. It wasn't hot.
8. Was it hot?
9. Wasn't it hot?
10. Why wasn't it hot?
11. They were cold.
12. They weren't cold.
13. Were they cold?
14. Weren't they cold?
15. When were they cold?
16. There'll be an orchestra.
17. There won't be an orchestra?
18. Will there be an orchestra.
19. Won't there be an orchestra?
20. How many orchestras will there be?

EXERCISE 4

Translate the following sentences. Change them to the negative, interrogative, and interrogative negative.

1. You know what makes the engine knock.
2. He knew what made the silver tarnish.
3. They'll find out what makes the ice melt.
4. We've found out what makes your watch stop.
5. She's going to see what makes the tub leak.
6. She was going to see what made the baby cry.
7. He likes to deal with Europeans.
8. They wanted to deal with Americans.
9. We dealt with the cowboys.
10. She should deal with honest men.

EXERCISE 5

Give the past tense and past participle of the following verbs.

satisfy	smell	spill	serve
save	smile (at)	stay	spoil
seem	smoke	suffer	shave
sew	snow	surprise	sharpen
shout (at)	sound	slice	step on

EXERCISE 6

Give the past tense and past participle of the following verbs.

go back	get away	get in	get old
go out	get better	get light	get on
go out of	get dark	get lost	get out of
go to bed	get drunk	get off	get ready
go to sleep	get hurt	get married	get rid of

EXERCISE 7

Verb Practice *Expand the following verb practice, using different tenses.*

1. If they heated the soup, it would taste better.
2. If they heated the soup, it wouldn't taste better.
3. If they had heated the soup, it would have tasted better.
4. If they had heated the soup, it wouldn't have tasted better.
5. If they could heat the soup, it would taste better.
6. If they could heat the soup, it wouldn't taste better.
7. If they were heating the soup, they'd be in the kitchen.
8. If they were heating the soup, they wouldn't be in the kitchen.

EXERCISE 8

Verb Practice *Make short sentences with forms of the verbs* **furnish, fold, bend, argue (about, with), quarrel, deal with, have (something) re-covered, dust, plaster, varnish, wax.** *Expand each verb practice to include different tenses, as in the exercise above. Use a different noun or pronoun with each verb. Use the interrogative words when it is possible.*

236

EXERCISE 9

Translate into Spanish.

1. What makes your sweater stretch?
2. Those are the rudest people that I've ever dealt with.
3. How much will it cost to have this chair re-covered?
4. One of these days we'll find out what makes our chickens die.
5. She doesn't know what makes her hands so red.
6. Don't hurry. Take your time. There's more than an hour left.
7. I want you to pick out some nice material to re-cover the sofa with.
8. I'm crazy about your new lamp shade.
9. Guess who I heard from today?
10. We'll eat as soon as the cook finishes heating the soup.
11. I plan to travel around the world before I die.
12. He's a hard person to get acquainted with.
13. How about helping me move next week?
14. We didn't get back until after sundown.
15. I can't stand her brother-in-law.

EXERCISE 10

Translate into English.

1. ¿(De) qué están discutiendo? Están discutiendo por dinero.
2. Si Ud. dobla sus trajes con cuidado antes de empacarlos, no se le arrugarán.
3. No podrás doblar más la hoja sin romperla.
4. Debe haberse peleado con su mujer.
5. No voy a amueblar este año la sala.
6. Ella quiere amueblar toda su casa en caoba.
7. No tiene chiste trabajar con gente que está siempre peleando.
8. Ellos no discutieron con el profesor, ni yo tampoco.
9. Su mamá va a mandar retapizar estos muebles el año próximo, ¿verdad?
10. Él hace todas las cosas al revés, y Estela también.

EXERCISE 11

Answer the following questions.

1. What makes him look so pale?

2. What made this water red?
3. What makes her so fat?
4. Did you have this birthday cake made?
5. Will you have your wedding dress made?
6. Have you had your shoes shined?
7. What's he showing off for?
8. What was he showing off for?
9. Did you hear from Martha?
10. Have you heard from the boss?
11. Did you hear about the fire?
12. Have you heard about the flood?
13. Do you plan to furnish the bedroom this fall?
14. Did you plan to take a trip last summer?
15. Do you plan to have your teeth pulled?

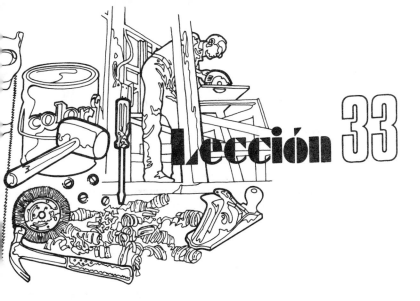

Vocabulary

1. **to explode, exploded, exploded** explotar
2. **to undress, undressed, undressed** desvestir (se)
3. **to refuse, refused, refused** rehusar, negarse a
4. **to supply (someone with), supplied (someone with), supplied (someone with)** surtir o abastecer (a alguien) (de)
5. **to limp, limped, limped** cojear
6. **to carve, carved, carved** tallar, cincelar; trinchar, cortar (*carne*)
7. **sculpture** escultura
8. **hammer** martillo
9. **saw** sierra
10. **nail** clavo
11. **lumber** madera aserrada
12. **cement** cemento

   concrete concreto
13. **depth** profundidad
14. **list** lista
15. **tack** tachuela
16. **screw** tornillo
17. **frame** marco
18. **chisel** cincel
19. **paintbrush** brocha, pincel
20. **pipe** tubo
   pipes tubería, tubos
21. **faucet** llave (*de agua*)
22. **wire** alambre
23. **turpentine** aguarrás
24. **(light) switch** apagador
25. **wall plug** contacto
   outlet contacto
26. **plumbing** plomería; tubería
27. **hardware store** ferretería
28. **wallet** cartera
29. **billfold** cartera

IDIOMS

1. **to be fond of** + **(gerund, objective pronoun, or noun)**
   tener cariño o afición (a), gustar, apreciar
   I'm very fond of her. Le tengo mucho cariño.
   He's very fond of swimming. Le gusta mucho nadar.
2. **to get in trouble** meterse en dificultades
3. **to keep a promise** cumplir una promesa
4. **a set of tools** un equipo de herramientas
5. **a coat of paint** una mano de pintura
6. **That makes me mad.** Eso me disgusta, Eso me da coraje.
7. **The sun sets at 6:30.** El sol se mete a las seis y media.
8. **The sun rises at 7:30.** El sol sale a las siete y media.
9. **neat** pulcro, bien arreglado y limpio
   neatly pulcramente
   Her house is very neat. Tiene su casa muy bien arreglada y limpia.
   She dresses neatly. Se viste pulcramente.

EXERCISE 1

Practice the following dialogue.

AT THE HARDWARE STORE

Clerk: If you're going to build a garage, you'll need more than a hammer and a saw and some nails. Tell me what you have on hand, and I'll tell you what we can supply you with here.

Customer: I already have all the lumber I need, and I have the cement for the concrete floor. I've got a list of things that I want to buy this morning. I'll need some tacks, screws, a screwdriver, and a chisel.

Clerk: What about paint? (¿Y pintura?)

Customer: I'll let you know later how much paint I'll need. I'll also need a paintbrush, some varnish, and some turpentine.

Clerk: How about the plumbing? (¿Y tubería?)

Customer: I've got all the pipe I need, but I don't have a faucet.

Clerk: Now, about the lighting. Do you know how much wire you'll need?

Customer: I think forty feet will be enough. The garage will have one light switch and one wall plug.

Clerk: Can you think of anything else you'll need this morning?
Customer: No, I can't think of anything else now. I'll have to make
            another trip into town this afternoon, and maybe I'll pick
            some more things up then. I want to talk to the carpenter
            first. I'll probably see you later.
Clerk: O. K. Good-bye.

EXERCISE 2

Learn these words.

HARDWARE TERMS

1. **ax** hacha
2. **bolt** perno
3. **brace** berbiquí
4. **bit** broca
5. **brick** ladrillo
6. **bricklayer** albañil
7. **carpenter** carpintero
8. **drill** berbiquí; taladro
9. **electrician** electricista
10. **fuse** tapón
11. **hoe** azadón, azada
12. **mason** albañil
13. **mouse trap** ratonera
14. **nut** tuerca
15. **pick** zapapico
16. **plaster of Paris** escayola,
    yeso para modelar
17. **pliers** alicates; pinzas
18. **plumber** plomero
19. **sawdust** aserrín
20. **shingle** tejamanil
21. **shovel** pala
22. **spade** laya
23. **spray** rociador, bomba,
    pulverizador
24. **sprayer** rociador, bomba,
    pulverizador
25. **tool** herramienta
26. **washer** rondana
27. **wrench** llave

EXERCISE 3

Translate the following sentences and practice reading them.

1. She used to dust the blinds.
2. She didn't use to dust the blinds.
3. Did she use to dust the blinds?
4. Didn't she use to dust the blinds?
5. When did she use to dust the blinds?
6. They'll have to collect the taxes.

7. They won't have to collect the taxes.
8. Will they have to collect the taxes?
9. Won't they have to collect the taxes?
10. When will they have to collect the taxes?
11. There have been many checking accounts.
12. There haven't been many checking accounts.
13. Have there been many checking accounts?
14. Haven't there been many checking accounts?
15. How many checking accounts have there been?
16. It'll be cold.
17. It won't be cold.
18. Will it be cold?
19. Won't it be cold?
20. When will it be cold?
21. They'll be hungry.
22. They won't be hungry.
23. Will they be hungry?
24. Won't they be hungry?
25. When will they be hungry?
26. What was the story about?
27. What was the picture about?
28. Who did you go with?
29. Who are you going to go with?
30. What did you cheat for?

EXERCISE 4

Translate the following sentences. Change them to the negative, interrogative, and interrogative negative.

1. He's fond of fried chicken.
2. Alice is fond of reading.
3. They were fond of children.
4. We ought to be fond of traveling.
5. Henry should be fond of his grandparents.
6. You used to be fond of painting.
7. I was fond of my mother-in-law.
8. They were fond of riding.
9. We're fond of Mexican food.
10. She's been fond of swimming for a long time.

242

EXERCISE 5

Give the past tense and past participle of the following verbs.

swallow	scratch	shock	stretch
sign	suggest	snore	serve
soak	sacrifice	skid	show off
smear	suppose	screw	starch
sterilize	seal	start back	stain

EXERCISE 6

Give the past tense and past participle of the following verbs.

get scared	give a dis-	go on	go up
get sick	count	go with	go down
get wet	go dancing	go shopping	get a haircut
get worse	go riding	grow	get a shave
give away	go swimming	grind	get a shine
			get burned

EXERCISE 7

Verb Practice *Expand the following verb practice, using different tenses.*

1. The pressure cooker used to explode, didn't it?
2. The pressure cooker didn't use to explode, did it?
3. Did the pressure cooker use to explode?
4. Didn't the pressure cooker use to explode?
5. When did the pressure cooker use to explode?

EXERCISE 8

Verb Practice *Make short sentences with forms of the verbs* **undress, refuse, supply (someone with), limp, carve, be fond of, get in trouble, keep a promise.** *Expand each verb practice to include different tenses, as in the exercise above. Use a different noun or pronoun with each verb. Use the interrogative words when it is possible.*

243

EXERCISE 9

Transalate into Spanish.

1. Didn't you use to be fond of dancing?
2. You're going to get in trouble if you aren't careful.
3. I can't stand people who can't keep promises.
4. Do you know what time the sun sets?
5. We'll have to give this room two coats of paint.
6. He says he's an engineer, but he doesn't look like one.
7. This material looks like satin.
8. The movie wasn't over until ten minutes to twelve.
9. I hope you have a good time in San Antonio.
10. He asked me if they had fun at the market, and I said I didn't think so.
11. I caught a mouse in that mouse trap, but he got away.
12. He got in trouble in California, and they sent him to jail.
13. If you make a promise, you must keep it.
14. I'm fond of having breakfast in bed.
15. When you finish ironing that shirt, please press my pants.
16. I can't read your handwriting. Why don't you write neatly?

EXERCISE 10

Translate into English.

1. ¿Por qué estás cojeando?
2. Le surtiremos todas las herramientas que necesite.
3. Usen un cuchillo filoso para cortar el pavo.
4. El sol se mete más temprano en enero que en julio, ¿verdad?
5. Le tengo mucho cariño a Estela, pero a su hermana no.
6. Si no hubiera sentido lástima por él, no le hubiera dado el dinero.
7. Le dije que se enfermaría si no se cuidaba.
8. Ellos tendrán que cobrar el dinero antes de la Pascua.
9. Ojalá que no se niegue a ayudarnos.
10. ¿Por qué no lo haces así? Será más fácil.

EXERCISE 11

Answer the following questions.

1. Are you fond of books?

244

2. Are you fond of the movies?
3. Are you fond of potato salad?
4. Did he keep his promise?
5. Will he keep his promise?
6. Has he kept his promise?
7. Did you get in trouble?
8. Will you get in trouble?
9. Have you got in trouble?
10. If he had come early, would he have seen you?
11. If they had gone yesterday, would they have taken you?
12. If it had rained on Monday, would you have gone to play football?
13. Did you get rid of your car?
14. Will you get rid of your car?
15. Have you got rid of your car?
16. Does she dress neatly?
17. Isn't her room neat?
18. Is her sister very neat?
19. Don't you think it's awfully hot?
20. It's pretty hot in Acapulco, isn't it?

Lección 3

Vocabulary

1. **to include, included, included**
   incluir
2. **to depend (on), depended (on), depended (on)**
   depender (de), contar (con)
3. **to appreciate, appreciated, appreciated** agradecer
4. **to accept, accepted, accepted**
   aceptar
5. **to mark, marked, marked**
   marcar, anotar; poner precio
6. **to demand, demanded, demanded** exigir
7. **tag** etiqueta (*para colgar*)
   price tag etiqueta de precio
8. **athlete** atleta
9. **athletics** atletismo
   sports deportes
10. **athletic equipment**
    equipo gimnástico
11. **(baseball) bat** bate, tolete
12. **water skis** esquíes acuáticos
13. **habit** costumbre

14. **(tennis) racket** raqueta
    (*de tenis*)
15. **baseball glove** manopla
    (*de béisbol*)
16. **helmet** casco
17. **shoulder pads** hombreras
18. **shin guards** protectores
    de espinilla
19. **track shoes** zapatos para
    carrera
20. **rod and reel** caña y carrete
    (*para pescar*)
21. **hook** anzuelo; gancho
    fishhook anzuelo
22. **crippled** inválido
23. **lame** cojo
    disabled imposibilitado
24. **fingerprints** huellas
    digitales
25. **bitter** amargo; amargado
26. **label** etiqueta (*para pegar*)
27. **unless** a menos que, a no
    ser que

246

28.	**sporting goods** artículos de deporte	29. **bathing cap** gorra de baño

IDIOMS

1. **to build a fire** prender fuego, hacer una fogata
   to set (something) on fire prender fuego (a algo)
2. **to knock (someone or something) down** derribar o tirar (a alguien o algo)
   to knock (someone) out noquear (a alquien)
3. **to name someone after someone** poner nombre igual al de una persona
   Who were you named after? ¿Cómo quién te llamas?
   They named him after his grandfather. El se llama como su abuelo.
   The child was named after George Washington. Le pusieron al niño George Washington.
4. **to come off** zafársele a uno, salírsele a uno, caérsele a uno
   His shoe came off. Se le zafó (salió, cayó) el zapato.
5. **to fall off** caerse, caérsele a uno
   The lamp fell off the table. La lámpara se cayó de la mesa.
6. **Beware of the dog.** Cuidado con el perro.
   (*used on signs*)
7. **The skate isn't on tight enough.** El patín no está bien ajustado (sujeto).

EXERCISE 1

Practice the following dialogue.

IN A SPORTING GOODS STORE

First Clerk: Did you put price tags on all that athletic equipment that came in yesterday?

Second Clerk: I put price tags on some of it, but there's still a lot to do.

First Clerk: How about that baseball equipment? Did you finish marking it?

Second Clerk: Yes, the balls, bats, and gloves are marked.

First Clerk: I think we'd better put a pair of roller skates and ice skates in the window. Take those water skis out of the window and put them against the wall.

Second Clerk: All this tennis equipment should be put on the same shelf—nets, balls, rackets, and shoes.

First Clerk: There won't be enough room unless you move these football helmets, shoulder pads, and shin guards.

Second Clerk: I fixed a place on the bottom shelf for all that football equipment. And put those track shoes down there too.

First Clerk: We don't have much fishing equipment on hand, do we?

Second Clerk: We're out of fishhooks, but there should be some in today. The rods and reels came in yesterday.

First Clerk: We'll have to get them on the shelves this afternoon. I'm going to lunch now. I'll see you later.

Second Clerk: Try to be back by one.

First Clerk: O. K. Good-bye.

EXERCISE 2

Learn these words.

WORDS CONNECTED WITH SPORTS

1. **to bowl** jugar boliche
   to go bowling ir al boliche
   bowling (*el deporte*) boliche
   bowling alley establecimiento donde se juega boliche
   (bowling) pin pino
2. **to box** boxear
   boxer boxeador
   boxing (*el deporte*) el box, el boxeo
   boxing match pelea
   boxing gloves guantes de box
   (boxing) ring ring
   the fights el box, las peleas
   opponent contrincante
   hook gancho
   left hook gancho de izquierda

   right hook gancho de derecha
   round round
3. **to dive** echar un clavado; bucear
   diver clavadista; buzo
   diving (*el deporte*) echar clavados
   diving board trampolín
4. **to fence** esgrimir
   fencing (*el deporte*) esgrimir, la esgrima
5. **to fish** pescar
   to catch a fish coger un pez
   to go fishing ir a pescar
   fishing (*el deporte*) pescar, la pesca
   bait carnada, cebo
6. **to play golf** jugar al golf
   golf golf
   golf ball pelota de golf

golf club palo de golf
golf course campo de golf
caddy caddy
7. to play billiards jugar
carambola
to play pool jugar al
billar, jugar pool
pool (*el deporte*) el billar,
el pool
pool hall establecimiento
donde se juega pool
8. to row remar
oar remo
rowing (*el deporte*) remar
9. to skate patinar
to go skating ir a patinar
skater patinador
skating (*el deporte*) patinar
skating rink pista de
patinar
a pair of ice skates
un par de patines de hielo
a pair of roller skates
un par de patines
10. to ski esquiar (*sobre la
nieve*)
to water-ski esquiar

(*sobre el agua*)
skiing (*el deporte*) esquiar
skis esquíes
skier esquiador
11. to play tennis jugar tenis
tennis tenis
tennis court cancha de tenis
12. to wrestle luchar
wrestler luchador
wrestling (*el deporte*) las
luchas, luchar
wrestling match lucha
13. batter bateador, toletero
pitcher pitcher, lanzador
catcher catcher, receptor
outfielder jardinero
fly (ball) elevado (*sust.*)
inning entrada
14. weightlifter levantador de
pesas
weightlifting (*el deporte*)
hacer pesas
bar bell mancuerna
weights pesas
15. team equipo
16. trophy trofeo

EXERCISE 3

Translate the following sentences and practice reading them.

1. There'd be a price tag.
2. There wouldn't be a price tag.
3. Would there be a price tag?
4. Wouldn't there be a price tag?
5. How many price tags would there be?
6. It's been cold.
7. It hasn't been cold.
8. Has it been cold?
9. Hasn't it been cold?

10. When has it been cold?
11. We've been afraid.
12. We haven't been afraid.
13. Have we been afraid?
14. Haven't we been afraid?
15. Why haven't we been afraid?
16. It used to be hot.
17. It didn't use to be hot.
18. Did it use to be hot?
19. Didn't it use to be hot?
20. Why did it use to be hot?
21. He used to be able to dance.
22. He didn't use to be able to dance.
23. Did he use to be able to dance?
24. Didn't he use to be able to dance?
25. When did he use to be able to dance?

EXERCISE 4

Translate the following sentences. Change them to the negative, inter-rogative, and interrogative negative.

1. He knows how to build a fire in the fireplace.
2. They built a fire in the kitchen.
3. We'll build a fire outside.
4. She's built a fire under the kettle.
5. You should be able to build a fire.
6. He tried to set the house on fire.
7. We set the grass on fire.
8. They set the wood on fire.
9. You'll set the woods on fire.
10. He's set the building on fire.

EXERCISE 5

Give the past tense and past participle of the following verbs.

strain	turn off	travel	taste
supply	turn on	try hard	taste like
talk	test	turn over	thank
translate	tie	trim your	tarnish
try	touch	mustache, beard	tip
			trust

250

EXERCISE 6

Give the past tense and past participle of the following verbs.

get excited
give a dis-
   count
go on a trip
go for a walk,
   ride
get a trim

get a per-
   manent
get a mani-
   cure
get a tan
get sun-
   burned

get run over
get well
get hurt
give out
go on a picnic
get beat
get a divorce

go on a diet
get fired
give (some-
   thing) back
have an ac-
   cident
have a flat

EXERCISE 7

Verb Practice   *Expand the following verb practice, using different tenses.*

1. This list includes everything, doesn't it?
2. This list doesn't include everything, does it?
3. Does this list include everything?
4. Doesn't this list include everything?
5. Why doesn't this list include everything?

EXERCISE 8

Verb Practice   *Make short sentences with forms of the verbs* depend (on), appreciate, accept, mark, demand, build a fire, set (something) on fire, knock (someone or something) down, knock (someone) out, name someone after someone, come off, fall off, box, dive, play golf, row, skate, go skating, ski, water-ski, wrestle, fence, play tennis, bowl, go bowling, play pool, play billiards, fish, go fishing, catch a fish. *Expand each verb practice to include different tenses, as in the exercise above. Use a different noun or pronoun with each verb. Use the interrogative words when it is possible.*

EXERCISE 9

Translate into Spanish.

1. He knocked him down, but he didn't knock him out.
2. We went to the fights last night, but there were so many people there we couldn't get in.

3. What set the skating rink on fire?
4. My oldest son was named after you.
5. Who were you named after?
6. Let's go fishing when we get to Acapulco.
7. That fisherman over there is having good luck. I wonder what kind of bait he uses.
8. There should be a law against wrestling.
9. He hasn't been able to play baseball since he got old.
10. I can't help it if your ice skates don't fit.
11. How come you didn't take any bait when you went fishing?
12. Let me know if you decide to go to the fights the day after tomorrow.
13. No wonder Logan was able to knock Berry out. He weighs about fifty pounds more.
14. Why did you tell me the phone was out of order?
15. This whistle I bought doesn't work. I'm going to take it back.

EXERCISE 10

Translate into English.

1. Prefiero ir a los toros que a las luchas.
2. Mis deportes predilectos son el boxeo, las luchas y la esgrima.
3. El jardinero debió haber cachado ese elevado.
4. Toma estas vitaminas para que no te enfermes.
5. Blake ganó el concurso de clavados como de costumbre.
6. Si puede Ud. estar lista a las diez, iremos a patinar.
7. Con razón se te cayó el patín. No estaba bien ajustado.
8. Derribó a su contrincante con un gancho de izquierda a la quijada.
9. El mejor jugador se lastimó durante el torneo de basketball.
10. No prendas una fogata cerca de la casa.

EXERCISE 11

Answer the following questions.

1. Did you build a fire?
2. Can you build a fire?
3. Will you be able to build a fire?
4. Did you set the house on fire?
5. Will you set the mattress on fire?

6. Will you set the sofa on fire?
7. How far is it from here to the filling station?
8. How far is it from here to the laundry?
9. How far is it from here to the hardware store?
10. How far is it to the filling station?
11. How far is it to the laundry?
12. How far is it to the hardware store?
13. If it had been cold, would you have worn your coat?
14. If you had collected the money, would you have paid him?
15. If the teacher had told you to memorize the verbs, would you have done it?
16. Did he knock him out?
17. What round did he knock him out in?
18. Did he knock him down?
19. What round did he knock him down in?
20. How many times did he knock him down?
21. Did your button fall off?
22. Did the picture fall off the wall?
23. Did her skate come off?
24. How come your ring fell off?
25. Doesn't the kitchen look neat?

Lección 3

Vocabulary

1. **to vote (for), voted (for), voted (for)** votar (por)
2. **to contain, contained, contained** contener
3. **to inspect, inspected, inspected** inspeccionar, revisar
4. **to pin (on), pinned (on), pinned (on)** prender (a)
   pin prendedor; alfiler
   safety pin seguro
5. **to perform, performed, performed** actuar
   performance actuación
6. **to whisper, whispered, whispered** cuchichear, susurrar
7. **medium** mediano
8. **tennis shorts** shorts para tenis
9. **sweat shirt** sudadera
10. **costume** disfraz
11. **custom** costumbre
12. **politeness** educación, cortesía
13. **population** población
14. **mercy** clemencia
15. **weed** hierba (mala)
16. **temporary** temporal
    temporarily temporalmente
17. **permanent** permanente
    permanently permanentemente
18. **show** función
19. **revenge** venganza
20. **thankful** agradecido
21. **helpful** útil, servicial
22. **problem** problema
23. **climate** clima
24. **headlines** encabezados
25. **superstition** superstición
    superstitious supersticioso
26. **landlord** dueño (*de casa alquilada*); arrendador
27. **strike** huelga

IDIOMS

1. **to let go (of someone or something)** soltar(se) (a alguien o algo)
   Let go. Suéltese.
   Let go of it. Suéltalo.
   He let go of me. El me soltó.
2. **to keep on + (gerund)** seguir + (gerundio)
   He kept on eating. El siguió comiendo.
3. **There are four of us.** Somos cuatro.
   There are two of them. Son dos.
   There were four of us. Eramos cuatro.
   There were two of them. Eran dos.
4. **to go on strike** ponerse o declararse en huelga
   to be on strike estar en huelga
5. **a pair of riding boots** unas botas para montar

EXERCISE 1

Practice the following dialogue.

AT THE SPORTING GOODS STORE

Clerk: Have you been waited on?
Customer: I'm looking for a pair of white tennis shorts.
Clerk: What size?
Customer: I think size 34 will fit me.
Clerk: Here's a size 34. Would you like to try them on?
Customer: Yes, I would.
Clerk: Go into the third booth on the left, please.
Customer: These are too big. I'd better try on a 32.
Clerk: Here's a 32. How do they fit?
Customer: They fit all right. Now let me try on a sport shirt while I'm here.
Clerk: We have three sizes of sport shirts—small, medium, and large. Which do you wear?
Customer: Medium.
Clerk: What color would you like?
Customer: White.
Clerk: What else would you like?
Customer: I want a pair of white wool socks and a sweat shirt.

Clerk: We have sweat shirts in red, white, and black. Which color would you prefer?

Customer: Give me a red one, size 38.

Clerk: Would you be interested in anything else?

Customer: No, thank you. I've bought enough for today. I'll probably be in again next month. Good-bye.

Clerk: Good-bye.

EXERCISE 2

Learn these words.

WORDS CONNECTED WITH THE CIRCUS

1. **animal trainer** entrenador de animales
2. **ape** gorila, chimpancé
3. **bearded lady** dama barbuda
4. **carnival** feria (*de diversiones*); carnaval
5. **circus** circo
6. **clown** payaso
7. **dwarf** enano
8. **fair** feria
9. **Ferris wheel** rueda de la fortuna
10. **fire-eater** tragafuegos
11. **fortuneteller** adivina, pitonisa
12. **freak** fenómeno
13. **giant** gigante
14. **gorilla** gorila
15. **knife-thrower** lanzador de cuchillos
16. **lion-tamer** domador
17. **matinee** matiné
18. **merry-go-round** caballitos; carrusel
19. **midget** enano
20. **popcorn** palomitas (*de maíz*), rosetas
21. **puppet** títere
22. **reserved seats** asientos reservados
23. **ring** pista
24. **ring master** (*in the circus*) maestro de ceremonias
25. **roasted peanuts** cacahuates dorados
26. **roller coaster** montaña rusa
27. **side show** diversiones alrededor del circo
28. **snake-charmer** encantadora de serpientes
29. **sword-swallower** tragasables
30. **tent** tienda de campaña; carpa
31. **trapeze** trapecio
32. **trapeze performer** trapecista
33. **trick** juego, suerte
34. **tights** mallas
35. **tunnel of love** túnel del amor

EXERCISE 3

Translate the following sentences and practice reading them.

1. There should be a circus.
2. There shouldn't be a circus.
3. Should there be a circus?
4. Shouldn't there be a circus?
5. Why should there be a circus?
6. It'd been rainy.
7. It hadn't been rainy.
8. Had it been rainy?
9. Hadn't it been rainy?
10. Why had it been rainy?
11. It'd be windy.
12. It wouldn't be windy.
13. Would it be windy?
14. Wouldn't it be windy?
15. Why would it be windy?
16. He'd be sleepy.
17. He wouldn't be sleepy.
18. Would he be sleepy?
19. Wouldn't he be sleepy?
20. Why wouldn't he be sleepy?
21. I've had to complain to his boss.
22. I haven't had to complain to his boss.
23. Have I had to complain to his boss?
24. Haven't I had to complain to his boss?
25. Why have I had to complain to his boss?

EXERCISE 4

Translate the following sentences. Change them to the negative, interrogative, and interrogative negative.

1. The batter let go of the bat.
2. She let go of the child.
3. I told him to let go of me.
4. The driver let go of the steering wheel.
5. The electrician should have let go of the wire.
6. I want you to keep on studying.
7. He kept on singing.

8. We kept on dancing after the music stopped.
9. The students went on strike.
10. The workers are going on strike.

EXERCISE 5

Give the past tense and past participle of the following verbs.

try (something) on	threaten	visit	want
tighten	turn loose	vomit	wash
telephone	use	varnish	work
tow (in)	unload	wait (for)	watch
type	undress	walk	wish

EXERCISE 6

Give the past tense and past participle of the following verbs.

get wrinkled	get back	hear	hit
get acquainted (with)	get nervous	hang	hurt
give (someone) a ring	get infected	have a good time	hang up
get stuck	get loose	have fun	have a wreck
	get in trouble	hide	hold
	have		

EXERCISE 7

Verb Practice *Expand the following verb practice, using different tenses.*

1. We've planned to vote for Mr. Wilson.
2. We haven't planned to vote for Mr. Wilson.
3. Have we planned to vote for Mr. Wilson?
4. Haven't we planned to vote for Mr. Wilson?
5. Why haven't we planned to vote for Mr. Wilson?

EXERCISE 8

Verb Practice *Make short sentences with forms of the verbs* contain, inspect, pin (on), perform, whisper, let go (of someone or something), keep on, go on strike, be on strike. *Expand each verb practice to include different tenses, as in the exercise above. Use a different noun or pronoun with each verb. Use the interrogative words when it is possible.*

EXERCISE 9

Translate into Spanish.

1. Let go of me.
2. How many are here? There're ten of us.
3. I told him to keep on playing the piano.
4. If you don't hurry up and get ready, we're going to be late for the party.
5. No wonder you can't translate these sentences. You haven't learned the vocabulary yet.
6. Dick said the record player was out of order and the radio wouldn't work.
7. Even though we knew the teacher was out of town, we went to school as usual.
8. I hope you don't get sick on your vacation.
9. He asked me if I thought he could make a living in the United States, and I told him I didn't think so.
10. We didn't want to pay so much rent for this apartment, but we couldn't help it. We had to have it.
11. Eva is too old to play with children.
12. If you're a good host, you can even make enemies feel at home.
13. I don't like the smell of paint. It makes me sick.
14. How long is your swimming lesson?
15. How long does it take to get to New York by plane?

EXERCISE 10

Translate into English.

1. ¿Para qué vas a votar por él?
2. Me he tenido que quejar con el dueño (de la casa) respecto a los hijos de mi vecino.
3. Quiero que revises esos animales cuidadosamente.
4. ¿Qué tan alto es este enano?
5. A Estela le gustaría ser trapecista del circo, pero a Hunter no.
6. Sólo éramos trece en la junta.
7. No sé lo que contiene el paquete, ni él tampoco.
8. Los payasos hubieran actuado para los niños si hubiera habido tiempo.
9. Le estoy muy agradecido por haberme ofrecido este empleo.
10. Por poco ese coche me atropella.
11. Él le prendió la flor a su vestido, ¿verdad?

EXERCISE 11

Answer the following questions.

1. How far is it to the lake?
2. How far is it to the movies?
3. How far is it to the market?
4. Whose boxing gloves are these?
5. Do you know whose boxing gloves these are?
6. Whose tennis racket is this?
7. Do you know whose tennis racket this is?
8. Whose golf balls are these?
9. Do you know whose golf balls these are?
10. Whose skates are these?
11. Do you know whose skates these are?
12. Whose hammer is this?
13. Do you know whose hammer this is?
14. Whose saw is this?
15. Do you know whose saw this is?
16. Do you know what time it is?
17. Do you know who he is?
18. Do you know where we are?
19. Did he let go of it?
20. Did she let go of you?
21. Did he keep on talking?
22. Did they keep on drinking?
23. Did everyone in the factory go on strike?
24. Are the newspapers on strike?
25. Is there going to be a railroad strike?

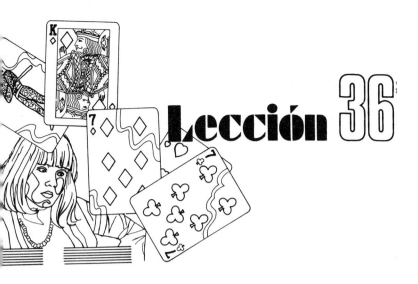

Vocabulary

1. **to gossip, gossiped, gossiped** chismear
   gossip chisme; chismoso (*sust.*)
2. **to gamble, gambled, gambled** jugar (*de dinero*)
   gambler jugador (*de dinero*); tahur
3. **to harm, harmed, harmed** hacer daño; perjudicar
   harm daño; perjuicio
4. **to support, supported, supported** mantener
5. **to locate, located, located** localizar
6. **to cool, cooled, cooled** enfriar
7. **card table** mesa de juego
   bridge table mesa de juego
8. **partner** compañero (*en el juego*); socio (*en los negocios*)
9. **diamonds** diamantes
   hearts corazones
   clubs tréboles
   spades espadas
10. **ace** as
    king rey
    queen reina
    jack jack
    joker comodín
    deuce dos
11. **trumps** triunfo
12. **suit** palo
13. **full house** full
14. **straight** corrida
15. **flush** flor
    royal flush corrida mayor
16. **solitaire** solitario
17. **bridge** bridge
18. **dummy** muerto (*bridge*)
19. **poker** póker (*el juego*)
20. **a pair** un par
    a pair of fives un par de cincos
21. **three of a kind** tercia
    three aces tercia de ases

261

22. **four of a kind** póker	*barajas*)
four sixes póker de seises	27. **graceful** gracioso,
23. **(poker) chip** ficha	garboso
24. **rummy** rummy	28. **nightmare** pesadilla
25. **trick** baza (*en el juego*)	29. **miser** (*noun*) avaro
26. **card trick** suerte (*con las*	30. **muddy** lodoso

IDIOMS

1. **to do your best** esmerarse
   He did his best. Él se esmeró.
2. **to play cards, bridge, poker, etc.** jugar a las barajas, bridge, póker etc.
3. **to deal (cards)** dar (cartas)
4. **to shuffle (cards)** barajar
5. **to take a trick** ganar una baza
6. **to cut (cards)** cortar
7. **to draw (cards)** sacar o robar (naipes)
8. **to shoot dice, craps** jugar a los dados
9. **to flip (a coin)** echar un volado
10. **heads or tails** águila o sol
11. **a deck of cards** una baraja
12. **I have a good hand.** Tengo buen juego.
    I have a bad hand. No tengo buen juego.
13. **What's the score?** ¿Cómo vamos? (*puntuación en el juego*)
14. **to bid** declarar (*en el juego*)
    How much do you bid? ¿Qué cantas? (*bridge*)
    He bids two hearts. Él canta dos corazones.

EXERCISE 1

Practice the following dialogue.

A CARD GAME

John: Shall we draw (cards) for partners?

Jim: O. K. The two highest will play against the two lowest.

Mary: John and I have the highest (cards), so we'll play against Jim and Ruth.

Ruth: Who's going to deal?

John: (to Jim) We'll flip a coin to see who deals. Heads, I deal; and
tails, you deal.
Ruth: It's heads, so it's John's deal.
Mary: Jim, you'll bid first then.
Jim: Yes, I get the first bid.
John: Are we going to play for money?
Jim: Yes, it makes the game more interesting.
Mary: Shuffle the cards and deal them, John.-
John: Cut the cards, Ruth.
Jim: You dealt me a bad hand. I can't bid on this. I pass.
Mary: Is it my bid?

_____

Ruth: What's the score?
John: I don't know exactly, but you and Jim are still ahead (van ade-
lante). And this is the last hand.
Mary: Ruth, you and Jim won.

EXERCISE 2

Learn these words.

WORDS CONNECTED WITH A BURIAL

1. **burial** entierro
2. **casket** ataúd
3. **cemetery** cementerio
4. **coffin** ataúd
5. **corpse** cadáver
6. **funeral** funeral
7. **funeral parlor** agencia mortuoria
8. **funeral procession** cortejo fúnebre
9. **grave** tumba
10. **graveyard** cementerio
11. **hearse** carroza
12. **mortician** encargado de ceremonias fúnebres
13. **obituary** noticia biográfica de una persona recién fallecida
14. **tomb** cripta; tumba
15. **tombstone** lápida
16. **undertaker** empresario de funeraria
17. **to cremate** incinerar
18. **to embalm** embalsamar

EXERCISE 3

Translate the following sentences and practice reading them.

1. I ought to be sleepy.

2. I shouldn't be sleepy.
3. Should I be sleepy?
4. Shouldn't I be sleepy?
5. Why shouldn't I be sleepy?
6. It should have been cold.
7. It shouldn't have been cold.
8. Should it have been cold?
9. Shouldn't it have been cold?
10. Why shouldn't it have been cold?
11. It should have been hot.
12. It shouldn't have been hot.
13. Should it have been hot?
14. Shouldn't it have been hot?
15. Why shouldn't it have been hot?
16. It was going to be hot.
17. It wasn't going to be hot.
18. Was it going to be hot?
19. Wasn't it going to be hot?
20. When was it going to be hot?
21. They're going to be afraid.
22. They aren't going to be afraid.
23. Are they going to be afraid?
24. Aren't they going to be afraid?
25. Why are they going to be afraid?

EXERCISE 4

Translate the following sentences. Change them to the negative, inter-rogative, and interrogative negative.

1. He said he would do his best.
2. I'm doing my best.
3. She always does her best.
4. We're going to do our best.
5. I told him to do his best.
6. They expect me to do my best.
7. You should always do your best.
8. They'd like to do their best.
9. We wanted him to do his best.
10. She'll be able to do her best.

264

EXERCISE 5

Give the past tense and past participle of the following verbs.

lie
worry (about)
wrap
weigh
whistle
laugh (at)

wash your
    mouth out
wonder
worship
wrinkle
waste

wink (at)
wrap (some-
    thing) up
wax
wrestle
whisper

x-ray
yell (at)
answer
ask
blush

EXERCISE 6

Give the past tense and past participle of the following verbs.

have an ac-
    cident
have (some-
    thing) made
have a hang-
    over
have a flat

have a blow-
    out
have (some-
    thing) re-
    covered
hold a crease
hear from

hear about
know
kneel (down)
keep
keep a prom-
    ise
keep on

cut a tooth
lay eggs
leave
let
lie down
strike

EXERCISE 7

Verb Practice *Expand the following verb practice, using different tenses.*

1. These people used to gossip, didn't they?
2. These people didn't use to gossip, did they?
3. Did these people use to gossip?
4. Didn't these people use to gossip?
5. Why didn't these people use to gossip?

EXERCISE 8

Verb Practice *Make short sentences with forms of the verbs* gamble, harm, support, locate, cool, be in mourning, play cards, deal (cards), shuffle (cards), cut (cards), draw (cards), shoot dice, flip (a coin), bid, do your best, cremate, embalm. *Expand each verb practice to include different tenses, as in the exercise above. Use a different noun or pronoun with each verb. Use the interrogative words when it is possible.*

EXERCISE 9

Translate into Spanish.

1. It wasn't my fault if we didn't beat them playing canasta. I did my best.
2. He dealt me a terrible hand.
3. Let's flip to see who has to pay for the drinks.
4. The Yankees beat the Dodgers yesterday, but I don't know what the score was.
5. Wherever he went, he always took a deck of cards.
6. Heads, I win; tails, you lose.
7. How many chips do you have left?
8. We kept on playing bridge after the others had quit.
9. There were six of us when we started, but only three of us finished the game.
10. I'm very fond of playing cards, but I don't like to shoot craps.
11. If you don't stop gambling, you're going to get in trouble.
12. Don't trust that man. He never keeps his promise, and his word isn't worth anything.
13. We built a fire in the fireplace and roasted peanuts.
14. Have you heard about this kind of material that you don't have to iron?
15. The last time I heard from him he was having all his teeth pulled.

EXERCISE 10

Translate into English.

1. ¿Cómo vamos? (*puntuación en un juego*)
2. ¿De qué están chismeando?
3. Su padre era un borracho y un jugador.
4. No me hubiera ganado todo el dinero si no hubiera hecho trampa.
5. Echamos un volado y perdí.
6. Debimos de haber jugado cinco juegos antes de que nos ganaran.
7. Tienes que tratar de esmerarte.
8. Cualquiera puede aprender a hacer esta suerte de baraja.
9. ¿Sabe Ud. cómo vamos? (*puntuación en un juego*)
10. Su negocio se encuentra en la parte norte de la ciudad.

EXERCISE 11

Answer the following questions.

1. Did you do your best?
2. Will you do your best?
3. Have you done your best?
4. Is this game worth playing?
5. Were the fights worth seeing?
6. Are the wrestling matches worth watching?
7. How long ago did you hear from him?
8. How long ago did you hear about the accident?
9. How long ago did you build the fire?
10. Would you rather play canasta or bridge?
11. Would they rather ice skate or roller skate?
12. Would you rather go to the fights or to the wrestling matches?
13. How often do you go swimming?
14. How often do you go dancing?
15. How often do you go riding?

Vocabulary

1. **to overflow, overflowed, overflowed** desbordarse; derramarse, rebosar
2. **to yawn, yawned, yawned** bostezar
3. **to brag (about), bragged (about), bragged (about)** jactarse (de)
4. **to balance, balanced, balanced** balancear (se), equilibrar (se)
5. **to deserve, deserved, deserved** merecer
6. **to improve, improved, improved** mejorar
7. **desk clerk** administrador en un hotel
8. **bellboy** botones
9. **reservation** reservación
10. **single room** cuarto sencillo

double room cuarto doble
inside room cuarto interior
11. **bag** maleta, veliz
12. **room service** servicio
13. **funny papers** monitos
    comics monitos
14. **comic book** revista de monitos
15. **crutch** muleta
16. **cable** cable
17. **handcuffs** esposas (*para presos*)
18. **saying** dicho, refrán
19. **portrait** retrato (*pintado*)
20. **program** programa
21. **museum** museo
22. **pottery** alfarería
23. **basement** sótano
24. **slums** barrio bajo
25. **chapter** capítulo

IDIOMS

1. **to be in charge (of)** estar encargado (de); tener el cargo (de)
2. **to face the street, park, sea, etc.** dar a la calle, parque, mar, etc.
3. **to check-in** tomar un cuarto (*en el hotel*)
4. **to check-out** dejar el cuarto (*en el hotel*)
   When is checking-out time? ¿A qué hora tenemos que dejar el cuarto?, ¿A qué hora vence el cuarto?
   Checking-out time is at 3:00 p. m. Tienen que dejar el cuarto a las tres, El cuarto vence a las tres.
5. **How + (adj. or adv.)!** ¡Qué + (adj. o adv.)!
   How pretty! ¡Qué bonito!
   How far (away) you live! ¡Qué lejos vive Ud!
6. **What (a) + noun!** ¡Qué + sustantivo!
   What a pretty girl! ¡Qué muchacha más linda!
   What pretty girls! ¡Qué muchachas más lindas!
   What weather! ¡Qué tiempo!
   (*If the noun is singular but has a plural form,* **what a** *is used.*
   If the noun has no plural form, **what** *is used. With all plural forms*
   what *is used.*)
7. **Everything went wrong.** Todo salió mal.
8. **on the other hand** por otra parte, en cambio

EXERCISE 1

Practice the following dialogue.

AT A HOTEL

Desk Clerk: Good evening. Do you have a reservation?

Guest: No, I don't. I didn't know that I'd be stopping here. Do you have a room?

Desk Clerk: We don't have any single rooms left. Would you like a double room?

Guest: Yes, that'll be all right if I can't get a single room.

Desk Clerk: Would you prefer an inside room or a room that faces the street?

Guest: It doesn't make any difference—whichever is cheaper.

Desk Clerk: (*to the bellboy*) Take Mr. Watson up to room 325. Here's the key.

Bellboy:	Do you want me to open both windows?
Guest:	Yes, please. And check the bathroom to see that there are plenty of towels and soap.
Bellboy:	Will there be anything else, sir?
Guest:	No, thank you.
Bellboy:	There's a dining room and a bar downstairs when you're ready to eat, sir.
Guest:	Thank you, but I think I'll just call room service and have something sent up to my room. I don't feel like dressing for dinner.
Bellboy:	Yes, sir. Good night.
Guest:	Good night. When is checking-out time?
Bellboy:	Checking-out time is at 3:00 p. m., sir. Would you like us to call you in the morning?
Guest:	Yes. Give me a ring about eight.

EXERCISE 2

Learn these words.

NAMES OF TREES

1. **beech** haya
2. **birch** abedul
3. **cedar** cedro
4. **cottonwood** álamo
5. **elm** olmo
6. **evergreen** siempreviva

7. **fir** abeto
8. **maple** maple, arce
9. **palm** palma
10. **pine** pino
11. **weeping willow** sauce llorón
12. **willow** sauce

EXERCISE 3

Translate the following sentences and practice reading them.

1. He left without paying.
2. He paid before leaving.
3. Besides paying his bill, he tipped the waiter.
4. Instead of paying me, he paid the cashier.
5. He paid me before paying you.
6. In spite of being sick, he worked today.
7. He plays pool, but I don't.

8. I don't play pool, but he does.
9. They bowl, but we don't.
0. We don't bowl, but they do.
1. You like to box, but they don't.
2. They don't like to box, but you do.
3. She plays cards, but I don't.
4. I don't play cards, but she does.
5. You're polite, but they aren't.
6. They aren't polite, but you are
7. I don't gamble, do you?
18. I didn't gamble, did you?
19. I'm not going to gamble. Are you?
20. I wasn't going to gamble. Were you?
21. I haven't gambled. Have you?
22. I wouldn't gamble. Would you?
23. I don't like to gamble. Do you?
24. I don't want to gamble. Do you?
25. I shouldn't gamble. Should you?

EXERCISE 4

Translate the following sentences. Change them to the negative, interrogative, and interrogative negative.

1. He was in charge of the office.
2. They were in charge here.
3. We'll be in charge of the books.
4. You've been in charge for many years.
5. She should be in charge of the money.
6. My apartment faces the street.
7. Their house faced the sea.
8. That building ought to face the south.
9. The school will face the park.
10. The new church is going to face the north.

EXERCISE 5

Give the past tense and past participle of the following verbs.

call	capture	count	comb your hair
change	carry	cover	complain (about)

clean	change your	cross	climb
close	mind	cry	charge
complete	clap	can	dent
correct	cook		taste like

EXERCISE 6

Give the past tense and past participle of the following verbs.

be fattening	get fat	make	make a trip
be in mourning	get paid	make a living	meet
be shocked	lose weight	make a mis-	mean
(at)	lose your	take	put
be on strike	temper	make fun of	put on
be sharp	let go (of)	make money	
fall asleep			

EXERCISE 7

Verb Practice *Expand the following verb practice, using different tenses.*

1. The rivers have been overflowing, haven't they?
2. The rivers haven't been overflowing, have they?
3. Have the rivers been overflowing?
4. Haven't the rivers been overflowing?
5. Why have the rivers been overflowing?

EXERCISE 8

Verb Practice *Make short sentences with forms of the verbs* yawn, brag (about), balance, deserve, improve, be in charge (of), face the street, *etc.,* check-in, check-out. *Expand each verb practice to include different tenses, as in the exercise above. Use a different noun or pronoun with each verb. Use the interrogative words when it is possible.*

EXERCISE 9

Translate into Spanish.

1. Stop bragging and tell us the truth.
2. You'll have to talk to Mr. Keller. Mr. Logan isn't in charge here any more.

272

3. What a day! Everything went wrong, and I didn't get anything done (no pude hacer nada).
4. I'd rather have a room that faces the street.
5. We've just finished the ninth lesson.
6. We got through before it got dark.
7. He used to brag about how well (de lo bien) he could speak English.
8. The house across the street is warmer than ours. It faces the south.
9. They made me deal the cards.
10. On the other hand, I don't know why anyone wants to play poker (no entiendo cómo hay gente a quien le gusta jugar póker).
11. What did you keep him from going to the circus for?
12. We plan to go swimming if we get through before it gets dark.
13. Stop bothering the children while they're trying to study.
14. It's a shame that you couldn't get rid of your furniture.
15. I'd rather go shopping in the morning than in the afternoon.

EXERCISE 10

Translate into English.

1. Le dijimos al administrador que queríamos un cuarto que diera a la calle.
2. ¡Qué alfarería más bonita! Debe ser de Guadalajara.
3. He estado viviendo en el Hotel West, pero me voy a cambiar.
4. Ha de estar saliéndose el agua de alguna tubería porque hay agua en el sótano.
5. Acostumbraba que le pintaran (a ella) su retrato todos los años.
6. ¡Qué muchacha más linda!
7. Tengo tres años de ver este programa de televisión.
8. ¿Si hubieras necesitado alguna cosa, hubieras llamado al botones?
9. Le pregunté que a dónde había ido la semana pasada y me dijo que a ninguna parte.
10. Habría adelantado mucho en inglés si hubiera estudiado más este año.

EXERCISE 11

Answer the following questions.

1. Who's in charge here?
2. Who was in charge last week?

3. Who'll be in charge of the money?
4. Did you go anywhere yesterday?
5. Did you go any place last night?
6. Will you go anywhere tomorrow?
7. Does your room face the street?
8. Does your house face the sea?
9. Does your room face the east?
10. How long has it been since you played bridge?
11. How long has it been since you played pool?
12. How long has it been since you went riding?
13. How far is it from here to the bowling alley?
14. How far is it from here to the skating rink?
15. How far is it from here to the bull ring?

Lección 38

Vocabulary

1. **to act, acted, acted** actuar, trabajar
2. **to stutter, stuttered, stuttered** tartamudear
3. **to drizzle, drizzled, drizzled** lloviznar
4. **to lean over, leaned over leaned over** inclinarse, doblarse
5. **to investigate, investigated, investigated** investigar
6. **to hire, hired, hired** contratar
7. **emotion** emoción
   emotional emotivo
8. **actor** actor
   actress actriz
9. **usher** acomodador
10. **theater** teatro
11. **stage** foro
12. **screen** pantalla
13. **aisle** pasillo
14. **newsreel** noticiero
15. **shorts** cortos
16. **cartoon** caricatura

17. **show** cine; función
18. **balcony** arriba (*en el cine*)
    first balcony primer piso
    second balcony segundo piso
19. **main floor** luneta, abajo (*en el cine*)
20. **role** papel
    leading role papel estelar
21. **musical** comedia musical
    comedy comedia
    tragedy tragedia
22. **producer** productor
    director director
23. **intermission** intermedio
24. **lobby** lobby, vestíbulo
25. **ticket window** taquilla
26. **hero** héroe
    heroine heroína
27. **leading man** protagonista
    leading lady protagonista
28. **villain** villano
29. **gangster** gangster

275

| 30. **detective** detective | 32. **trailers** avances |
| 31. **plot** argumento; complot | **coming attractions** avances |

IDIOMS

1. **to put (something) off** aplazar (algo)
   He put his trip off. Aplazó su viaje.
2. **to keep (doing something)** seguir o continuar (haciendo algo)
   He kept going to Mexico every year. Siguió yendo a México cada año.
   She kept hitting the man. Siguió pegándole al hombre.
3. **to play (take) the part of a** hacer, desempeñar el papel de, hacerla de
   He played (took) the part of a gangster. Hizo el papel de un gangster. La hizo de gangster.
4. **to put on a play** montar una obra teatral
5. **How far down do you want to sit?** ¿Qué tan cerca quieres sentarte?
6. **Let's sit halfway down.** Sentémonos en medio.
7. **standing room only** sólo parados
8. **It sounds right.** Suena (bien).
   It doesn't sound right. No suena (bien).
9. **Move over.** Hazte a un lado, Córrete.
10. **My nose is running.** Me está fluyendo (moqueando) la nariz.

EXERCISE 1

Practice the following dialogue.

AT THE MOVIES

Boy: Would you rather sit in the balcony or on the main floor?
Girl: I'd rather sit on the main floor if there are any seats left.
Usher: How many, please?
Boy: Two.
Usher: How far down?
Boy: About halfway.
Usher: There are only seats in the front row.
Girl: Are there any seats in the balcony?
Usher: No, there won't be any seats until the movie is over.

Boy: When will the movie be over?
Usher: There'll be an intermission at 8:40.
Boy: (*to the girl*) It's only twenty minutes until the movie ends. Do
       you want to sit in the lobby until the next one starts?
Girl: Yes, I'd rather do that than sit in the front row.
Boy: O. K. We'll wait then.

EXERCISE 2

Learn these words.

WORDS CONNECTED WITH A FARM AND RANCH

1. **agriculture** agricultura
2. **brand** marca
3. **branding iron** hierro de marcar
4. **breed** raza (*animales*)
5. **bridle** brida
6. **corral** corral
7. **girth** cincha
8. **halter** almartigón
9. **harness** guarnición; arnés
10. **horseshoe** herradura
11. **lariat** reata
12. **lawn mower** segadora (*de césped*)
13. **plow** arado
14. **pitchfork** horca; bieldo
15. **rein** rienda
16. **rake** rastrillo
17. **riding crop** fuete
18. **saddle** silla de montar
19. **English saddle** albardón
20. **saddlebag** alforja
21. **saddleblanket** mantilla, sudadera
22. **stirrup** estribo
23. **tractor** tractor
24. **wagon** carreta
25. **well** pozo
26. **windmill** molino de viento
27. **to brand** marcar con hierro
28. **to buck** reparar
29. **to plow** arar
30. **to rope** lazar
31. **to shoe** herrar

EXERCISE 3

Translate the following sentences and practice reading them.

1. He voted. I did too.
2. He didn't vote. I didn't either.
3. I'll vote. He will too.
4. I won't vote. He won't either.
5. They voted. We did too.

6. They didn't vote. We didn't either.
7. We'll be able to vote. They will too.
8. We won't be able to vote. They won't either.
9. She's been able to vote. You have too.
10. She hasn't been able to vote. You haven't either.
11. You'd be able to vote, and she would too.
12. You wouldn't be able to vote, and she wouldn't either.
13. They'd be able to vote, and I would too.
14. They wouldn't be able to vote, and I wouldn't either.
15. I should vote, and they should too.
16. I shouldn't vote, and they shouldn't either.
17. You're voting, and we are too.
18. You aren't voting, and we aren't either.
19. You were going to vote, and he was too.
20. You weren't going to vote, and he wasn't either.

EXERCISE 4

Translate the following sentences. Change them to the negative, interrogative, and interrogative negative.

1. They put their wedding off until June.
2. You should put this work off until tomorrow.
3. We'll have to put the party off until next week.
4. I can put this appointment to the dentist off again.
5. He'll put the meeting off until next week.
6. Mr. Jones always puts everything off.
7. The boss has put my vacation off twice.
8. He kept going to school.
9. They kept going after we told them to stop.
10. We told her to keep swimming.

EXERCISE 5

Give the past tense and past participle of the following verbs.

chase	cure	collide	combine
chew	cheat	criticize	carve
cause	congratulate	copy	contain
cough	crush	consist (of)	cool
commit suicide	change clothes	collect	shuffle (cards)

278

EXERCISE 6

Give the past tense and past participle of the following verbs.

pay	run	run after	see
pay attention (to)	run away	run over	sell
put on make-up	run around	ride	set
quit	run out of	rise	set the table
read	run a business	say	sit (down)

EXERCISE 7

Verb Practice *Expand the following verb practice, using different tenses.*

1. She used to be able to act.
2. She didn't use to be able to act.
3. Did she use to be able to act?
4. Didn't she use to be able to act?
5. When did she use to be able to act?

EXERCISE 8

Verb Practice *Make short sentences with forms of the verbs* **stutter, drizzle, lean over, investigate, hire, put (something) off, play (take) the part of, put on a play, keep (doing something), buck, plow, rope, shoe.** *Expand each verb practice to include different tenses, as in the exercise above. Use a different noun or pronoun with each verb. Use the interrogative words when it is possible.*

EXERCISE 9

Translate into Spanish.

1. Move over. These girls want to sit down here.
2. Humphrey Bogart played the part of a gangster in his last movie.
3. The Crown Club put on a show last night, but it wasn't very good.
4. It was a lot of fun to put on plays when we were in high school.
5. There've been so many floods lately that I'm afraid we'll have to put our trip off until the weather is better.
6. Would you like to play the part of an old man when we put on our next play?
7. Do you have a kleenex? My nose is running.

8. Don't stop at the next corner if there's a red light. Keep going.
9. We'd better keep going if you plan to get to Mexico City before sundown.
10. You should never put anything off until tomorrow that you can do today.
11. You shouldn't criticize the students if they're doing their best.
12. We built a fire in the yard.
13. If your horse is hard to handle, be sure not to let go of the reins.
14. The soldiers got in trouble because they were caught shooting dice.
15. I have found out that this person can't keep a promise; therefore, I refuse to recommend him.

EXERCISE 10

Translate into English.

1. Quisiera contratar un buen vendedor por unos doscientos dólares al mes.
2. Si nos hubiéramos sentado en el primer piso, ¿hubiéramos podido ver a los actores?
3. ¿Prefieres sentarte abajo o arriba?
4. ¿Te gusta más el cine que el teatro?
5. ¿Qué tan cerca nos debemos sentar si queremos ver bien?
6. Ya tiene tres días de lloviznar. Ojalá dejara de llover.
7. Quizá podamos hablar a los actores durante el intermedio.
8. Me dijo que su niño mayor tartamudeaba.
9. Seguíamos yendo al cine aunque subieron los precios.
10. Le dijo que no llegara tarde si quería ver la caricatura.

EXERCISE 11

Answer the following questions.

1. Did they put the meeting off?
2. Will they put the picnic off?
3. Have they put the wedding off?
4. Did she play the part of an old woman?
5. Will she play the part of a young girl?
6. Has she played the part of a maid?
7. Did they put on a play?
8. Will they put on a play?

9. Have they put on a play?
0. Do you know what time it is?
1. Do you know where my book is?
2. Do you know how old he is?
3. Do you know whose comic book this is?
4. How far down do you like to sit at the movies?
5. How far back do you like to sit at the movies?

Lección 3

Vocabulary

1. **to rob, robbed, robbed** robar
   to get robbed, got robbed
   got robbed robarle a uno
2. **to sting, stung, stung**
   picar (*con aguijón*)
3. **to sprinkle, sprinkled,**
   sprinkled rociar
4. **to crawl, crawled, crawled**
   arrastrarse; gatear
5. **to crochet, crocheted,**
   crocheted tejer (*a gancho*)
6. **to deny, denied, denied** negar
7. **information desk** mesa de
   informes, información
8. **ticket office** oficina de boletos
   ticket agent agente de boletos
9. **sleeper (coach)** coche cama
10. **Pullman** Pullman
    Pullman ticket boleto de
    coche cama
    (Pullman) porter mozo
11. **baggage room** sala de equipajes
    baggage locker casillero

para equipaje
baggage agent agente de
equipaje
baggage check talón de
equipaje
12. **railroad** ferrocarril
    railroad track vía, riel
13. **morning train** tren de la
    mañana
    noon train tren del mediodía
    afternoon train tren de la
    tarde
    night train tren de la
    noche
    midnight train tren de la
    medianoche
14. **berth** litera, cama
    upper berth cama alta
    lower berth cama baja
15. **engine** máquina
    steam engine máquina de
    vapor
    locomotive locomotora

16. **monthly** mensual, mensualmente
    weekly semanal, semanalmente
    daily diario, diariamente
    hourly a cada hora
17. **train station** estación de ferrocarril
    railroad station estación de ferrocarril
    depot estación de ferrocarril
18. **freight train** tren de carga
    express (train) expreso
19. **timetable** horario (*de llegadas y salidas*)
20. **redcap** mozo (*de estación*)
21. **conductor** conductor
22. **platform** andén, plataforma
23. **diner** coche comedor
    dining car coche comedor
24. **engineer** maquinista
25. **track** vía, carril; huella (*de pie*)
26. **suitcase** maleta, veliz

IDIOMS

1. **to have your picture taken** retratarse
2. **to have the film developed** mandar revelar el rollo
3. **to hate (something)** chocarle a uno (algo)
4. **to get in line** hacer cola
   Please get in line. Favor de hacer cola.
5. **to meet someone (at the station, airport, etc.)** esperar a alguien en la estación, aeropuerto, etc.)
   I'm going to meet him at the station. Lo voy a esperar en la estación.
   to see (someone) off ir a despedir (a alguien)
   I saw my father off. Fui a despedir a mi papá.
6. **How much of a layover is there between trains?** ¿Cuánto se tiene que esperar entre tren y tren?
   There's a two hour layover. Se tiene que esperar dos horas.
7. **All aboard!** ¡Vámonos! (*en el tren*)
8. **right there** ahí mismo
   He lives right there. Vive ahí mismo.
9. **on tonight's (today's, yesterday's) train** en el tren de esta noche (de hoy, de ayer)
10. **round-trip ticket** boleto de ida y vuelta, boleto de viaje redondo
11. **one-way ticket** boleto sencillo
12. **It's good for six months.** Vale por seis meses.

EXERCISE 1

Practice the following dialogue.

A TRIP BY TRAIN

Passenger: I want a ticket to Mexico City, please.

Ticket Agent: One-way or round-trip?

Passenger: How long is a round-trip ticket good for?

Ticket Agent: It's good for three months, and you save fifteen percent that way.

Passenger: No, I can't use it. How much is a one-way ticket?

Ticket Agent: Eighty-seven twenty, including the tax.

Passenger: When does the next train leave for Mexico City?

Ticket Agent: There isn't a direct train to Mexico City. You'll have to change at Chicago and again at Laredo to get the *Aguila Azteca*. Both run daily.

Passenger: How much of a layover is there between trains?

Ticket Agent: An hour in Chicago and a half hour in Laredo.

Passenger: Do the trains have a sleeper?

Ticket Agent: Yes, and a diner, too.

Passenger: That's good. I'd hate to eat sandwiches all the way.

Ticket Agent: Here's a timetable. You can get a Pullman reservation at window No. 7.

Passenger: Where all those people are?

Ticket Agent: Yes, right there.

Passenger: Thank you.

Passenger: Will you please give me an upper berth all the way to Mexico City?

Ticket Agent: I can only give you a Pullman reservation as far as Chicago. You'll have to make your other Pullman reservation when you get there.

Passenger: I see. How much is the Pullman?

Ticket Agent: The upper berth is five dollars, but I have only two lower berths left. They're six-fifty.

Passenger: O. K. Give me a lower. Where can I check my baggage while I get something to eat?

Ticket Agent: Over there—in the baggage room or in the baggage lockers.

Passenger: Thank you.

EXERCISE 2

Learn these words.

NAMES OF STORMS

1. **blizzard** ventisca
2. **cloudburst** chaparrón
3. **cyclone** ciclón
4. **dust storm** tolvanera
5. **earthquake** terremoto
6. **flood** inundación
7. **hail storm** granizada
8. **hurricane** huracán
9. **landslide** deslave, derrumbamiento (*de tierra*)
10. **lightning** relámpago
11. **rain storm** aguacero
12. **sleet** mezcla de agua y nieve
13. **snow storm** tormenta de nieve
14. **tornado** tornado
15. **thunder** trueno
16. **volcano** volcán
17. **whirlwind** torbellino, remolino (*de viento*)
18. **wind storm** tormenta de viento

EXERCISE 3

Translate the following sentences and practice reading them.

1. It rains.
2. It doesn't rain.
3. Does it rain?
4. Doesn't it rain?
5. When does it rain?
6. It rained.
7. It didn't rain
8. Did it rain?
9. Didn't it rain?
10. When did it rain?
11. It's raining.
12. It isn't raining.
13. Is it raining?
14. Isn't it raining?
15. Why is it raining?
16. It was raining.
17. It wasn't raining.
18. Was it raining?
19. Wasn't it raining?
20. When was it raining?
21. It'll rain.
22. It won't rain.
23. Will it rain?
24. Won't it rain?
25. When will it rain?
26. It's rained.
27. It hasn't rained.
28. Has it rained?
29. Hasn't it rained?
30. When has it rained?

EXERCISE 4

Translate the following sentences. Change them to the negative, interrogative, and interrogative negative.

1. He had his picture taken.

285

2. She'll have her picture taken.
3. You're going to have your picture taken.
4. They want to have their picture taken.
5. We hate to play cards.
6. He hates sleeveless sweaters.
7. They hate to swim in cold water.
8. She hates gangster pictures.
9. They'll have these pictures developed.
10. He had the pictures developed.

EXERCISE 5

Give the past tense and past participle of the following verbs.

cremate	drop	disappear	dial
crawl	dance	discover	dream (about)
crochet	dent	dress	direct
deny	die	drown	dry up
dictate	die down	describe	destroy

EXERCISE 6

Give the past tense and past participle of the following verbs.

sit (down)	shake	spend	spread
sleep	shake hands	stand in line	sit at a table
speak	with	swim	sit at the
stand up	shine	sink	counter
sweat	shoot	strike a	set your watch
stick	sing	match	(clock)

EXERCISE 7

Verb Practice *Expand the following verb practice, using different tenses*

1. The thieves should have robbed the bank.
2. The thieves shouldn't have robbed the bank.
3. Should the thieves have robbed the bank?
4. Shouldn't the thieves have robbed the bank?
5. When should the thieves have robbed the bank?

286

EXERCISE 8

Verb Practice *Make short sentences with forms of the verbs* rob, get robbed, sting, sprinkle, crawl, crochet, deny, have your picture taken, have the pictures developed, hate (something), get in line, meet someone (at the station, airport, etc.), see (someone) off. *Expand each verb practice to include different tenses, as in the exercise above. Use a different noun or pronoun with each verb. Use the interrogative words when it is possible.*

EXERCISE 9

Translate into Spanish.

1. I hate to stand in line.
2. We had our picture taken on our wedding day.
3. They plan to go by train.
4. Don't bother me now. I've got to finish this work.
5. The policeman made us get in line.
6. They look alike.
7. A woman has a right to change her mind.
8. How much is your ring worth?
9. How long ago did he go?
0. That house isn't worth painting.
1. How old were you when you fell in love the first time?
2. We made a big mistake when we got rid of that car.
3. Shut up. I don't want to discuss it any more.
4. I had to go shopping with my mother on Tuesday.
5. Don't take a shower in cold water if you have a cold.
6. I got robbed last week, but the police caught the thieves.

EXERCISE 10

Translate into English.

1. Me picó una abeja.
2. Si hubiéramos visto las huellas de ese animal en la nieve, las hubiéramos seguido.
3. No debió haber negado que te ayudó con tu tarea.
4. Puede que ese insecto que se está arrastrando en el piso te pique.
5. Desde que me robaron, siempre tengo una buena cerradura en la puerta.

6. No se te olvide **rociar estas** camisas antes de plancharlas.
7. ¿Sabes leer el horario de ferrocarriles?
8. Le dije al agente de boletos que no me diera una cama alta.
9. No podremos desayunar en el tren porque no hay coche comedor
10. Tal vez lleguen en el tren de esta noche.

EXERCISE 11

Answer the following questions.

1. Did you have your picture taken?
2. Will you have your picture taken?
3. Have you had your picture taken?
4. Do you hate to get up early?
5. Do you hate to shave every morning?
6. Do you hate to learn irregular verbs?
7. Did you have your pants made?
8. Will you have your riding boots made?
9. Have you had your cowboy boots made?
10. Did you feel sorry for her?
11. Did you lose your temper?
12. Did you miss the bus?
13. Did you run over the dog?
14. Did you hear from John?
15. Did you hear about the accident?
16. Did you have a layover between trains?
17. How much of a layover did you have?
18. What did you do during your layover in Chicago?
19. Did all the people get in line?
20. Are you going to get in that line?

Lección 40

Vocabulary

1. **to land, landed, landed**
   aterrizar
   landing aterrizaje
2. **to take off, took off,
   taken off** despegar
   take off despegue
3. **to allow, allowed, allowed**
   permitir, dejar
4. **to fasten fastened,
   fastened** abrocharse
5. **to refuel, refueled, refueled**
   poner gasolina
   (*reabastecer de gasolina*)
6. **to buzz, buzzed, buzzed**
   tocar (*timbre*); zumbar
   buzzer timbre
7. **to crash (into), crashed
   (into), crashed (into)**
   estrellarse (contra)
   chocar (con, contra)
   plane crash accidente aéreo
8. **airport** aeropuerto
9. **airsick** mareado

   airsickness mareo
10. **pilot** piloto
    co-pilot copiloto
11. **flight** vuelo
    nonstop flight vuelo directo
12. **space** lugar
13. **steward** sobrecargo,
    aeromozo
    stewardess sobrecargo,
    aeromoza
14. **insurance** seguro
    life insurance seguro de
    vida
15. **available** disponible
16. **effective** efectivo
17. **plus** más
18. **(chewing) gum** chicle
19. **side street** calle transversal
20. **fan** aficionado
    baseball fan aficionado
    al béisbol
21. **naked** desnudo
22. **slang** caló

289

23. **cross-eyed** bizco	piernas torcidas hacia
24. **bowlegged** (*adj.*) de	adentro
piernas torcidas en arco	26. **pigeon-toed** (*adj.*) con los
25. **knock-kneed** (*adj.*) de	pies torcidos hacia adentro

IDIOMS

1. **to get along (with)** llevarse bien (con); congeniar (con)
   Do you get along with him? ¿Te llevas bien con él?
2. **to get airsick** marearse
3. **to make a stop** hacer una escala
4. **to be overweight** tener exceso de peso; estar demasiado pesado
   to be underweight faltar peso
5. **to be booked-up** no tener lugar
   This flight is all booked-up. No hay lugar en este vuelo.
6. **It's (It takes) one hour to Cuernavaca.** Se hace una hora a Cuernavaca.
7. **Please fasten your seat belts.** Favor de abrocharse los cinturones de seguridad.
8. **just in case** por si acaso
9. **I'll think it over.** Lo pensaré.
10. **We're about to take off.** Estamos para despegar.

EXERCISE 1

Practice the following dialogue.

TRAVELING BY PLANE

Passenger:	Can you tell me at what time your next flight to Mexico City leaves?
Ticket Agent:	Let's see. There's one at 10:40—that's in about half an hour—but it's all booked-up. We have space on Flight 347 at 1:30 this afternoon.
Passenger:	Is it nonstop?
Ticket Agent:	No, it makes a thirty minutes stop at Dallas to refuel and pick up passengers. But it takes only two hours longer than the nonstop flight.
Passenger:	When is the next nonstop flight?

Ticket Agent:	At 3:45 p.m., but there aren't any seats available on that flight either.
Passenger:	Oh, well, give me a seat on the 1:30 flight. How much is the ticket?
Ticket Agent:	$99.50 plus ten per cent tax makes it $109.45. Do you want any insurance?
Passenger:	On my baggage? I thought that was included in the price of the ticket.
Ticket Agent:	It is. We pay up to $200.00. But I mean life insurance.
Passenger:	No, I'm covered by my own company.
Ticket Agent:	Well, here's your ticket and your change. Now if you'll get in line, they'll weigh your baggage for you.

Baggage Attendant:	You're sixteen pounds overweight.
Passenger:	How come? I wasn't overweight when I flew up from Mexico. How much weight am I allowed?
Baggage Attendant:	You're allowed sixty pounds on first class flights. You must have come on one of those. You're flying down on a tourist flight now. It's cheaper; but, of course, that's why you're allowed only forty-four pounds.
Passenger:	How much do I owe you?
Baggage Attendant:	It's one dollar for every pound overweight, so that'll be sixteen dollars.
Passenger:	Here you are.
Baggage Attendant:	Thank you.

Stewardess:	Please fasten your seat belts. We're about to take off. Once in the air, you can loosen you seat belts and smoke.
Passenger:	Excuse me, stewardess. I always get airsick. Do you have paper bags—just in case?
Stewardess:	Surely. Here you are. But why don't you take two of these pills? They're very effective against airsickness.
Passenger:	Thank you. My ears are buzzing, too.
Stewardess:	Try chewing gum. That'll keep your ears from both-

Passenger: ering you. Blowing your nose also helps.
            I'm feeling better already.
Stewardess: I knew you would. If you need me again, just press
            the buzzer on the side of your seat.

EXERCISE 2

Learn these words.

SUPPLEMENTARY VOCABULARY

1. **adjustment** ajuste
2. **advancement** adelanto
3. **appreciation** apreciación
4. **argument** pleito, discusión
5. **collection** colección, colecta
6. **collision** choque
7. **combination** combinación
8. **contents** contenido
9. **critic** crítico
10. **criticism** crítica
11. **damage** daño
12. **decoration** decoración
13. **disappointment** desilusión, desengaño
14. **discouraging** desalentador
15. **embarrassing** penoso
16. **embarrassment** pena
17. **explosion** explosión
18. **inspection** inspección
19. **inspector** inspector
20. **location** ubicación, colocación
21. **performance** actuación; función
22. **protection** protección
23. **recognition** reconocimiento
24. **registration** inscripción
25. **ruins** ruinas
26. **shock** choque (*mental*); toque (*eléctrico*)
27. **threat** amenaza

EXERCISE 3

Translate the following sentences and practice reading them.

1. It should have been cold.
2. It shouldn't have been cold.
3. Should it have been cold?
4. Shouldn't it have been cold?
5. It should have been hot.
6. It shouldn't have been hot.
7. Should it have been hot?
8. Shouldn't it have been hot?

9. They may get in line.
10. They may not get in line.
11. They might build a fire.
12. They might not build a fire.
13. Maybe they'll keep their promise.
14. Maybe they won't keep their promise.
15. Perhaps they'll have their picture taken.
16. Perhaps they won't have their picture taken.
17. Maybe they sleep here.
18. Maybe they don't sleep here.
19. Perhaps they sleep here.
20. Perhaps they don't sleep here.
21. I had to be polite. So did he.
22. I didn't have to be polite. He didn't either.
23. She used to be fond of dancing. So did he.
24. She didn't use to be fond of dancing. He didn't either.
25. They were well off, and so were we.
26. They weren't well off, and we weren't either.
27. You'll be successful, and so will I.
28. You won't be successful, and I won't either.

EXERCISE 4

Translate the following sentences. Change them to the negative, inter-rogative, and interrogative negative.

1. She gets along with her mother-in-law.
2. They got along with us very well.
3. You'll have to get along with your teacher.
4. We'll be able to get along with him.
5. I've got along with her for five years.
6. We want you to get along with us.
7. You should get along with Mary better.
8. He used to get along with everybody.
9. Helen would like to get along with her parents.
10. Mr. Banks tried hard to get along with the owner.

EXERCISE 5

Give the past tense and past participle of the following verbs.

develop   damage   disturb   demand

drill	decorate	deposit	dive
deliver	disappoint	deserve	drizzle
dye	drip	dust	deny
discuss	discourage	depend (on)	fasten

EXERCISE 6

Give the past tense and past participle of the following verbs.

say good-bye (to)	shoot dice,	think of	take off
say hello (to)	craps	take (some-	tear
shrink	sting	thing) away	throw
set (some-	take	take a bath	throw away
thing) on	tell	take a shower	take place
fire	think	take care of	take charge (of)

EXERCISE 7

Verb Practice *Expand the following verb practice, using different tenses.*

1. The pilot should have landed by this time.
2. The pilot shouldn't have landed.
3. Should the pilot have landed by this time?
4. Shouldn't the pilot have landed by this time?
5. Why should the pilot have landed?

EXERCISE 8

Verb Practice *Make short sentences with forms of the verbs* **take off, allow, fasten, refuel, buzz, crash (into), get along (with), get airsick, make a stop, be overweight, be underweight.** *Expand each verb practice to include different tenses, as in the exercise above. Use a different noun or pronoun with each verb. Use the interrogative words when it is possible.*

EXERCISE 9

Translate into Spanish.

1. The train made two stops between Monterrey and Laredo.
2. How did you get along with the class you had last year?

294

3. I'll be glad when the plane lands. I'm beginning to get airsick.
4. We've had to brand all the cattle.
5. What did you tell them to put the picnic off for?
6. What did the dentist fill your tooth with?
7. You should wind the clock before you go to bed.
8. We may varnish the chairs and wax the floors tomorrow.
9. We went for a ride on Sunday.
10. Do you know how many people in the United States committed suicide last year?
11. How many cans of paint did you say were missing?
12. I wonder where my wedding ring is. I put it on the dressing table last night.
13. We plan to take a trip to Mexico this summer, but we don't plan to stay very long.
14. Don't walk on the floor, I've just waxed it.
15. You shouldn't let them take advantage of you.

EXERCISE 10

Translate into English.

1. Quizá el sobrecargo le traiga una cobija si tiene frío.
2. Se mató en un accidente aéreo.
3. ¿Crees que los aviones son más peligrosos que los trenes?
4. ¿Cree que podrá cobrar su seguro?
5. Leí en el periódico que se estrelló un avión contra una montaña y sesenta y seis personas murieron.
6. Viajar por ferrocarril es tan seguro como viajar por avión.
7. La sobrecargo le dijo que tocara el timbre si se le ofrecía algo.
8. Me da miedo volar, y a él también.
9. Debiste haberles dicho que nos esperaran a las seis y media en el aeropuerto.
10. Hubiera llegado al aeropuerto a tiempo si el camión no se hubiese retrasado.

EXERCISE 11

Answer the following questions.

1. Did you get along with your boss?
2. Will you get along with your in-laws?

3. Have you got along with them all right?
4. Did the plane crash?
5. Will the plane crash?
6. Has the plane crashed?
7. How long has it been since the plane took off?
8. How long has it been since the plane landed?
9. How long has it been since the plane crashed?
10. How far is it to the airport?
11. How far is it to the ticket office?
12. How far is it to the baggage room?
13. How long have you been waiting?
14. How long have you been working here?
15. How long have you been living here?

Leccion 41

Vocabulary

1. **to board, boarded, boarded**
   ir a bordo, abordar
2. **to dock, docked, docked**
   atracar
   dock muelle
3. **to haul, hauled, hauled**
   transportar (*mercancía*)
4. **to stack, stacked, stacked**
   amontonar
5. **to sail, sailed, sailed**
   salir (*barco*); zarpar;
   navegar
6. **to rock, rocked, rocked**
   balancearse, mecerse
7. **first-class (passage)**
   (pasaje) de primera clase
   second-class (passage)
   (pasaje) de segunda clase
   tourist-class (passage)
   (pasaje) de clase turista
8. **stateroom** camarote
9. **purser** sobrecargo (*barco*)
10. **crossing** travesía
11. **tide** marea
    high tide marea alta
    low tide marea baja
12. **ton** tonelada
    tonnage tonelaje
13. **sailor** marinero
14. **stowaway** polizón
15. **shipwreck** naufragio
16. **pier** muelle
    wharf muelle
17. **deck** cubierta
18. **deck chair** silla de cubierta
19. **anchor** ancla
20. **port (side)** a babor
    starboard (side) a estribor
21. **stern** popa
22. **bow** proa
23. **hold** bodega (*de barco*)
24. **cargo** carga
25. **gangplank** pasarela;
    escalerilla
26. **lifeboat** lancha salvavidas
    life preserver salvavidas

297

life belt cinturón de salvamento	28. **liner** barco de una línea, transatlántico
life jacket chaleco salvavidas	29. **tentative** provisional (*fecha, cita, etc.*)
27. **seasickness** mareo	30. **repair** reparación

IDIOMS

1. **to get used to + (gerund)** acostumbrarse a + (inf.)
   I can't get used to getting up early. No me puedo acostumbrar a levantarme temprano.
   I got used to it. Me acostumbré.
2. **to be used to + (gerund)** estar acostumbrado a + (inf.)
   I'm used to getting up early. Estoy acostumbrado a levantarme temprano.
   I'm used to it. Estoy acostumbrado.
3. **I finish work at six.** Acostumbro (suelo) salir de mi trabajo a las seis.
   I finished (used to finish) work at six. Acostumbraba (solía) salir de mi trabajo a las seis.
4. **to write (something) down** apuntar (algo)
5. **to be seasick** estar mareado
   to get seasick marearse
6. **to be shipwrecked** naufragar, ser náufrago
   He was shipwrecked on an island. El naufragó y estuvo en una isla.
7. **to go ashore** ir a tierra
8. **at sea** en el mar
   We were at sea for five days. Estuvimos en el mar cinco días.
9. **You can still find them in.** Todavía los puede encontrar.
10. **I'll keep the reservation open for you.** Le guardaré su reservación.
11. **I'd appreciate it.** Se lo agradezco.

EXERCISE 1

Practice the following dialogue.

TRAVELING BY SHIP

Passenger: When does the next ship leave for France?
Ticket Agent: The *La France* sails about two weeks from today. The

	sailing date is tentative because it's still at sea. When she docks, it'll depend on how much cargo we have to load, what repairs she needs. etc.
Passenger:	I see. Well, can I make my reservation now?
Ticket Agent:	Certainly. Would you like first-class, second-class, or tourist-class passage?
Passenger:	Second-class, please.
Ticket Agent:	Let me see. In second-class the only thing I have left is a lower berth in stateroom twelve on C Deck.
Passenger:	May I see a plan of the ship?
Ticket Agent:	Of course. Here it is. All these other staterooms were taken weeks ago. But look, your stateroom is nice. You're close to the dining room and bar.
Passenger:	What's the fare?
Ticket Agent:	One hundred and seventy dollars, plus ten per cent tax.
Passenger:	And what's the first stop?
Ticket Agent:	Le Havre. And then from the Mediterranean it goes on to England.
Passenger:	How long will the crossing take?
Ticket Agent:	Four days to Le Havre if the weather is good.
Passenger:	Thank you. By the way, will I need a visa from the French consulate before you can sell me my ticket?
Ticket Agent:	Yes, you will. But if you hurry, you can still find them in. They close at five, I'll write the address down for you.
Passenger:	Thank you. I'll be back tomorrow
Ticket Agent:	You're welcome. Then I'll expect you tomorrow, and I'll keep that reservation open for you.
Passenger:	Thank you. I'd appreciate it. Good-bye.

EXERCISE 2

Learn these words.

WORDS CONNECTED WITH A FIRE DEPARTMENT

1. **asbestos** asbesto
2. **artificial respiration** respiración artificial
3. **fire alarm** alarma contra incendios
4. **fire chief** jefe de bomberos
5. **fire engine** carro de incendios
6. **fire department** servicio de bomberos
7. **fire hydrant** toma de agua para incendios
8. **fireman** bombero

9. **first degree burns** quemaduras de primer grado
10. **flames** llamas, flamas
11. **hose** manguera
12. **ladder** escalera
13. **oxygen tent** cámara de oxígeno
14. **second degree burns** quemaduras de segundo grado
15. **siren** sirena
16. **to asphyxiate** asfixiar
17. **to burn down** quemarse
    The building burned down. El edificio se quemó.
18. **to choke** asfixiar, estrangular
19. **to smother** sofocar, asfixiar
20. **to suffocate** asfixiar

EXERCISE 3

Translate the following sentences and practice reading them.

1. Maybe they had an accident.
2. Maybe they didn't have an accident.
3. Perhaps the plane has crashed.
4. Perhaps the plane hasn't crashed.
5. The ship might have sunk.
6. The ship might not have sunk.
7. I've had to refuse.
8. I haven't had to refuse.
9. They'll have to change clothes.
10. They won't have to change clothes.
11. He'd have to forgive her.
12. He wouldn't have to forgive her.
13. Would he have to forgive her?
14. Wouldn't he have to forgive her?
15. Why wouldn't he have to forgive her?
16. We'd have liked to discuss it.
17. We wouldn't have liked to discuss it.
18. Would we have liked to discuss it?
19. Wouldn't we have liked to discuss it?
20. Why wouldn't we have liked to discuss it.
21. We should have moved.
22. We shouldn't have moved.
23. Should we have moved?
24. Shouldn't we have moved?
25. When should we have moved?

*ranslate the following sentences. Change them to the negative, inter-
ngative, and interrogative negative.*

1. He'll get used to the noise.
2. They got used to an early class.
3. We're getting used to the new teacher.
4. She got used to being alone.
5. You're going to get used to working.
6. He's used to the noise.
7. They were used to an early class.
8. We're used to the new teacher.
9. She was used to being alone.
0. You were used to working.

XERCISE 5

ive the past tense and past participle of the following verbs.

oard	rock	fill	follow
ock	burn down	finish	fry
aul	asphyxiate	fix	fine
tack	smother	fill a tooth	file your finger-
il	form	loan	nails
hoke	fail		

XERCISE 6

ive the past tense and past participle of the following verbs.

et up early	give a discount	take a walk,	take (some-
et used to	go ashore	ride	thing) back
o to bed late	take your	take a sun	take off
e used to	pulse	bath	understand
write (some-	take your	take advan-	wake up
thing) down	blood pres-	tage of	wear
e seasick	sure	take your	wear out
et seasick	take a trip	order	withdraw
e shipwrecked			

301

EXERCISE 7

Verb Practice *Expand the following verb practice, using different tenses*

1. He'd like to board the ship.
2. He wouldn't like to board the ship.
3. Would he like to board the ship?
4. Wouldn't he like to board the ship?
5. What time would he like to board the ship?

EXERCISE 8

Verb Practice *Make short sentences with forms of the verbs* **dock, haul, stack, sail, rock, get used to, be used to, write (something) down, be seasick, get seasick, be shipwrecked, go ashore, burn down, asphyxiate, choke, smother, suffocate.** *Expand each verb practice to include different tenses, as in the exercise above. Use a different noun or pronoun with each verb. Use the interrogative words when it is possible.*

EXERCISE 9

Translate into Spanish.

1. Do you think he'll ever get used to the sea?
2. I'm used to sailing now. I never get seasick any more.
3. We were shipwrecked on an island in the Pacific during the war.
4. We were at sea for five days before we were rescued.
5. The barn burned down before the firemen got there.
6. I'd appreciate it if you'd describe your costume to me.
7. We wrote down all the names so we could remember them.
8. I got so seasick I thought I'd die.
9. Are you bothered with seasickness?
10. I hate to travel by ship.
11. Move over. I need a little more room.
12. We might not be able to go ashore when we get to the next port.
13. Let's go down to the pier and say good-bye to the sailors.
14. Let go of my sleeve.
15. Have you heard from the agency about your reservation?

EXERCISE 10

Translate into English.

1. ¿Para qué estás transportando cemento en tu camión?

2. Si hubiésemos amontonado los libros en (against) la pared, no se habrían caído.
3. Dice (él) que no le molesta madrugar porque está acostumbrado.
4. Quizá el barco no se balancee tanto después que pasemos la tormenta.
5. ¿Qué haría Ud. si el barco se hundiera?
6. ¿Cuánto se hace a Europa por barco?
7. Nunca me he mareado, ni él tampoco.
8. Después de un rato nos acostumbramos al balanceo del barco.
9. ¿Has pasado alguna tormenta en el mar?
10. Prefiero ir a Europa por barco más que (than) por avión.
11. En mi casa acostumbramos comer a las dos y media.

EXERCISE 11

Answer the following questions.

1. Did you get used to the ship?
2. Will you get used to the ship?
3. Have you got used to the ship?
4. Did you write the message down?
5. Will you write the message down?
6. Have you written the message down?
7. Are you seasick?
8. Were you seasick?
9. Have you ever been seasick?
10. Do you get seasick?
11. Did you get seasick?
12. Have you got seasick?
13. Would you like to travel by ship?
14. Would you like to travel by plane?
15. Would you like to travel by car?
16. Can you get used to getting up so early?
17. Will you be able to get used to getting up so early?
18. Is she used to going to bed late?
19. Was she used to going to bed late?
20. Was he used to seeing so many people?
21. Aren't you used to it?
22. Are you used to the cold weather?
23. Was she used to the heat?
24. Did he get used to the cold?
25. Will they get used to it?

Lección 4

Vocabulary

1. **to loosen, loosened, loosened** soltar, aflojar
2. **to distribute, distributed, distributed** distribuir
3. **to embrace, embraced, embraced** abrazar
4. **to intend, intended, intended** pensar, planear
5. **to search (for), searched (for), searched (for)** registrar; esculcar; buscar
6. **photostatic copy** copia fotostática
7. **responsibility** responsabilidad
8. **photograph** fotografía **photo** fotografía
9. **document** documento
10. **passport** pasaporte **passport photograph** fotografía de pasaporte
11. **birth certificate** acta de nacimiento **vaccination certificate** certificado de vacuna
12. **border** frontera
13. **customs** aduana
14. **will power** fuerza de voluntad
15. **bald-headed** calvo
16. **extension** extensión
17. **single** (*adj.*) soltero, a **married** (*adj.*) casado, a **widowed** (*adj.*) viudo, a **divorced** (*adj.*) divorciado, a
18. **diplomat** (*noun*) diplomático **diplomatic service** servicio diplomático
19. **pleasure trip** viaje de placer **business trip** viaje de negocios
20. **visa** visa
21. **consulate** consulado **consul** cónsul
22. **embassy** embajada **ambassador** embajador

23. **crop** cosecha	25. **mood** humor
24. **lump** chipote	26. **scholarship** beca

IDIOMS

1. **to blow up** explotar
   to blow (something) up volar (algo)
2. **to get a visa** sacar una visa
3. **to prevent someone from** + **gerund** impedir a alguien + inf.
   He prevented me from going. Me impidió ir (que fuera).
4. **to have a scholarship** tener beca, estar becado
   to be on a scholarship tener beca, estar becado
   to go on a scholarship ir becado
5. **I got my passport stamped.** Me sellaron el pasaporte.
6. **What difference does it make?** ¿Qué importa?
7. **Just what kind do you want?** ¿Precisamente qué clase quiere?
8. **I'm just going for pleasure.** Voy solamente por placer.
9. **for business or pleasure** de negocios o de placer
10. **I don't know what that's got to do with it.** No sé qué tiene eso que ver.
11. **It was a tie.** Hubo empate.
    They tied. Empataron.
12. **with all expenses paid** con todos los gastos pagados

EXERCISE 1

Practice the following dialogue.

GETTING A VISA

Traveler: Good morning.

Clerk: Good morning. May I help you?

Traveler: Yes. I'd like to know how I can get a visa to the United States.

Clerk: Well, just what kind of a visa do you want? Do you intend to work, to study? Is it for business or pleasure—or what?

Traveler: Well, what difference does it make?

Clerk: Oh, a great deal of difference. You see, the documents that you'll need will depend mainly on what kind of visa you want.

Traveler: Oh, I'm just going for pleasure. I'll only be there for about a month.

305

Clerk: In that case you'll need only your passport and a bank statement.

Traveler: What's the bank statement for?

Clerk: To prove that you've got enough money to cover your expenses while in the United States. This way we're sure that you won't be dependent on the American Government.

Traveler: Oh, I see. And can I get an extension if I decide to stay longer?

Clerk: Yes. That won't be difficult. Now here's this form. Fill it out and bring it back when you've got your passport.

Traveler: Thank you.

EXERCISE 2

Learn these words.

WORDS CONNECTED WITH INSTITUTIONS

1. **asylum** asilo
2. **cell** celda
3. **criminal** criminal
4. **insane asylum** manicomio
5. **institution** institución
6. **jail** cárcel
7. **matron** celadora
8. **orphan** huérfano
9. **orphanage** orfanato
10. **penitentiary** penitenciaría
11. **psychiatrist** psiquiatra
12. **psychology** psicología
13. **playground** campo de recreo
14. **prison** prisión
15. **prison guard** guardia
16. **reform school** reformatorio
17. **reformatory** reformatorio
18. **sanatorium** sanatorio
19. **strait jacket** camisa de fuerza
20. **warden** encargado de la prisión

MISCELLANEOUS IDIOMATIC VERBS

1. **(to) break down** descomponer
   My car broke down yesterday. Ayer se me descompuso el coche.
2. **(to) call for (someone or something)** pasar por (alguien o algo)
   I'll call for you at seven. Paso por ti a las siete.
3. **(to) call (something) off** cancelar (algo)
   The picnic was called off. Cancelaron el día de campo.
4. **(to) call (someone) up** telefonear (a alguien)
   He called me up at two o'clock. Me telefoneó a las dos.

306

5. **(to) drop (someone or something) off** dejar (a alguien o algo)
   He dropped me off at my house. Me dejó en la casa.
6. **(to) get in touch with** comunicarse con
   How can I get in touch with you? ¿Cómo me puedo comunicar con Ud.?
7. **(to) keep in touch with** mantener comunicación con
   I'll always keep in touch with you. Siempre mantendré comunicación con Ud.
8. **(to) make up your mind** decidirse
   Please make up your mind. Por favor, decídete.
9. **(to) put (something) away** guardar (algo)
   I'm putting my summer clothes away. Estoy guardando mi ropa de verano.
10. **(to) put up with** aguantar, soportar
    He put up with his mother-in-law for ten years. Aguantó a su suegra diez años.
11. **(to) sharpen a pencil** sacarle punta a un lápiz
    Please sharpen this pencil for me. Favor de sacarle punta a este lápiz.
12. **(to) tie your shoes, tie, etc.** amarrarse los zapatos, hacerse el nudo de la corbata, etc.
    Please tie my shoes for me. Por favor, amárrame los zapatos.
13. **(to) tear (something) up** romper (algo), rasgar, desgarrar
    They tore the check up. Rompieron el cheque.

EXERCISE 3

Translate the following sentences and practice reading them.

1. He used to haul cattle.
2. He didn't use to haul cattle.
3. Did he use to haul cattle?
4. Didn't he use to haul cattle?
5. Why did he use to haul cattle?
6. They used to be able to wrestle.
7. They didn't use to be able to wrestle.
8. Did they use to be able to wrestle?
9. Didn't they use to be able to wrestle?
10. When did they use to be able to wrestle?
11. It would have been hot.
12. It wouldn't have been hot.

13. Would it have been hot?
14. Wouldn't it have been hot?
15. When would it have been hot?
16. It should have been cold.
17. It shouldn't have been cold.
18. Should it have been cold?
19. Shouldn't it have been cold?
20. When should it have been cold?

EXERCISE 4

Translate the following sentences. Change them to the negative, interrogative, and interrogative negative.

1. The pressure cooker blew up.
2. The building has blown up.
3. The factory will blow up.
4. The stove would have blown up.
5. The ship is going to blow up.
6. They blew the bridge up.
7. We should have blown the factory up.
8. He's going to blow the mine up.
9. They'll blow the oil tanks up.
10. They've blown the railroad track up.

EXERCISE 5

Give the past tense and past participle of the following verbs.

loosen	call for	tie your shoes,	fire
distribute	(someone or	tie, etc.	flatter
intend	something)	fill a prescription	file
search (for)	call (some-	faint	fade
prevent	thing) off	float	fold
embrace	call (some-	furnish	sharpen a
	one) up		pencil

EXERCISE 6

Give the past tense and past participle of the following verbs.

blow up	keep in touch with	put up with	be late

blow (some-thing) up	be crazy about (something)	tear (some-thing) up	be about
blush	make up your	wind a watch,	be polite
get a visa	mind	(clock)	go swimming
break down	put (something)	write (some-thing) down	go dancing
get in touch with	away	be early	go hunting
			go on strike

EXERCISE 7
Verb Practice *Expand the following verb practice, using different tenses.*

1. You'll have to loosen the screws.
2. You won't have to loosen the screws.
3. Will you have to loosen the screws?
4. Won't you have to loosen the screws?
5. Why will you have to loosen the screws?

EXERCISE 8

Verb Practice *Make short sentences with forms of the verbs* distribute, embrace, intend, search (for), prevent someone from, get a visa, have a scholarship, be on a scholarship, go on a scholarship, blow up, blow (something) up. *Expand each verb practice to include different tenses, as in the exercise above. Use a different noun or pronoun with each verb. Use the interrogative words when it is possible.*

EXERCISE 9

Translate into Spanish.

1. What did the soldiers blow the bridge up for?
2. What made the pressure cooker blow up?
3. No one won. It was a tie.
4. If my car broke down, I'd call a mechanic.
5. Did you hear that they were going to call the wedding off?
6. Put those toys away and don't play with them any more.
7. I don't know why she puts up with her husband.
8. She told me to call for her at about seven-thirty.
9. We've kept in touch with each other for twenty years.
10. Why don't you call me up tomorrow?
11. Don't tear those letters up. They might be worth something.

12. Tie that boy's tie.
13. How long does it take to get a visa?
14. We can't put the meeting off any longer.
15. Have you done your best to learn Spanish?

EXERCISE 10

Translate into English.

1. ¿Cree Ud. que puede aflojar la reata un poco?
2. Debió haber hecho frío en diciembre, pero no hizo.
3. Si hubiera distribuido los papeles, le hubiera dado uno.
4. ¿Para qué registraron tu apartamiento?
5. ¿Es Ud. soltera o casada? Soy divorciada.
6. Traté de decirle que no sacara su visa hoy.
7. Apunté los números y él también.
8. ¿Qué hubieras hecho si él hubiera tenido una pistola?
9. No podemos acostumbrarnos a levantarnos tan temprano.
10. ¿Todavía no está Ud. acostumbrado a la altura?

EXERCISE 11

Answer the following questions.

1. Did they blow the factory up?
2. Will they blow the factory up?
3. Have they blown the factory up?
4. Did the stove blow up?
5. Will the stove blow up?
6. Has the stove blown up?
7. Did the bus break down?
8. Will the bus break down?
9. Has the bus broken down?
10. Did they call the dance off?
11. Will they call the dance off?
12. Have they called the dance off?
13. Did you put your books away?
14. Will you put your books away?
15. Have you put your books away?
16. What time are you going to call for her?
17. Did they call the party off?

18. Can you call me up tomorrow evening?
19. Did you drop my suit off at the cleaners?
20. Have you got in touch with Mr. Parks yet?
21. Will you keep in touch with me?
22. Has he made up his mind yet?
23. When are you going to put all those clothes away?
24. How long are you going to put up with him?
25. Did she sharpen all the pencils?
26. Who tied Johnny's shoes for him?
27. How did she tear her dress?
28. Did she get used to getting up early?
29. Have they got used to Mexico?
30. Do you think she'll be able to get used to it?

Vocabulario inglés-español

A

absolutely not desde luego que no, de ninguna manera
accelerator acelerador

(to) accept aceptar
    accepted
    accepted
accordion acordeón
accountant contador
accounting contabilidad
ace as
aquamarine aguamarina

(to) act actuar, trabajar
    acted
    acted
actor actor
actress actriz
adding machine sumadora

(to) address poner nombre y dirección, rotular
    addressed
    addressed

adhesive tape tela adhesiva
(to) adjust ajustar
    adjusted
    adjusted
adjustment ajuste
adopted child hijo adoptivo
adopted children hijos adoptivos
adopted daughter hija adoptiva
adopted son hijo adoptivo
(to) advance avanzar
    advanced
    advanced
advancement adelanto
adventure aventura
Africa África
African africano
afternoon train tren de la tarde
agricultural engineer ingeniero agrónomo
agriculture agricultura

313

a half dollar cincuenta centavos
air-mail correo aéreo
airport aeropuerto
airsick mareado
airsickness mareo
aisle pasillo
Alaska Alaska
alcoholic alcohólico
alexandrine alejandrina
algebra álgebra
alike parecido; igual
alive vivo
alley callejón
alligator caimán
(to) allow permitir; dejar
   allowed
   allowed
almond almendra
altar altar
alteration compostura
altogether por todo
aluminum aluminio
ambassador embajador
ambulance ambulancia
amethyst amatista
(to) analyze analizar
   analyzed
   analyzed
anchor ancla
anemia anemia
anemic anémico
animal trainer entrenador de animales
ankle tobillo
anniversary aniversario
announcement aviso; notificación
ant hormiga
anxious ansioso
ape gorila, chimpancé

apiece cada uno
(to) apologize (to) disculparse (con)
   apologized (to)
   apologized (to)
apology disculpa
appendicitis apendicitis
appetite apetito
apple sauce puré de manzana
applicant solicitante
(to) apply for solicitar, hacer una solicitud para
   applied for
   applied for
appointment cita (*business*)
(to) appreciate reconocer, agradecer
   appreciated
   appreciated
appreciation apreciación; agradecimiento
apricot chabacano
apron delantal
archbishop arzobispo
architect arquitecto
architecture arquitectura
(to) argue (about) discutir (*de, por*), argüir, alegar, pelear (se)
   argued (about)
   argued (about)
argument pleito
arithmetic aritmética
(to) arrange arreglar; acomodar
   arranged
   arranged
arrangement arreglo
arrest arresto
(to) arrest arrestar
   arrested

arrested
(to) arrive (in, at) llegar (a)
arrived (in, at)
arrived (in, at)
arthritis artritis
artichoke alcachofa
artificial respiration
    respiración artificial
asbestos asbesto
ashes cenizas
ashtray cenicero
Asia Asia
Asiatic asiático
as long as con tal que
asparagus (sing.) espárragos
(to) asphyxiate asfixiar
asphyxiated
asphyxiated
aspirin aspirina
asylum asilo
athlete atleta
athletic equipment
    equipo gimnástico

athletics atletismo
Atlantic Ocean Océano
    Atlántico
atmosphere atmósfera;
    ambiente
(to) attend asistir a
attended
attended
attendance asistencia
attractive atractivo
Australia Australia
Australian australiano
available disponible
aviation aviación
avocado aguacate
awful terrible, horrible,
    pésimo
awfully muy; terriblemente
awkward desgarbado,
    torpe
ax hacha

B

back seat asiento trasero
backwards al revés; hacia
    atrás
bacon tocino
bag veliz, maleta
baggage equipaje
baggage agent agente de
    equipajes
baggage check talón de
    equipaje
baggage locker casillero de
    equipaje
baggage room sala de
    equipaje

bait carnada; cebo
(to) bake hornear
baked
baked
baked potatoes papas al
    horno
baker panadero
bakery panadería
baking powder polvo de
    hornear
(to) balance balancear (se),
    equilibrar (se)
balanced
balanced

balcony arriba
        (*en el cine*)
bald calvo
ball pelota
banana plátano
band banda
bandage venda
band-aid curita
band leader director de
        banda
bangs fleco
banquet banquete
bank account cuenta (*en
        un banco*)
bank draft giro (*bancario*)
bank statement estado de
        cuenta
baptism bautismo; bautizo
(to) baptize bautizar
        baptized
        baptized
bar cantina
bar bell mancuerna
barber peluquero
barber shop peluquería
(to) bark ladrar
        barked
        barked
barrel barril
bartender cantinero
(baseball) bat bate, tolete
baseball fan
        aficionado al béisbol
baseball glove manopla (*de
        béisbol*)
basement sótano
bashful tímido, cohibido,
        vergonzoso
bass bajo
bat murciélago
bathrobe bata

bathtub tina
baton batuta
batter bateador, toletero
battery batería
battle batalla
(to) bawl (someone) out
        regañar (a alguien)
        bawled (someone) out
        bawled (someone) out
beach playa
beach chair silla para playa
bead cuenta (*de collar*)
        abalorio
(to) be all gone acabarse
        was, were all gone
        been all gone
bear oso
beard barba
bearded lady dama barbuda
(to) beat batir
        beat
        beaten
(to) beat someone ganar a
        alguien
        beat someone
        beaten someone
beauty operator cultor(a)
        de belleza
beauty parlor salón de
        belleza
beauty shop salón de
        belleza
beaver castor
(to) be booked-up no tener
        lugar
        was, were booked up
        been booked up
(to) be crazy about
        estar loco por, gustar
        muchísimo, encantarle
        a uno

316

was, were crazy about
been crazy about
bedbug chinche
bedroom set juego de recámara
bedspread colcha
bee abeja
beech haya
beef carne de res
beehive colmena
beer cerveza
beer on tap cerveza de barril
beet betabel
beetle escarabajo
(to) be fattening engordar
was, were fattening
been fattening
(to) be fond of tener cariño a, gustar, apreciar
was, were fond of
been fond of
(to) beg suplicar, rogar; pedir limosna
begged
begged
beggar mendigo
beige beige
(to) be in estar (*en casa, oficina*)
was, were in
been in
(to) be in charge (of) estar encargado (de); tener el cargo (de)
was, were in charge (of)
been in charge (of)
(to) be in mourning estar de luto (de duelo)
was, were in mourning
been in mourning
(to) belch eructar

belched
belched
Belgian Belga
bellboy botones
(to) belong pertenecer
belonged
belonged
belt buckle hebilla para cinturón
(to) be missing faltar
was, were missing
been missing
(to) bend doblar (*metales, el cuerpo*)
bent
bent
(to) be on a diet estar a dieta
was, were on a diet
been on a diet
(to) be on strike estar en huelga
was, were on strike
been on strike
(to) be operated on ser operado
was, were operated on
been operated on
(to) be out no estar (*en casa, oficina*)
was, were out
been out
(to) be out of something acabársele a uno algo
was, were out of something
been out of something
(to) be overweight tener exceso de peso
was, were overweight
been overweight
(to) be polite tener educación
was, were polite
been polite

317

Berlin Berlín
berth litera, cama
(to) be seasick estar mareado
    was, were seasick
    been seasick
(to) be sharp tener filo
    was, were sharp
    been sharp
(to) be shipwrecked naufragar,
    ser náufrago
    was, were shipwrecked
    been shipwrecked
(to) be shocked (at) escandalizarse
    (de)
    was, were shocked (at)
    been shocked (at)
best man padrino (*en la
    iglesia*)
(to) be successful tener éxito
    was, were successful
    been successful
(to) be supposed + **(infinitive)**
    deber + (infinitivo)
    was, were supposed
    been supposed
(to) be underweight faltar peso
    was, were underweight
    been underweight
(to) be used to estar
    acostumbrado a
    was, were used to
    been used to
(to) be well off
    ser acomodado, tener
    buena posición
    was, were well off
    been well off
Bible Biblia
(to) bid declarar (*en las
    barajas*)
    bid

    bid
big toe dedo gordo (*del pie*)
bill decreto; cuenta (*de un
    restaurant*)
billfold cartera
biology biología
birch abedul
birth certificate acta de
    nacimiento
biscuit bizcocho
bishop obispo
bit poco
bite mordida
(to) bite moder
    bit
    bitten
bitter amargo; amargado
blackboard pizarrón
black widow spider araña
    capulina; viuda negra
blade hoja de un cuchillo
(to) bleach teñir, pintar (*pelo*);
    blanquear
    bleached
    bleached
bleached muslin bramante
    blanqueado
blemish mancha (*de piel*)
blender licuadora
(to) bless bendecir
    blessed
    blessed
blinds persianas
blister ampolla
blizzard ventisca
blond, blonde rubio, a
blood pressure presión
    arterial
(to) bloom florecer; abrir (*flor*)
    bloomed
    bloomed

blossom flor de árbol frutal
blotter secante
blouse blusa
(to) blow (something) up volar
    (algo)
    blew (something) up
    blown (something) up
(to) blow up explotar
    blew up
    blown up
(to) blow your horn tocar el
    claxon
    blew your horn
    blown your horn
(to) blow your nose sonarse
    blew your nose
    blown your nose
blue jeans pantalones
    vaqueros
bluing azul (añil)
(to) blush ruborizar
    blushed
    blushed
(to) board abordar, ir a bordo
    boarded
    boarded
board and room cuarto con
    asistencia
boarding house casa de
    asistencia
bobby pins pasadores
bologna mortadela
bolt perno
bookcase librero
bookstore librería
boot bota
booth caseta; vestidor
border frontera
bore (noun) aburrido,
    aburrición
(to) bore aburrir

bored
bored
boring (ser) aburrido
(to) borrow pedir o tomar
    prestado
borrowed
borrowed
boss jefe, patrón
botanist botánico
botany botánica
bottle botella
bottle of aspirins un frasco
    de aspirinas
bottle of hand lotion un
    frasco de crema
    (líquida) para las manos
bottle of perfume un frasco
    de perfume
bottle of perfume
bow arco de violín; proa
bowl tazón (para sopa)
(to) bowl jugar boliche
    bowled
    bowled
bowlegged (adj.)
    de piernas torcidas en
    arco
bowling el boliche (el
    deporte)
bowling alley establecimiento
    donde se juega boliche
(to) box boxear
    boxed
    boxed
boxer boxeador
boxing el box, el boxeo
    (el deporte)
boxing gloves guantes de
    box
boxing ring ring
box office taquilla

319

box spring box spring
boyfriend novio
brace berbiquí; freno
    (*de dientes*)
bracelet pulsera
(to) brag (about) jactarse (de)
    bragged (about)
    bragged (about)
(to) braid your hair hacerse trenzas
    braided your hair
    braided your hair
braids trenzas
brake freno
branch sucursal
brand marca
(to) brand marcar (con hierro)
    branded
    branded
branding iron hierro para
    marcar
brass latón
(to) break down descomponer
    broke down
    broken down
(to) break out brotar; estallar;
    salirle a uno
    broke out
    broken out
breed raza (*de animales*)
brick ladrillo
bricklayer albañil
bride novia (*en la boda*)
bridesmaid dama de honor
bridge puente; bridge (*el
    juego*)
bridge table mesa de juego
bridle brida
brooch prendedor, broche
broom escoba
brunet, burnette moreno, a
brush cepillo; brocha

(to) brush cepillar
    brushed
    brushed
(to) brush your teeth lavarse los
    dientes
    brushed your teeth
    brushed your teeth
Brussels sprouts colecitas de
    Bruselas
(to) buck reparar
    bucked
    bucked
buckle hebilla
bud botón, capullo
buffet aparador
bug insecto, bicho
(to) build a fire prender fuego,
    hacer una fogata
    built a fire
    built a fire
(to) build you up reconstituirle
    a Ud.
    built you up
    built you up
bulb foco; bulbo
bull toro
bullet bala
bullfight corrida de toros
bullfighter torero, matador
bullring arena
bumper defensa
bun chongo
bunch manojo, racimo;
    montón
bundle bulto
burglar ladrón (*el que se
    mete en casa ajena*)
burial entierro
(to) burn down quemar (se)
    burned down
    burned down

bus driver chofer de camión
bush arbusto, matorral
bushel canasta
business trip viaje de
    negocios
bus stop parada de camión
butcher carnicero
butcher knife cuchillo de
    carnicero
butcher shop carnicería
butterfly mariposa

butterknife cuchillo
    mantequillero
button botón
buttonhole ojal
(to) buzz tocar (*timbre*); zumbar
    buzzed
    buzzed
buzzard buitre
buzzer timbre
by heart de memoria
by means of por medio de

C

cabbage col
cabin cabaña
cable cable
caddy caddy
calculus cálculo
calendar calendario
calf becerro; pantorrilla
(to) call for (someone or
    something) pasar (por
    alguien o algo)
    called for (someone or
        something)
    called for (someone or
        something)
(to) call (something) off
    cancelar (algo)
    called (something) off
    called (something) off
(to) call (someone) up telefonear
    (a alguien)
    called (someone) up
    called (someone) up
    callus callo
    cameo camafeo
    can lata; bote
(to) can enlatar; envasar; hacer
    conservas de alimentos

    canned
    canned
Canada Canadá
Canadian canadiense
can afford tener (dinero)
    con que; poder costear,
    convenir
    could afford
    been able to afford
canal canal (*natural*)
cancer cáncer
candle vela
candleholder palmatoria
candlestickholder candelero
candy dulces
cane bastón
can opener abrelatas
cantaloupe melón
canvas lona
cape cabo, capa
carbon paper papel carbón
carburetor carburador
cardinal cardenal
cards naipes, barajas
card table mesa de juego
card trick suerte (*con las
    barajas*)

cargo cargo
carnation clavel
carnival carnaval; feria
carpenter carpintero
carrot zanahoria
carton paquete, cartón
cartoon caricatura
car trouble avería o
    desperfecto de un
    coche
(to) carve tallar; trinchar;
    cincelar; cortar
    (*carne*)
    carved
    carved
case caso
cash efectivo; en efectivo;
    al contado
(to) cash a check cambiar
    (*cobrar*) un cheque
    cashed a check
    cashed a check
cashew nut nuez de la
    India
cashier cajero(a)
cashier's box caja
    registradora
casket féretro, ataúd
(to) catch a fish coger un pez
    caught a fish
    caught a fish
catcher catcher, receptor
caterpillar oruga
Catholic católico
catsup salsa de tomate
cattle ganado
cauliflower coliflor
cause causa
(to) cause causar
    caused
    caused

caviar caviar
cavity caries, muela picada
cedar cedro
celery apio
cell celda
cello viloncelo
cement cemento
cemetery cementerio
centipede ciempiés
century siglo
cereal cereal
chalk gis
(to) change clothes cambiarse de
    ropa
    changed clothes
    changed clothes
channel canal (*construido*)
chapter capítulo
charge cargo, acusación
(to) charge cobrar
    charged
    charged
(to) charge a battery cargar una
    batería
    charged a battery
    charged a battery
charge account cuenta de
    crédito
(to) chase perseguir
    chased
    chased
(to) cheat hacer trampa, ser
    tramposo; engañar
    cheated
    cheated
check cheque; cuenta (*en
    un restaurante*)
checked a cuadros
(to) check-in tomar un cuarto
    checked-in
    checked-in

checking account cuenta
    de cheques
(to) ckeck-out dejar el cuarto
    checked-out
    checked out
(to) check the oil, gas, tires, etc.
    revisar el aceite,
    gasolina, llantas, etc.
    checked the oil, gas,
    tires, etc.
    checked the oil, gas,
    tires, etc.
check-up examen médico
    general
cheek mejilla
chemical engineer ingeniero
    químico
chemist químico
chemistry química
cherry cereza
chest pecho
chestnut castaña
chest of drawers cómoda
(to) chew masticar
    chewed
    chewed
(chewing) gum chicle
chicken pox varisela
chigger nigua
china vajilla de lujo
China China
china closet vitrina
Chinese chino
chip ficha
chisel cincel
choice selección
choir coro
(to) choke asfixiar; estrangular
    choked
    choked

Christian cristiano
cigar puro
cigarette cigarro, cigarrillo
cigarette butt colilla
cigarette holder boquilla
(cigarette) lighter
    encendedor
cinnamon canela
circus circo
citizen ciudadano
citrus fruit fruta cítrica
clarinet clarinete
classroom salón de clase
clay barro
cleansing cream crema
    limpiadora
clear claro
clerk empleado, dependiente
clever listo
climate clima
(to) climb subir, escalar
    climbed
    climbed
clinic clínica
clippers máquina para
    cortar el pelo
cloudburst chaparrón
clown payaso
clubs tréboles
clutch cluch, embrague
cockroach cucaracha
cocktail cocktail
cocktail shaker coctelera
coconut coco
coffeepot cafetera
coffee table mesa para café
coffin féretro, ataúd
coin moneda
Coke coca
cold cream cold cream

cold cuts carnes frías
collar cuello (de una
    camisa)
collateral garantía (para
    préstamo bancario)
(to) collect coleccionar; cobrar
    collected
    collected
    collection colecta, colección
    college universidad
(to) collide chocar
    collided
    collided
    collision choque
    colt potro
    comb peine
(to) comb your hair peinarse
    combed your hair
    combed your hair
    combination combinación
(to) combine combinar
    combined
    combined
    combustion combustión
    comedy comedia
(to) come down bajar (se)
    (viniendo hacia abajo)
    came down
    come down
(to) come off zafársele a uno,
    salírsele a uno, caérsele
    a uno
    came off
    come off
(to) come up subir (se)
    (viniendo hacia arriba)
    came up
    come up
    comic book revista de
    monitos
(to) commit suicide suicidarse

committed suicide
committed suicide
communion comunión
communism comunismo
communist comunista
Communist (partido)
    comunista
company compañía
(to) complain (about) quejar(se)
    (de)
    complained (about)
    complained (about)
complaint queja
complexion cutis, tez
composer compositor
concrete concreto
conductor director (de
    orquesta)
conference conferencia
confession confesión
confessional booth
    confesionario
(to) congratulate felicitar
    congratulated
    congratulated
congratulations felicitaciones
congress congreso
congressman diputado
conservative conservatorio
(to) consist of consistir en,
    constar de
    consisted of
    consisted of
consul cónsul
consulate consulado
(to) contain contener
    contained
    contained
contents contenido
continent continente
contract contrato

convent convento
cook cocinero (a)
cooky galleta (*dulce*)
cool fresco
(to) cool enfriar
    cooled
    cooled
cop policía
co-pilot copiloto
copper cobre
copy copia, ejemplar
(to) copy copiar
    copied
    copied
coral coral
cord cuerda, mecate
corduroy pana
corkscrew sacacorcho
corn elote, maíz; callo (*del pie*)
corn bread pan de maíz
cornet corneta
corn meal harina de maíz
corn (on the cob) elote
corpse cadáver
corral corral
corsage corsage
cosmetics cosméticos
costume vestido de fantasía
costume jewelry joyería de fantasía
cot catre, cama de campaña
cotton algodón
cottonwood álamo
cough tos
(to) cough toser
    coughed
    coughed
count conde
countess condesa
court corte

cover charge derecho de mesa
cowboy boots botas vaqueras
coyote coyote
crab cangrejo
cracker galleta (*salada*)
cranberries arándanos
craps dados
(to) crash (into) chocar (con, contra); estrellarse (contra)
    crashed (into)
    crashed (into)
(to) crawl arrastrar (se)
    crawled
    crawled
cream pitcher cremera
crease raya (*del pantalón*)
(to) cremate incinerar
    cremated
    cremated
cricket grillo
criminal criminal
crippled inválido
critic crítico
criticism crítica
(to) criticize criticar
    criticized
    criticized
(to) crochet tejer con gancho
    crocheted
    crocheted
crop cosecha
cross cruz
cross-eyed (*adj.*) bizco
crossing travesía; crucero
(to) cross yourself persignarse; santiguarse
    crossed yourself
    crossed yourself
crow gentío, multitud

crowded atestado, concurrido

(to) crush machacar; machucar; aplastar

crushed

crushed

crutch muleta

Cuba Cuba

Cuban cubano

cucumber pepino

cuff valenciana; puño

cuff link mancuerna

cup taza

cupboard aparador

cup cake panqué

(to) cure curar, sanar

cured

cured

curious curioso

curl rizo

(to) curl rizar

curled

curled

curly rizado, chino

curly hair pelo chino

curtain rod cortinero

custard flan

customer cliente, parroquiano

customs aduana

(to) cut (cards) cortar

cut (cards)

cut (cards)

(to) cut a stencil sacar un estencil

cut a stencil

cut a stencil

(to) cut a tooth salirle un diente

cut a tooth

cut a tooth

cute mono (*adj.*)

cuticle cutícula

cyclone ciclón

D

daddy papacito

daily diario, diariamente

daisy margarita

damage daño

(to) damage dañar

damaged

damaged

damp húmedo

dance band orquesta de baile

dandruff caspa

Dane (*noun*) danés

Danish (*adj.*) danés

dark blue azul oscuro

dark-complexioned (*adj.*) de piel morena

dashboard tablero (*del coche*)

dashboard light luz del tablero

date (*social and with the opposite sex*) cita; dátil

daughter-in-law nuera

day off día libre, día de descanso

(to) deal (cards) dar (naipes)

dealt (cards)

dealt (cards)

(to) deal with tratar con

dealt with

dealt with

deck cubierta

deck chair silla de cubierta

deck of cards una baraja

(to) decorate decorar, adornar; condecorar
decorated
decorated
decoration decoración; condecoración
deed escritura
deep profundo
deep freeze congelador
delighted encantado
(to) deliver entregar
delivered
delivered
delivery entrega
delivery truck camión de entrega
(to) demand exigir
demanded
demanded
democracy democracia
Democrat (partido) demócrata
democratic democrático
Denmark Dinamarca
dent abolladura
(to) dent abollar
dented
dented
dentist dentista
dentistry odontología
(to) deny negar
denied
denied
deodorant desodorante
(to) depend on contar con depender de
depended on
depended on
deposit depósito
(to) deposit depositar
deposited

deposited
deposit slip esqueleto para depositar dinero
depot estación de ferrocarril
depth profundidad
(to) describe describir
described
described
desert desierto
(to) deserve merecer
deserved
deserved
design diseño
desk escritorio
desk clerk administrador en un hotel
desk drawer cajón (de un escritorio)
dessert postre
(to) destroy destruir
destroyed
destroyed
destruction destrucción
detective detective
detour desviación
deuce dos (de naipes)
(to) develop desarrollar
developed
developed
development desarrollo
devil diablo
(to) dial marcar (en el teléfono)
dialed
dialed
dialogue diálogo
diamond diamante, brillante
dice dado
dictator dictador
diet dieta
(to) dim your lights bajar o disminuir las luces

dimmed your lights

dimmed your lights

dime moneda de diez
    centavos

diner comedor (*de un tren*)

dining car coche comedor

diplomat diplomático

diplomatic service servicio
    diplomático

diphteria difteria

(to) **direct** dirigir
    directed
    directed

direction dirección

director director

disabled deshabilitado

(to) **disappoint** desilusionar
    disappointed
    disappointed

disappointment desilusión,
    desengaño

discount descuento

(to) **discourage** desanimar,
    desalentar
    discouraged
    discouraged

discouraging desalentador

(to) **discuss** discutir, hablar de
    discussed
    discussed

disease enfermedad
    (*infecciosa y
    transmisible*)

disgrace deshonra,
    desprestigio, vergüenza

disgraced deshonrado,
    desprestigiado,
    avergonzado

dishcloth toalla de cocina
    (*de platos*)

dishes platos, trastes

dishonest no honrado

dishpan tina para lavar platos

dishrag trapo para cocina

dishtowel toalla de cocina

desinfectant desinfectante

(to) **distribute** distribuir
    distributed
    distributed

district distrito

(to) **disturb** molestar
    disturbed
    disturbed

(to) **dive** echar clavados
    dived
    dived

diver clavadista

dividend dividendo

diving (*el deporte*) echar
    clavados

diving board trampolín

divorce divorcio

divorced (*adj.*) divorciado(a)

(to) **divorce someone** divorciarse
    de alguien
    divorced someone
    divorced someone

dizzy mareado

dock muelle

(to) **dock** atracar
    docked
    docked

document documento

doll muñeca

doorbell timbre (*de la
    puerta*)

door handle manija

dope narcótico

dormitory dormitorio

dot punto

double boiler baño María

double-breasted cruzado (*traje*)

double room cuarto doble

dough masa

doughnut dona

downhill cuesta abajo

down payment enganche

downstairs abajo (*en un edificio*)

(to) do your best esmerarse

    did your best

    done your best

dozen docena

dramatics el estudio del drama

drape cortina

(to) draw (cards) sacar o robar naipes

    drew (cards)

    drawn (cards)

drawing dibujo

dream sueño

(to) dream (about) soñar (con)

    dreamed (about)

    dreamed (about)

dressing room vestidor

dressing table tocador

drill taladro

(to) drill taladrar; perforar

    drilled

    drilled

drip gotera

(to) drip chorrear; gotear (*refiriéndose al líquido*)

    dripped

    dripped

driver's license licencia para manejar

(to) drizzle lloviznar

    drizzled

    drizzled

(to) drop (someone or something) off dejar (a alguien o algo)

    dropped (someone or something) off

    dropped (someone or something) off

drug droga; medicamento

druggist farmacéutico

drugstore farmacia, botica

drum tambor

drummer el que toca el tambor; baterista

dry seco

dry cleaned lavado en seco

dry cleaners tintorería

dryer secadora

(to) dry up secarse (*plantas*)

    dried up

    dried up

duchess duquesa

duck pato

duet dueto

duke duque

dull aburrido (*ser*); sin filo, desafilado

dummy muerto (*bridge*)

duplicate duplicado

dust polvo

dust sacudir

(to) dusted

    dusted

    dusted

dust cloth sacudidor, trapo para quitar el polvo

dust storm tolvanera

dusty polvo

Dutch holandés

Dutchman (*noun*) holandés

duty derecho aduanal; deber

dwarf enano
dye tinte
(to) dye teñir, pintar (*el pelo*)

dyed
dyed
dysentery disentería

E

eagle águila
earring arete
earthquake terremoto
earth worm lombriz de tierra
economical económico
economics economía
effective efectivo, eficaz
effort esfuerzo
egg beater batidor
eggplant berenjena
eggwhite clara (*de huevo*)
eggyolk yema
elbow codo
electrical engineer ingeniero
    electricista
electrician electricista
electric razor máquina de
    rasurar eléctrica
elementary school primaria
elm olmo
(to) elope fugarse
    eloped
    eloped
(to) embalm embalsamar
    embalmed
    embalmed
(to) embarrass apenar
    embarrassed
    embarrassed
embarrassing penoso
embarrassment pena
embassy embajada
(to) embrace abrazar
    embraced
    embraced

emerald esmeralda
emery board lima de cartón
emotion emoción
emotional emotivo
employee empleado
employer patrón
employment empleo
enamel esmalte
end fin
(to) end terminar
    ended
    ended
(to) endorse a check endosar un
        cheque
    endorsed a check
    endorsed a check
engagement ring anillo de
        compromiso
engine máquina
engineer ingeniero
engineering ingeniería
England Inglaterra
English inglés
English cut corte inglés
Englishman (*noun*) inglés
English saddle albardón
Englishwoman (*noun*)
        inglesa
(to) enjoy gozar de, disfrutar de
    enjoyed
    enjoyed
envelope sobre
envious envidioso
(to) envy envidiar

330

envied
envied
equator ecuador
equipment equipo
(to) erase borrar
erased
erased
eraser borrador; goma
Eskimo esquimal
estimate presupuesto
evening gown traje de noche
evergreen siempreviva
ever since desde que
executive ejecutivo
expensive caro; costoso

expert experto, perito
(to) explode explotar, volar,
        estallar
exploded
exploded
explosion explosión
express (train) expreso
extension extensión
extra extra
eyebrow ceja
eyebrow pencil lápiz de cejas
eyelash pestaña
eye shadow sombra para
        los ojos

F

(to) face the street, park, sea, etc.
        dar a la calle, parque,
        mar, etc.
    feced the street, park, sea,
        etc.
    faced the street, park, sea,
        etc.
    facial masaje facial
    factory fábrica
(to) fade despintar
    faded
    faded
(to) faint desmayarse
    fainted
    fainted
    fair feria
(to) fall asleep dormirse
        (conseguir dormirse)
    fell asleep
    fallen asleep

(to) fall off caerse, caérsele a
        uno
    fell off
    fallen off
    false falso
    false teeth dentadura
        postiza
    fan aficionado
    fare tarifa, pasaje
    fashion designer diseñador
        de modas
    fashion designing diseño de
        modas
    fast-colored de colores firmes
(to) fasten abrochar (se)
    fastened
    fastened
    father-in-law suegro
    faucet llave (de agua)
    feather duster plumero

(to) feel like (present participle) tener ganas de (infinitivo)
    felt like
    felt like
(to) feel sorry for sentir pena por; compadecer (se)
    felt sorry for
    felt sorry for
    felt fieltro
    female hembra
(to) fence esgrimar
    fenced
    fenced
    fencing (*el deporte*) la esgrima
    fender salpicadera
    Ferris wheel rueda de la fortuna
    fever calentura, fiebre
    fig higo
(the) fights el box, las peleas
    filbert avellana
(to) file archivar
    filed
    filed
(to) file your (finger)nails limarse las uñas
    filed your (finger)nails
    filed your (finger)nails
(to) fill a prescription surtir una receta
    filled a prescription
    filled a prescription
(to) fill a tooth tapar un diente
    filled a tooth
    filled a tooth
    filling empaste, obturación; relleno
    filling station gasolinera

(to) fill out a form llenar un esqueleto
    filled out a form
    filled out a form
    filter filtro; boquilla
    fine multa
(to) fine multar
    fined
    fined
    (finger)nail uña de la mano
    (finger)nail file lima para las uñas
    (finger)nail polish barniz para las uñas
    fingerprint huella digital
    finger tip yema, punta del dedo
    Finland Finlandia
    fir abeto
(to) fire despedir (*del empleo*)
    fired
    fired
    fire alarm alarma contra incendios
    fire chief jefe de bomberos
    firecracker cohete
    fire department servicio de bomberos
    fire-eater tragafuegos
    fire engine carro de incendios
    fire hydrant toma de agua para incendios
    fireman bombero
    fireplace chimenea
    fireworks fuegos artificiales
    first balcony primer piso
    first class de primera clase
    first degree burns quemaduras de primer grado
(to) fish pescar

fished
fished
fisherman pescador
fishhook anzuelo
fishing la pesca (*el deporte*)
fist puño
(to) fit quedar, ajustar
fit
fit
five-room apartment departamento de cinco piezas
(to) fix a flat reparar una ponchadura
fixed a flat
fixed a flat
flag bandera
flames llamas; flamas
flannel franela
(to) flatter halagar
flattered
flattered
flavor sabor
flea pulga
flight vuelo
flint piedra
(to) flip (a coin) echar un volado
flipped (a coin)
flipped (a coin)
(to) float flotar
floated
floated
flood inundación
floor lamp lámpara de pie
floor show variedad (*de un club nocturno*)
Florence Florencia
flour harina
flu influenza
flush flor (*de póker*)
flute flauta

fly mosca; bragueta
fly (ball) elevado
fog niebla
(to) fold doblar (*tela, papel*)
folded
folded
folding chair silla plegadiza
footstool taburete
forehead frente
(to) forgive perdonar
forgave
forgiven
fortuneteller adivino
foster parents padres adoptivos
four of a kind póker
four sixes póker de seises
frame marco
France Francia
frankfurter salchicha
frayed raído, luído
freak fenómeno
freckle peca
freight train tren de carga
French (*adj.*) francés
French cuff puño doblado
French fried potatoes papas fritas (*al estilo francés*)
French fries papas fritas (*al estilo francés*)
Frenchman francés
Frenchwoman francesa
fresh del día (*pan*), fresco
friendship amistad
frog rana
front seat asiento delantero
frosting betún
(to) fry freír
fried
fried
frying pan sartén

full house full
full skirt falda amplia
funds fondos
funeral funeral
funeral parlor agencia
    mortuoria
funeral procession cortejo
    fúnebre

funny papers monitos
fur piel (*para abrigo*)
fur coat abrigo de piel
(to) furnish amueblar
    furnished
    furnished
fuse tapón, fusible

G

gabardine gabardina (*tela*)
(to) gain weight subir de peso
    gained weight
    gained weight
gallon galón
(to) gamble jugar (*dinero*)
    gambled
    gambled
gambler jugador (*de dinero*);
    tahur
gangplank pasarela;
    escalerilla
gangster gangster
garbage basura
garbage can basurero,
    bote de basura
garden huerta; jardín
gardenia gardenia
garlic ajo
garnet granate
garter liga
(gas) attendant despachador
    (*de una gasolinera*)
(gas) tank tanque
(to) gather (up) juntar y recoger
    gathered (up)
    gathered (up)
gauze gasa

gears velocidades
gear shift palanca de cambio
    de velocidades
Geneva Ginebra
genius genio
gentleman caballero
geography geografía
geologist geólogo
geology geología
geometry geometría
German alemán
german measles rubéola
Germany Alemania
(to) get acquainted with llegar a
    conocer; conocer;
    ambientarse con;
    relacionarse con
    got acquainted with
    got acquainted with
(to) get a divorce divorciarse
    got a divorce
    got a divorce
(to) get a haircut cortarse el
    pelo, cortarle a uno
    el pelo
    got a haircut
    got a haircut

(to) get airsick marearse (*en el aire*)
    got airsick
    got airsick
(to) get along with llevarse bien, congeniar con
    got along with
    got along with
(to) get a manicure hacerse el manicure
    got a manicure
    got a manicure
(to) get a permanent (a cold wave) hacerse el permanente (en frío)
    got a permanent (a cold wave)
    got a permanent (a cold wave)
(to) get a shave rasurarse, rasurarle a uno
    got a shave
    got a shave
(to) get a shine bolearle a uno (*los zapatos*)
    got a shine
    got a shine
(to) get a tan broncearse
    got a tan
    got a tan
(to) get a trim emparejarse el pelo, emparejarle a uno el pelo
    got a trim
    got a trim
(to) get a visa sacar una visa
    got a visa
    got a visa
(to) get back regresar
    got back
    got back

(to) get beat ser derrotado por alguien
    got beat
    got beat
(to) get behind atrasarse
    got behind
    got behind
(to) get burned quemarse
    got burned
    got burned
(to) get excited emocionarse; excitarse
    got excited
    got excited
(to) get fat engordar
    got fat
    got fat
(to) get fired ser despedido de un empleo
    got fired
    got fired
(to) get gored ser empitonado, ser corneado, ser cogido
    got gored
    got gored
(to) get hurt lastimarse
    got hurt
    got hurt
(to) get infected infectarse
    got infected
    got infected
(to) get in line hacer cola
    got in line
    got in line
(to) get in touch (with) comunicarse (con)
    got in touch (with)
    got in touch (with)
(to) get in trouble meterse en dificultades

got in trouble
got in trouble
(to) get loose soltarse
got loose
got loose
(to) get nervous ponerse nervioso
got nervous
got nervous
(to) get paid cobrar (*salario*)
got paid
got paid
(to) get robbed robarle a uno
got robbed
got robbed
(to) get run over ser atropellado
got run over
got run over
(to) get seasick marearse (*en el mar*)
got seasick
got seasick
(to) get a shock darle a uno toques
got a shock
got a shock
(to) get stuck atascarse, atorarse
got stuck
got stuck
(to) get sunburned quemarse (*por el sol*)
got sunburned
got sunburned
(to) get up early madrugar
got up early
got up early
(to) get used to acostumbrarse a
got used to
got used to
(to) get well mejorarse, aliviarse
got well
got well

(to) get wrinkled arrugarse
got wrinkled
got wrinkled
(to) get your ticket sacar su boleto
got your ticket
got your ticket
ghost fantasma
giant gigante
gin ginebra
giraffe jirafa
girdle faja (*de mujer*)
girlfriend novia
girth cincha
(to) give a discount hacer un descuento
gave a discount
given a discount
(to) give out repartir
gave out
given out
(to) give (someone) a ring llamar (a alguien) por teléfono
gave (someone) a ring
given (someone) a ring
(to) give (something) back devolver (algo)
gave (something) back
given (something) back
gladiola gladiola
glasses anteojos
glassware cristalería
glove compartment cajuela interior
glue cola, pegamento, goma líquida
go adelante, siga, continúe
(to) go ashore ir a tierra
went ashore
gone ashore
goat chivo (a), cabra

goddaughter ahijada
godfather padrino
godmother madrina
(to) go down bajar (se) (*yendo hacia abajo*)
    went down
    gone down
godparents padrinos
godson ahijado
(to) go for a walk, ride dar un paseo a pie o en coche
    went for a walk, ride
    gone for a walk, ride
gold oro
golf golf
golf ball pelota de golf
golf course campo de golf
golf club palo de golf
(to) go on a diet ponerse a dieta
    went on a diet
    gone on a diet
(to) go on a picnic ir a un día de campo
    went on a picnic
    gone on a picnic
(to) go on a trip ir de viaje
    went on a trip
    gone on a trip
(to) gore empitonar, cornear, coger
    gored
    gored
gorilla gorila
gossip chisme; chismoso (*sust.*)
(to) gossip chismear
    gossiped
    gossiped
(to) go to bed late desvelarse, acostarse tarde
    went to bed late
    gone to bed late
(to) go to the bullfights ir a los toros
    went to the bullfights
    gone to the bullfights
(to) go up subir(se) (*yendo hacia arriba*)
    went up
    gone up
government gobierno
governor gobernador
graceful gracioso, garboso
grade año escolar; calificación
grandchild nieto
grandchildren nietos
granddaughter nieta
grandson nieto
granite granito
grape uva
grapefruit toronja
grasshopper saltamontes, chapulín
grave tumba
graveyard cementerio
gravy salsa, jugo (*de carne*)
gray gris
(to) grease engrasar
    greased
    greased
great-grandchild bisnieto
great-grandchildren bisnietos
great-granddaughter bisnieta
great-grandfather bisabuelo
great-grandmother bisabuela
great-grandparents bisabuelos
great-grandson bisnieto
Greece Grecia
greedy codicioso
Greek griego
green beans ejotes

green light siga, pase
(*semáforo*)
greeting saludo
(to) **grind** moler
ground
ground
grippe gripa
grocer abarrotero
groceries abarrotes
grocery store tienda de
abarrotes
groom novio (*en la boda*)
ground meat carne molida

guarantee garantía
(to) **guarantee** garantizar
guaranteed
guaranteed
guess conjetura
(to) **guess** adivinar
guessed
guessed
guest huésped; invitado
guitar guitarra
gums encías
gun pistola
gutter arroyo (*en la calle*)

H

habit costumbre
had better más vale, sería
mejor
hail granizo
hail storm granizada
haircut corte de pelo
hair-do peinado
hair dresser peinador (a)
hair net red para el pelo
hair oil aceite para el pelo
half-brother medio hermano
half a dollar moneda de 50
centavos
half-moons medias lunas
half-sister media hermana
halfway down en medio
hall corredor; pasillo
halter almartigón
ham jamón
hamburger hamburguesa
hammer martillo
handcuffs esposas (*para
presos*)
handful puñado, manojo
handle mango (*de olla*)

(to) **handle** manejar (*personas,
negocios*)
handled
handled
hand lotion crema (*líquida*)
para las manos
handmade hecho a mano
handwriting letra
hanger gancho (*para ropa*)
hangnail padrastro
(to) **hang up** colgar
hung up
hung up
harbor puerto, bahía
hardware store ferretería
hardwood floor piso de
madera
harm daño; perjuicio
(to) **harm** hacer daño; perjudicar
harmed
harmed
harmonica organillo
harmony armonía

harness guarnición; arnés
harp arpa
(to) hate odiar
    hated
    hated
(to) hate (something) chocarle
    a uno (algo)
    hated (something)
    hated (something)
(to) haul transportar (*mercancía*)
    hauled
    hauled
    Havana Habana
(to) have a blowout poncharse
    una llanta
    had a blowout
    had a blowout
(to) have a flat tener una
    ponchadura
    had a flat
    had a flat
(to) have a hangover estar crudo
    had a hangover
    had a hangover
(to) have an accident tener un
    accidente
    had an accident
    had an accident
(to) have (get) a tooth filled
    taparle a uno una
    muela
    had (got) a tooth filled
    had (got) a tooth filled
(to) have (get) a tooth pulled
    sacarle a uno una
    muela
    had (got) a tooth pulled
    had (got) a tooth pulled
(to) have on hand tener en
    existencia
    had on hand

    had on hand
(to) have pictures developed
    mandar revelar el rollo
    had pictures developed
    had pictures developed
(to) have (something) made
    mandarse a hacer
    (algo)
    had (something) made
    had (something) made
(to) have (something) re-covered
    mandar retapizar
    (algo)
    had (something) re-covered
    had (something) re-covered
(to) have your picture taken
    retratarse
    had your picture taken
    had your picture taken
    hawk gavilán
    hazelnut avellana
    headlight faro
    headlines encabezados
    heads or tails sol o águila
    head waiter capitán, jefe
    de meseros
(to) heal cicatrizar; sanar
    healed
    healed
    health salud
    healthy saludable; sano
(to) hear about saber de, oír de
    heard about
    heard about
(to) hear from (*persons*) saber de,
    oír de
    heard from
    heard from
    hearse carroza
    heart attack ataque al
    corazón

heart disease enfermedad del corazón
hearts corazones
heart trouble enfermedad del corazón
(to) **heat** calentar
heated
heated
heaven cielo
heavy beard barba cerrada
heavy weight material tela gruesa
heel talón; tacón
height altura
hell infierno
helmet casco
helpful servicial, útil
hem bastilla, dobladillo
hemorrhage hemorragia
hen gallina
herb hierba
hero héroe
heroine heroína
herring arenque
high chair silla alta para niño
high heels tacones altos
high-heeled (*adj.*) de tacón alto
high school escuela secundaria
high tide marea alta
hip cadera
hippopotamus hipopótamo
(to) **hire** contratar
hired
hired
historian historiador
history historia
(to) **hit a car** chocar con un coche

hit a car
hit a car
hoarse ronco
hobby pasatiempo
hoe azadón
hold bodega (*de un barco*)
(to) **hold** sostener
held
held
(to) **hold a crease** no arrugarse (*pantalón*)
held a crease
held a crease
holiday día de fiesta
Holland Holanda
holy sagrado
holy water agua bendita
honest honrado
honey miel
honeydew melon melón valenciano
honeymoon luna de miel
hood cofre
hook gancho
horn cuerno
horsepower caballo de fuerza
horseshoe herradura
hose manguera
hospital hospital
host anfitrión
hostess anfitriona; encargada (*en un restaurant*)
hourly cada hora
house coat bata de mujer
housekeeper ama de llaves
(**house**) **slippers** chancletas, pantuflas
housewife ama de casa
hub cap tapón (*de coche*)
human being ser humano

340

hurricane huracán
hut choza

hydraulic hidráulico
hymn himno

I

ice cream helado
ice cream cone barquillo
ice cream soda soda
(ice cream) sundae sundae
ice cube cubo de hielo
ice skate patín
ice tray charola de hielo
ice water agua helada
icing betún
illness enfermedad
imagination imaginación
(to) imagine imaginar (se);
        explicarse
    imagined
    imagined
(to) improve mejorar
    improved
    improved
(to) include incluir
    included
    included
    including incluso
(to) increase aumentar
    increased
    increased
indelible indeleble
industry industria
infection infección
informal sin ceremonia
information desk mesa de
        informes, informes
ink tinta
in-laws parientes políticos
inlay incrustación

(inner) tube cámara (de
        llanta)
inning entrada
insane asylum manicomio
insect insecto, bicho
inside out (clothes) al revés
inside room cuarto interior
(to) inspect inspeccionar,
        registrar
    inspected
    inspected
inspection inspección
inspector inspector
installment plan a plazos
instep empeine
institution institución
in stock en existencia
instrument instrumento
insurance seguro
(to) insure a package certificar
        un paquete
    insured a package
    insured a package
(to) intend pensar, planear
    intended
    intended
interior decorating decoración
interior decorator decorador
intermission intermedio
intestines intestinos
(to) introduce presentar;
        introducir
    introduced
    introduced

341

introduction presentación; introducción
(to) investigate investigar
    investigated
    investigated
Ireland Irlanda
Irish irlandés
Irishman (*noun*) irlandés
iron hierro; plancha
(to) iron planchar
    ironed
    ironed

island isla
Israeli israelí
(to) issue expedir
    issued
    issued
Italian italiano
Italy Italia
(to) itch tener comezón
    itched
    itched
ivory marfil

J

jack jack; gato
jacket chamarra, chaqueta; saco
jade jade
jail cárcel
jam mermelada
janitor portero
Japan Japón
jar frasco
jar of cold cream frasco de cold cream
jaw mandíbula
jeep jeep
jelly jalea
jersey jersey
Jesus Christ Jesús Cristo
Jew (*noun*) judío
jeweler joyero
jewelry joyería; alhajas
jewelry shop joyería

jewelry store joyería
Jewish (*adj.*) judío
job empleo, puesto
joint coyuntura, articulación
joint account cuenta mancomunada
joint checking account cuenta mancomunada de cheques
joke chiste, broma
(to) joke bromear
    joked
    joked
joker comodín
judge juez
juice jugo
juicy jugoso
juke box sinfonola
jury jurado

K

karat quilate
(to) keep a promise cumplir una promesa

kept a promise
kept a promise
(to) keep (doing something)

342

seguir o continuar
haciendo algo
kept (doing something)
kept (doing something)
(to) keep going seguir
kept going
kept going
(to) keep in touch with estar en
contacto con
kept in touch with
kept in touch with
(to) keep on + (present participle)
seguir + (gerundio)
**kept on + (present
participle)**
**kept on + (present
participle)**
kettle olla (*de metal*)
kick patada
(to) kick patear
kicked
kicked
kid cabritilla
kidneys riñones
(to) kill yourself matarse,
suicidarse
killed yourself

killed yourself
kind marca
king rey
king size tamaño regio
knee rodilla
(to) kneel arrodillarse
knelt
knelt
knife-thrower lanzador de
cuchillos
knock-kneed (*adj.*) de
piernas torcidas hacia
adentro
**(to) knock (someone or
something) down**
derribar o tirar (a
alguien o algo)
**knocked (someone or
something) down**
**knocked (someone or
something) down**
(to) knock (someone) out
noquear (a alguien)
knocked (someone) out
knocked (someone) out
knuckle nudillo

L

label etiqueta (*para pegar*)
lace encaje
(to) lack faltar
lacked
lacked
ladder escalera (*de mano*)
lady dama
lamb cordero
lamb chops chuletas de
cordero

lame cojo
lamp lámpara
lamp shade pantalla para
lámpara
(to) land aterrizar
landed
landed
landing aterrizaje
landlord dueño (*de casa
rentada*)

landslide deslave, derrumbamiento (*de tierra*)

lard manteca

lariat reata, lazo

lately últimamente

laundry lavandería; ropa sucia

laundry slip nota de la lavandería

lavatory baño, sanitario

lavender (*color*) lila

law leyes; derecho

lawn chair silla para jardín

lawn mower segadora (*de césped*)

lawyer abogado

layer piso (*de pastel*)

layover tiempo entre un transporte y otro

lead plomo; puntilla (*de lápiz*)

leading lady protagonista

leading man protagonista

leading role papel estelar

(to) leak gotear, salirse (*refiriéndose al objeto de donde sale*)

leaked

leaked

lean limpio y sin grasa; magro

(to) lean (against, on) apoyarse (en)

leaned (against, on)

leaned (against, on)

(to) lean back recargarse

leaned back

leaned back

(to) lean over doblarse, agacharse

leaned over

leaned over

leather piel; cuero

leather heel tacón de cuero

leather sole suela de cuero

lemon limón

lemonade limonada

length longitud

Lent Cuaresma

leopard leopardo

(to) let go (of) soltar

let go (of)

let go (of)

letterhead membrete

lettuce lechuga

liar(*noun*) mentiroso

library biblioteca

lice piojos

license licencia

license plate placa

(to) lie mentir

lied

lied

life belt chaleco salvavidas

lifeboat bote salvavidas

life insurance seguro de vida

life jacket cinturón de salvamento

life preserver salvavidas

(to) light a match encender un cerillo

lit a match

lit a match

light blue azul claro

light-complexioned (*adj.*) de piel clara; güero

lighter encendedor

lighter fluid combustible para encendedor

lightning relámpago

(light) switch apagador

344

light weight material tela
 ligera
lilac lila
lily lirio
lime limón verde
(to) limp cojear
 limped
 limped
line línea
linen lino
liner barco de una línea
lingerie ropa interior (*de
 mujer*)
lining forro (*de ropa*)
lion-tamer domador
lipstick lápiz labial
liquid líquido
list lista
literature literatura
little finger dedo meñique
little toe dedo chico del pie
liver hígado
(to) load cargar
 loaded
 loaded
loan préstamo
(to) loan prestar
 loaned
 loaned
lobby lobby, vestíbulo
lobster langosta (*del mar*)
(to) locate localizar; encontrarse,
 hallarse
 located
 located
location ubicación,
 colocación

lock candado, cerradura;
 chapa
(to) lock cerrar con llave
 locked
 locked
locomotive locomotora
locust langosta (*de la tierra*)
London Londres
long distance larga distancia
(to) look around curiosear
 looked around
 looked around
loose suelto, flojo
(to) loosen soltar, aflojar
 loosened
 loosened
loose pieces piezas sueltas
(to) lose weight perder peso
 lost weight
 lost weight
(to) lose your temper perder la
 paciencia
 lost your temper
 lost your temper
lotion loción
louse piojo
lower berth cama baja
low heels tacones bajos
low-heeled (*adj.*) de tacón
 bajo
low tide marea baja
loyal leal
lumber madera aserrada
lump chipote; terrón
lunch comida ligera al
 mediodía
lungs pulmones

M

magazine revista

magic mágico

magician mago
mahogany caoba
maid criada
maid of honor madrina (*en la boda*)
(to) **mail** mandar por correo
mailed
mailed
mailbox buzón
main principal
main floor luneta; abajo (*en el cine*)
(to) **make a stop** hacer una escala
made a stop
made a stop
(to) **make a trip** hacer un viaje
made a trip
made a trip
(to) **make someone fat** engordar o hacer engordar a alguien
made someone fat
made someone fat
(to) **make up your mind** decidirse a
made up your mind
made up your mind
malaria paludismo
male macho
(**malted**) **milk shake** leche malteada
manager gerente
mandolin mandolina
manner manera
maple maple, arce
maple syrup miel de maple (arce)
marble mármol
mare yegua

(to) **mark** marcar, anotar; poner precio
marked
marked
maroon marrón
married (*adj.*) casado
(to) **marry** casarse con
married
married
mascara rimel
(to) **mash** machacar
mashed
mashed
mashed potatoes puré de papas
mason albañil
match cerillo, fósforo
(to) **match** hacer juego (con)
matched
matched
material tela; casimir
mathematics matemáticas
matinee matiné
matron celadora
matter asunto
mattress colchón
mayonnaise mayonesa
meanwhile mientras tanto
measles sarampión
(to) **measure** medir
measured
measured
meat ball albóndiga
meat loaf albondigón
mechanic mecánico
mechanical engineer ingeniero mecánico
mechanics mecánica
medicine medicina
medicine cabinet botiquín (*del baño*)

346

medium mediano
(to) meet someone (at the
        station, airport, etc.)
        esperar a alguien (en la
        estación, aeropuerto,
        etc.)
      met someone (at the
        station, airport, etc.)
      met someone (at the
        station, airport, etc.)
(to) melt derretir
      melted
      melted
    memorandum memorándum
(to) memorize memorizar
      memorized
      memorized
    menu menú
(to) mention mencionar
      mentioned
      mentioned
    mercy clemencia
    merry-go-round los
      caballitos
    mesh malla, tejido
    message recado
    Mexico México
    middle centro, en medio de
    midget enano
    midnight train tren de
      medianoche
    mild suave (*tabaco*);
      templado
    miner minero
    mining minería
    minister ministro
    mink mink
    mirror espejo
    miser (*noun*) avaro
(to) miss (somebody) echar de
      menos (a alguien)

    missed (somebody)
    missed (somebody)
(to) miss (the train, boat, plane,
      etc.) perder (el tren,
      barco, avión, etc.)
    missed (the train, boat,
      plane, etc.)
    missed (the train, boat,
      plane, etc.)
    mist neblina
(to) mix mezclar
      mixed
      mixed
    mixer batidora
    mixture mezcla
    model modelo
    modeling estudio para ser
      modelo
    moist húmedo
    mold moho
    moldy mohoso
    mole lunar
    monastery monasterio
    money order giro (*postal*)
    monk monje
    monkey chango, mono
    monthly mensual,
      mensualmente
    monument monumento
    mood humor
    moose alce
    morning train tren de la
      mañana
    mortgage hipoteca
(to) mortgage hipotecar
      mortgaged
      mortgaged
    mortician encargado de
      ceremonias fúnebres
    Moscow Moscú
    mosquito mosquito, mosco

347

moss musgo
moth palomilla, polilla
mother-in-law suegra
motor motor
mountain climber alpinista
mourning luto
mouse trap ratonera
mouthful (*adj.*) bocado;
      bocanada
(to) move cambiarse (*de casa*),
      mudarse (*de casa*)
      moved

moved
mud lodo
muddy lodoso
mumps paperas
muscle músculo
museum museo
mushroom hongo
musical comedia musical
musician músico
mustache bigote(s)
mustard mostaza
mutton carnero

N

nail clavo; uña
naked desnudo
(to) name someone after someone
      poner nombre igual al
      de alguna persona
      named someone after
        someone
      named someone after
        someone
napkin servilleta
narcotics narcóticos
navy blue azul marino
nearly casi
neat pulcro, bien arreglado
      y limpio
neatly pulcramente
necklace collar (*joyería*)
(to) neglect descuidar
      neglected
      neglected
negligee camisón transparente
Negro negro (*raza*)
nervous nervioso
newsreel noticiero
nickel quinto (*moneda*)
nickname apodo

nightgown camisón
night letter carta nocturnal
nightmare pesadilla
night table buró
night train tren de la noche
nonstop flight vuelo directo
noon train tren del
      mediodía
no parking prohibido
      estacionarse
normal normal
North America América del
      Norte
North American
      norteamericano
North Pole Polo Norte
Norway Noruega
Norwegian noruego
note nota; apunte; recado
nun monja
nurse enfermera
nursing enfermería
nut nuez
nutmeg nuez moscada
nylon nylon

348

O

oar remo
oatmeal avena
obituary noticia biográfica de una persona recién fallecida
octopus pulpo
odor olor
offer oferta
(to) **offer** ofrecer
   offered
   offered
office boy muchacho mandadero, mozo
oil aceite; petróleo
old-fashioned anticuado
olive aceituna
one-way ticket boleto sencillo
onion skin paper papel cebolla
opal ópalo
(to) **open a busines** poner un negocio
   opened a business
   opened a business
open-toed (*adj.*) de punta descubierta
(to) **operate on** operar
   operated on
   operated on
ophthalmologist oftalmólogo
ophthalmology oftalmología
optician óptica
optometrist optometrista
optometry optometría
orange naranja
orchestra orquesta

orchestra leader director de orquesta
orchid orquídea
order pedido, orden
(to) **order** pedir (*en un restaurant*); ordenar
   ordered
   ordered
organ órgano
organdy organdí
original original
orphan huérfano
orphanage orfanatorio
orthodox ortodoxo
outfielder jardinero (*béisbol*)
outlet contacto
oven horno
overalls overol
overdrawn sobregirado
(to) **overflow** desbordarse; derramarse, rebosar
   overflowed
   overflowed
(to) **oversleep** quedarse dormido (*no despertar*)
   overslept
   overslept
overtime tiempo extra
ounce onza
(to) **owe** deber
   owed
   owed
owl lechuza
ownership papers documentos de propiedad
ox buey
oxfords choclos

oxygen tent cámara de oxígeno

oyster ostión

P

Pacific Ocean Océano Pacífico
(to) **pack** empacar
  packed
  packed
package paquete
padding guata
pain dolor
paintbrush pincel; brocha
painter pintor
pair of blue jeans pantalones vaqueros
pair of garters un par de ligas
pair of (house) slipper un par de pantuflas
pair of suspenders unos tirantes
pair of supporters un par de ligas
pale pálido
palm palma
pan charola para hornear
pants pantalones
paper clip clip
parade desfile
paradise paraíso
paragraph párrafo
parcel post servicio de paquetes postales
Paris París
(to) **park** estacionarse
  parked
  parked
parsley perejil

partner socio, compañero
(to) **part your hair** hacerse la raya
  parted your hair
  parted your hair
passenger pasajero
passport pasaporte
passport photograph fotografía de pasaporte
paste engrudo
(to) **patch** parchar
  patched
  patched
patent leather charol
patient paciente
pea chícharo
peacock pavo real
peanut cacahuate
pear pera
pearl perla
pecan nuez encarcelada
penance penitencia
penitentiary penitenciaría
penny centavo
pepper pimiento
pepper shaker pimentero
per cent porcentaje
percolator cafetera de vapor
(to) **perform** actuar
  performed
  performed
performance función; actuación
perfume perfume

permanent permanente
permanently
    permanentemente,
    definitivamente
peroxide agua oxigenada
(to) perspire sudar
    perspired
    perspired
pew banco de iglesia
pharmacist farmacéutico
pharmacy farmacia
(to) phone telefonear, hablar
    por teléfono
    phoned
    phoned
phone book directorio
phone booth caseta
    telefónica
photograph fotografía
physical education
    educación física
physics la física
pianist pianista
piano piano
pick zapapico
(to) pick (a person) up pasar por
    (alguien)
    picked (a person) up
    picked (a person) up
pickle pepino encurtido
picnic día de campo
pie pay
pie crust pasta (del pay)
pier muelle
pigeon pichón, paloma
pigeon-toed (adj.) con los
    pies torcidos hacia
    dentro
pijamas pijamas
pile montón

pilgrim peregrino
pilgrimage peregrinación
pill píldora
pillowcase funda (de cojín
    o almohada)
pilot piloto
pimple grano, barro
pin alfiler; prendedor
pine pino
pineapple piña
(to) pin (on) prender
    pinned (on)
    pinned (on)
pin-striped de mil rayas
pipe pipa; tubo
pipe cleaners limpiapipas
pipes tubos, tubería
pistachio pistache
pistol pistola
pitcher pitcher, lanzador;
    jarro
pitchfork horca; bieldo
plaid escocés (tela)
plain sencillo; sin dibujo
plain handled (adj.) de
    mango sin dibujo
(to) plan planear
    planned
    planned
plane crash accidente aéreo
plant planta
(to) plant plantar; sembrar
    planted
    planted
plaster yeso
(to) plaster enyesar
    plastered
    plastered
plaster of Paris escayola;
    yeso para modelar

platform andén, plataforma
platform shoes zapatos con
   plataforma
platinum platino
platter platón
(to) play billiards jugar carambola
   played billiards
   played billiars
(to) play cards, bridge, poker,
   etc.
     jugar a la baraja,
     bridge, póker, etc.
   played cards, bridge,
   poker, etc.
   played cards, bridge,
   poker, etc.
(to) play golf jugar al golf
   played golf
   played golf
   playground campo de recreo
(to) play pool jugar al billar
   played pool
   played pool
(to) play (take) the part of
     hacer o desempeñar el
     papel de, hacerla de
   played (took) the part of
   played (taken) the part of
(to) play tennis jugar tenis
   played tennis
   played tennis
(to) play the piano, etc. tocar el
     piano, etc.
   played the piano, etc.
   played the piano, etc.
pleasant agradable
pleasure placer, gusto
pleasure trip viaje de placer
pleat pliegue
pliers pinzas, alicates
plot argumento; complot

plow arado
(to) plow arar
   plowed
   plowed
(to) pluck your eyebrows
     depilarse las cejas
   plucked your eyebrows
   plucked your eyebrows
plum ciruela
plumber plomero
plumbing plomería; tubería
plus más
pneumonia pulmonía
poison veneno
(to) poison envenenar
   poisoned
   poisoned
poker póker (*el juego*)
(poker) chip ficha
police policía
policeman policía
(police) officer policía
police station delegación
polio poliomielitis
polish grasa; barniz
(to) polish bolear, sacar brillo;
     pulir
   polished
   polished
politeness cortesía
political party partido
   político
polka dot (*adj.*) moteado
pomegranate granada
pool alberca; el billar, el
   pool (*el juego*)
pool hall (*el establecimiento*)
   los billares
popcorn palomitas (*de maíz*)
pope papa
population población

pork carne de puerco
pork chops chuletas de
    puerco
port puerto
portrait retrato (*pintado*)
port (side) babor
Portugal Portugal
Portuguese portugués
post card tarjeta postal
postmaster administrador
    de correos
post office oficina de
    correos
post-office clerk empleado
    postal
pot olla
potato chips hojuelas de
    papa
potato salad ensalada de
    papa
pot holder agarradera
pottery alfarería
pound libra
(to) pour servir o vaciar
    (*líquido*)
    poured
    poured
(to) pour (something) out tirar
    (algo) (*líquido*)
    poured (something) out
    poured (something) out
powder polvo
powder base base de polvo
(to) pray rezar
    prayed
    prayed
prayer oración
prayer book devocionario,
    breviario
preacher predicador
precious stone piedra preciosa

prescription receta
    (*medicina*)
press prensa
(to) press planchar
    pressed
    pressed
pressure cooker olla express
pretty muy, bastante
pretty good muy bien
    (bueno), bastante
    bien (bueno)
(to) prevent someone from
    impedir a alguien + inf.
    prevented someone from
    prevented someone from
price precio
price tag etiqueta (*de
    precio*)
priest sacerdote
primary primaria
prince príncipe
princess princesa
principal director
(to) print imprimir
    printed
    printed
printer impresor
prison prisión, carcel
prison guard guardia
private particular, privado
private secretary secretario(a)
    particular
prize premio
problem problema
producer productor
professional profesional
professor profesor
profit utilidad, ganancia
program programa

promise promesa
(to) promise prometer
promised
proposal of marriage petición
matrimonial
(to) propose (to) proponer;
proponer matrimonio
proposed (to)
proposed (to)
(to) protect proteger
protected
protected
protection protección
Protestant protestante
prune ciruela pasa
psalm salmo
psychiatrist psiquiatra
psychology psicología
pudding pudín
(to) pull a tooth sacar una
muela
pulled a tooth
pulled a tooth
Pullman pullman
(Pullman) porter mozo
Pullman ticket boleto de
coche cama
pulpit púlpito
pulse pulso

pumpkin calabaza
pumps zapatillas
puppet títere
purgatory purgatorio
purple morado
purser sobrecargo (barco)
(to) put on a play montar una
obra teatral
put on a play
put on a play
(to) put on make-up ponerse
maquillaje
put on make-up
put on make-up
(to) put (something) away
guardar algo
put (something) away
put (something) away
(to) put (something) off aplazar
(algo)
put (something) off
put (something) off
(to) put up with tolerar, soportar
put up with
put up with
(to) put your hair up hacerse
anchoas
put your hair up
put your hair up

Q

quality calidad
quantity cantidad
quarrel disgusto
(to) quarrel reñir; pelear
quarreled
quarreled
quart cuarto
quarter cuarto; moneda de
25 centavos

quartet cuarteto
quartz cuarzo
queen reina
(to) quit dejar (el empleo); dejar
de; renunciar a
quit
quit
quite muy, bastante

R

rabbi rabí
racket raqueta
radiator radiador
radio announcer locutor de
    radio
radish rábano
railroad ferrocarril
railroad station estación
    de ferrocarril
railroad track riel, vía
rainbow arco iris
rain storm tormenta
raise aumento
(to) raise alzar, levantar;
    cultivar; criar
    raised
    raised
raisin pasa
rake rastrillo
rare raro
rash erupción cutánea,
    salpullido; urticaria
rat rata
rattlenaske serpiente
    cascabel
raw crudo; poco cocido, a
    la ingiesa, rojo
rayon rayón
razor navaja; rastrillo
razor blade hoja de rasurar
reading lectura
reasonable razonable
receiver audífono
recognition recognición
(to) recognize reconocer
    recognized
    recognized
(to) recommend recomendar
    recommended
    recommended

recommendation
    recomendación
record disco; record
redcap mozo (*de ferrocarril*)
red light luz roja (*semáforo*)
(to) reduce reducir; bajar de
    peso, adelgazar
    reduced
    reduced
reformatory reformatorio
reform school reformatorio
refrigerator refrigerador
(to) refuel poner gasolina
    (*rebastecer de gasolina*)
    refueled
    refueled
(to) refuse rehusar
    refused
    refused
(to) register inscribir (se);
    certificar
    registered
    registered
registered letter carta
    certificada
registration inscripción
reins riendas
reindeer reno
religion religión
religious religioso
(to) remind someone (of)
    recordarle a uno
    reminded someone (of)
    reminded someone (of)
(to) remove quitar
    removed
    removed
(to) remove the stale make-up
    quitarse el maquillaje
    anterior

removed the stale make-up
removed the stale make-up
repair reparación
(to) repent arrepentirse
    repented
    repented
reporter periodista
representative diputado
republic república
republican republicano
Republican (*partido*)
    republicano
(to) rescue rescatar
    rescued
    rescued
reservation reservación
reserved seat asiento
    reservado
(to) resign renunciar
    resigned
    resigned
resignation renuncia
responsibility responsabilidad
restaurant restaurante
rest room baño, sanitario
result resultado
retail al menudeo
return address remitente;
    remite
revenge venganza
rheumatism reumatismo
rhinestones piedras falsas
rhinoceros rinoceronte
rhubarb ruibarbo
rhythm ritmo
ribs costillas
rice arroz
riding boots botas de montar
riding crop fuete
rifle rifle
right here ahí mismo

rime rima
ring anillo; pista
(to) ring sonar, tocar, timbrar
    rang
    rung
ring master (*in the circus*)
    maestro de ceremonias
(to) rinse enjuagar
    rinsed
    rinsed
riot motín
ripe maduro (*fruta*)
(to) rise levantarse, subir, salir
    (*el sol*)
    rose
    risen
roast asado
(to) roast asar
    roasted
    roasted
roasted peanuts cacahuates
    dorados
roaster asador
(to) rob robar
    robbed
    robbed
(to) rock mecerse, balancearse
    rocked
    rocked
rocking balanceo
rocking chair silla mecedora
rod and reel caña y carrete
    (*para pescar*)
role papel
roll bolillo
(to) roll rodar
    rolled
    rolled
roller coaster montaña rusa
roller skates patines

roll of adhesive tape rollo de
   de tela adhesiva
Rome Roma
roommate compañero de
   cuarto
room service servicio de
   cuarto
rooster gallo
(to) **rope (an animal)** lazar
   un animal)
      roped (an animal)
      roped (an animal)
   rose rosa
   rose bush rosal
(to) **rot** pudrirse
      rotted
      rotted
   rotten podrido (*estar*)
   .**rouge** colorete
   round round
   round trip ticket boleto de
      ida y vuelta, boleto
      de viaje redondo
   row fila
(to) **row** remar
      rowed
      rowed
   rowing (*el deporte*) remar
   royal flush corrida mayor
(to) **rub** frotar; aplicar
      (*frotando*)
      rubbed
      rubbed
   rubber boots botas de hule
   rubber heel tacón de hule
   rubbers zapatos de hule
      (*para la lluvia*)
   rubber sole suela de hule

ruby rubí
rude grosero, mal educado
rudeness mala educación,
   falta de educación
(to) **ruin** arruinar; echar a perder
      ruined
      ruined
   ruins ruinas
   rum ron
   rummy rummy
(to) **run a business** manejar un
      negocio
      ran a business
      run a business
(to) **run after** perseguir
      ran after
      run after
(to) **run around** pasearse, salir a
      pasear; andar juntos;
      recorrer
      ran around
      run around
   run-down agotado
(to) **run out of** terminársele a
      uno
      ran out of
      run out of
(to) **run over** atropellar
      ran over
      run over
(to) **run the risk** correr el
      peligro
      ran the risk
      run the risk
   Russia Rusia
   Russian ruso
   rust moho
   rusty oxidado; mohoso

S

(to) sacrifice sacrificar
    sacrificed
    sacrificed
  saddle silla de montar
  saddlebag alforja
  saddleblanket mantilla
    para caballo
  safety pin seguro
(to) sail navegar; zarpar, salir
    (*barco*)
    sailed
    sailed
  sailor marinero
  saint santo
  salad ensalada
  salad bowl ensaladera
  salad fork tenedor para
    ensalada
  salad spoon cuchara para
    ensalada
  salary salario
  sale venta; barata
  saleslady vendedora;
    dependienta
  salesman vendedor;
    dependiente
  salmon salmón, salmones
  salt shaker salero
  salve ungüento
  sample muestra
  sanatorium sanatorio
  sand arena
  sandals sandalias
  sapphire zafiro
  sardine sardina
  satin satín
  sauce salsa
  saucer plato para café
  sauerkraut col agria

  sausage salchicha vienesa
  savings account cuenta de
    ahorros
  saw sierra
  sawdust serrín
  saxophone saxofón
(to) say good-bye (to) despedirse
    (de)
    said good-bye (to)
    said good-bye (to)
  saying dicho, refrán
  scales báscula; balanza;
    escamas
  scarce escaso
  scarf bufanda
  scarlet fever fiebre
    escarlatina
  scene escena; panorama
  scenery paisaje
  scholarship beca
  science ciencia
  score puntuación (*en el
    juego*)
  scorpion escorpión, alacrán
  Scotch escocés
  Scotchman (*noun*) escocés
  Scotland Escocia
(to) scratch rascar; rasguñar
    scratched
    scratched
  screen pantalla (*dél cine*)
  screw tornillo
(to) screw something in atornillar
    algo
    screwed something in
    screwed something in
  screwdriver desarmador
  sculpture escultura
  sea food mariscos

(to) seal cerrar (*carta*)
    sealed
    sealed
    sea level nivel del mar
(to) search buscar
    searched
    searched
    seasickness mareo en el mar
    seat cover cubreasiento
    second balcony segundo
        piso
    second class de segunda
        clase
    second cousin primo segundo
    second degree burns
        quemaduras de
        segundo grado
    secret secreto
    secretary secretario (a)
    security seguridad
    seed semilla
    seedless sin semilla
    semiprecious stones piedras
        semipreciosas
    Senate Senado
    senator senador
    sense sentido
    serious serio
    sermon sermón
    servant sirviente (a)
(to) serve servir
    served
    served
    service servicio
(to) set (something) on fire
        prender fuego a (algo)
    set (something) on fire
    set (something) on fire
(to) set the alarm poner el
        despertador
    set the alarm

    set the alarm
    setting montadura
(to) set your watch, clock poner
        su reloj
    set your watch, clock
    set your watch, clock
    shack choza
    shampoo champú
    shape forma; figura; horma
    share acción
    shark tiburón
(to) sharpen sacar punta; afilar
    sharpened
    sharpened
(to) sharpen a pencil sacarle
        punta a un lápiz
    sharpened a pencil
    sharpened a pencil
(to) shave rasurar(se)
    shaved
    shaved
    shaving cream crema de
        afeitar
    shaving lotion loción de
        afeitar
    shaving soap jabón de afeitar
    sheep oveja (s)
    sheet sábana
    shell concha
    shift turno (*de trabajo*)
(to) shift (gears) cambiar
        velocidades
    shifted gears
    shifted gears
    shin espinilla
    shin guards protectores de
        espinillas
    shine boleada
    shingle tejamanil
    shiny brillante
    shipment embarque

shipwreck naufragio
shock golpe (*mental*);
toque (*eléctrico*)
(to) shock escandalizar
shocked
shocked
shock absorber amortiguador
(to) shoe herrar
shoed
shoed
shoehorn calzador
shoelaces agujetas
shoe polish grasa de los
zapatos
(to) shoot dice, craps jugar a los
dados
shot dice, craps
shot dice, craps
(to) shoot off firecrackers echar
cohetes
shot off firecrackers
shot off firecrackers
shore orilla, playa, ribera
shorthand taquigrafía
shorts calzoncillos; shorts;
cortos (*del cine*)
shot inyección
shoulder pads hombreras
shovel pala
show función; cine
shower regadera
shower curtain cortina para
baño
(to) show off presumir
showed off
showed off
shrimp (*sing.*) camarón,
camarones
shrine santuario, lugar
sagrado

(to) shrink encoger
shrank
shrunk
(to) shuffle (cards) barajar
shuffled (cards)
shuffled (cards)
shy tímido, cohibido
sickness enfermedad
sideburns patillas
side show diversiones
alrededor del circo
side street calle transversal
sifter cernedor
sign letrero, rótulo
(to) sign firmar
signed
signed
signal señal
signature firma
silent silencioso; callado
silk seda
silly (*adj.*) tonto
silver plata
silverware (*sing.*) cubiertos
sin pecado
(to) sin pecar
sinned
sinned
sincere sincero
single (*adj.*) soltero (a)
single bed cama sencilla
single-breasted (*adj.*)
abierto, recto (*traje*)
single room cuarto sencillo
sink fregadero
(to) sink hundir (se)
sank
sunk
sinner pecador
siren sirena

(to) sit (down) at a table sentarse a una mesa
    sat (down) at a table
    sat (down) at a table
(to) sit at the counter sentarse en la barra
    sat at the counter
    sat at the counter
size tamaño
(to) skate patinar
    skated
    skated
skater patinador
skating (*el deporte*) patinar
skating rink pista de patinar
skeleton esqueleto
(to) ski esquiar
    skied
    skied
(to) skid derraparse (*coche*); resbalarse (*personas*)
    skidded
    skidded
skier esquiador
skies esquíes
skiing (*el deporte*) esquiar
skull cráneo
skunk zorrillo
slacks pantalón sport
slang caló
sleeper (coach) coche cama
sleeping pills pastillas para dormir
sleet mezcla de agua y nieve
sleeve manga
sleeveless sweater chaleco, sweater sin mangas
slice rebanada; lonja
(to) slice rebanar
    sliced
    sliced

sliced rye pan de centeno rebanado
slight leve
slip fondo (*de mujer*)
slipper pantufla, chancleta
slow down despacio
(to) slow down disminuir la velocidad
    slowed down
    slowed down
slums barrio bajo
smallpox viruela negra
(to) smear embarrar; rayar (se) (*pintura fresca*)
    smeared
    smeared
(to) smother sofocar, asfixiar
    smothered
    smothered
snow storm tormenta de nieve
(to) soak remojar; empapar
    soaked
    soaked
soap jabón
sociology sociología
soda soda
soda fountain fuente de soda
sole suela
solid color color liso
solitaire solitario
solo solo
son-in-law yerno
soprano soprano
sore (*adj.*) adolorido
sore (*noun*) llaga o úlcera
(soup) ladle cucharón (*para sopa*)
South America América del Sur
South American sudamericano

South Pole Polo Sur
souvenir recuerdo
space espacio; lugar
spade laya
spades espadas (*de naipes*)
Spain España
Spaniard español
sparerib costilla de puerco
    (*casi descarnada*)
spare time tiempo libre
spare (tire) llanta de
    refacción
spark plug bujía
special delivery entrega
    inmediata
(to) speed llevar mucha velocidad
    (*manejando*)
    speeded
    speeded
speed limit velocidad máxima
speedometer velocímetro
spelling ortografía
spider araña
spinach espinacas
spine espina dorsal
(to) spoil echar (se) a perder;
    consentir
    spoiled
    spoiled
spoonful cucharada
sport deporte
sport coat saco sport
sporting goods artículos de
    deportes
sport shirt camisa sport
spot mancha
spray rociador; bomba,
    pulverizador
sprayer rociador, bomba,
    pulverizador
(to) spread extender (se); aplicar
    (*frotando*)

spread
spread
spring resorte; muelle (*del
    coche*)
(to) sprinkle rociar
    sprinkled
    sprinkled
squash calabacitas
squirrel ardilla
(to) stack amontonar
    stacked
    stacked
stage foro
stain mancha
(to) stain manchar
    stained
    stained
stainless steel (*adj.*) acero
    inoxidable
stairs escaleras
stale duro (*de pan y pastel*)
stamp estampilla, timbre
stamped envelope sobre
    timbrado
staple grapa
(to) staple engrapar
    stapled
    stapled
stapler engrapadora
starboard (side) a estibor
starch almidón
(to) starch almidonar
    starched
    starched
(to) start back emprender el
    regreso, salir de regreso
    started back
    started back
(to) start your motor arrancar
    el motor
    started your motor
    started your motor

stateroom camarote
stationery papel y sobre
stationery store papelería
station wagon camioneta
statue estatua
steak bistec
steam vapor
steam bath baño de vapor
steam engine locomotora
steel acero
steep empinado
(steering) wheel volante
stenographer taquígrafo
stenography taquigrafía
stenotyping
     taquimecanografía
stenotypist taquimecanógrafo(a)
stepbrother hermanastro
stepfather padrastro
stepmother madrasta
(to) step on pisar
    stepped on
    stepped on
(to) step on the brake frenar
    stepped on the brake
    stepped on the brake
stepsister hermanastra
sterilization estelirización
(to) sterilize esterilizar
    sterilized
    sterilized
steward sobrecargo,
    aeromozo
stewardess sobrecargo,
    aeromoza
(to) stick pegar
    stuck
    stuck
(to) stick something on pegar algo
    stuck something on
    stuck something on

stiff tieso
(to) sting picar (*con aguijón*)
    stung
    stung
stingy tacaño
stirrup estribo
stock acciones (*de la bolsa*)
stock exchange bolsa (*de*
    valores)
stockholder accionista
stock market bolsa (*de*
    valores)
stole rebozo
stool taburete
stop light alto, pare
    (*semáforo*)
stowaway polizón
straight derecho; lacio (*pelo*);
    corrida (*de naipes*)
straight whiskey whisky
    solo
(to) strain colar
    strained
    strained
strainer coladera
strait jacket camisa de fuerza
straw paja; popote
strawberry fresa
streetcar tranvía
(to) stretch estirar (se);
    extender (se)
    stretched
    stretched
(to) strike a match encender un
    cerillo
    struck a match
    struck a match
string cordón
string beans ejotes
string of pearls, beads un
    hilo de perlas, cuentas

stripe franja; raya
striped rayado
strong fuerte (*tabaco*)
stub talón
stubborn terco
(to) stutter tartamudear
    stuttered
    stuttered
style estilo; moda
subject materia; asunto
success éxito
suddenly de repente
suds espuma (*de jabón*)
suede gamuza
(to) suffocate asfixiar
    suffocated
    suffocated
sugar bowl azucarera
(to) suggest sugerir
    suggested
    suggested
suggestion sugerencia
suit palo (*de naipes*)
suitcase maleta, veliz
sun bath baño de sol
sundown anochecer
sunny de sol (*día*); asoleado
sunup amanecer
super market super mercado
superstition superstición
superstitious supersticioso
supply abastecimiento,
    provisión
(to) supply (someone with)
    abastecer o surtir (a
    alguien) (de)
    supplied (someone with)
    supplied (someone with)

(to) support mantener
    supported
    supported
supporters ligas (*para
    hombre*)
(to) suppose suponer
    supposed
    supposed
Supreme Court Suprema
    Corte
surface superficie
suspenders tirantes
swallow golondrina
(to) swallow tragar
    swallowed
    swallowed
swan cisne
(to) sweat sudar
    sweat
    sweat
sweat shirt sudadera
Swede (*noun*) sueco
Sweden Suecia
Swedish sueco
sweetheart novio(a)
sweet potato camote
swimming pool piscina
Swiss suizo
Switzerland suiza
sword-swallower tragasables
symphony orchestra
    orquesta sinfónica
synagogue sinagoga
synthetic sintético
syrup jarabe; almíbar

T

tablecloth mantel
tablespoon cuchara
tack tachuela
taffeta tafeta
tag etiqueta (*para colgar*)
taillight calavera (*de coche*)
tailor sastre
(to) take advantage of
     aprovecharse de
     took advantage of
     taken advantage of
(to) take a steam bath tomar un
     baño de vapor
     took a steam bath
     taken a steam bath
(to) take a sun bath tomar un
     baño de sol
     took a sun bath
     taken a sun bath
(to) take a trick ganar una baza
     took a trick
     taken a trick
(to) take a trip hacer un viaje
     took a trip
     taken a trip
(to) take a walk, ride dar un
     paseo a pie, en coche
     took a walk, ride
     taken a walk, ride
(to) take charge (of) encargarse (de)
     took charge (of)
     taken charge (of)
(to) take communion comulgar
     took communion
     taken communion
take off despego
(to) take off despegar; quitarse
     took off
     taken off

(to) take place tener lugar,
     suceder, ocurrir
     took place
     taken place
(to) take (something) back
     devolver (algo)
     took (something) back
     taken (something) back
(to) take your blood pressure
     tomar la presión
     arterial
     took your blood pressure
     taken your blood pressure
(to) take your order tomar su
     orden
     took your order
     taken your order
(to) take your pulse tomar el pulso
     took your pulse
     taken your pulse
(to) take your temperature
     tomar la temperatura
     took your temperature
     taken your temperature
(to) take your tonsils out sacar
     las amígdalas
     took your tonsils out
     taken your tonsils out
tame manso
tangerine mandarina
tap llave de agua
(to) tarnish opacarse, oxidarse
     (*metal*)
     tarnished
     tarnished
taste gusto; sabor
(to) taste probar; saber
     tasted
     tasted

365

(to) taste like saber a
    tasted like
    tasted like
tax impuesto; contribución
taxi libre
taxi cab libre
team equipo
teapot tetera
tear lágrima
(to) tear (something) up rasgar
    (algo), desgarrar (algo),
    romper (algo) (*suave*)
    tore (something) up
    torn (something) up
teaspoon cucharita
teaspoonful cucharadita
telegram telegrama
(to) telephone hablar por
    teléfono
    telephoned
    telephoned
telephone book directorio
telephone booth caseta
    telefónica
teller pagador, cajero (*en el
    banco*)
temper genio
temperature temperatura
temporarily temporalmente
temporary temporal
tender suave (*carne*)
tennis tenis
tennis court cancha de tenis
tennis racket raqueta de
    tenis
tennis shoes zapatos tenis
tennis shorts shorts de tenis
tenor tenor
tent tienda de campaña
tentative provisional (*cita,
    fecha*)

terrible terrible
Testament Testamento
(to) thank dar las gracias,
    thanked
    thanked
thankful agradecido
theater teatro
the fights las luchas
thermometer termómetro
thigh muslo
threat amenaza
(to) threaten amenazar
    threatened
    threatened
three aces tercia de ases
three-cent stamp timbre de
    tres centavos
three of a kind tercia
thumb pulgar
thumb tack chinche
thunder trueno
tick garrapata
ticket agent agente de
    boletos
ticket window taquilla
tide marea
tie pin fistol; pisacorbata
(to) tie your shoes, tie, etc.
    atarse los zapatos,
    corbata, etc.
    tied your shoes, tie, etc.
    tied your shoes, tie, etc.
tiger tigre
(to) tighten apretar
    tightened
    tightened
tights mallas
tile azulejo
tile floor piso de azulejo
timetable horario (*de llegadas
    y salidas*)

tip propina
(to) tip dar propina
    tipped
    tipped
tire llanta
tiresome cansado, fastidioso
tissue kleenex, pañuelo
    desechable
toast pan tostado
toaster tostador
tobacco tabaco
toenails uñas (*de los pies*)
Tokyo Tokio
tomb tumba; cripta
tombstone lápida
ton tonelada
tongue (*of shoe*) lengüeta
tonnage tonelaje
tonsillitis amigdalitis
tonsils amígdalas
tool herramienta
toothbrush cepillo de
    dientes
toothpaste pasta de dientes
toothpowder polvo de
    dientes
topaz topacio
tornado tornado
tough dura (*carne*)
tourist turista
tourist class clase turista
tournament torneo
(to) tow (a car) in remolcar un
    coche
    towed (a car) in
    towed (a car) in
tow car remolcador, grúa
towel toalla
tower torre
track vía, carril; huella (*del
    pie*)

track shoes spikes
tractor tractor
trade in cambalache,
    trueque
(to) trade in cambiar (*el coche*)
    traded in
    traded in
traffic tránsito
traffic cop agente de tránsito
traffic light semáforo
traffic violation infracción
    de tránsito
tragedy tragedia
(to) train enseñar; instruir,
    adiestrar; entrenar
    trained
    trained
training entrenamiento;
    enseñanza, instrucción,
    adiestramiento
train station estación de
    ferrocarril
trapeze trapecio
trapeze performer trapecista
travelers check cheque de
    viajero
traveling salesman agente
    viajero
tray charola
trial juicio por corte
trick baza (*de barajas*);
    juego; suerte (*de
    barajas*)
(to) trim your mustache, beard
    emparejarse el bigote,
    la barba
    **trimmed your mustache,
    beard**
    **trimmed your mustache,
    beard**
triplets triates

trombone trombón
trophy trofeo
trouble dificultad
trousers pantalones
trout trucha
truck camión (*de carga*)
trumpet, trompeta
trumps triunfo (*las barajas*)
trunk baúl; cajuela
(to) trust confiar en, fiarse (de)
    trusted
    trusted
(to) try (something) on probarse
    (algo)
    tried (something) on
    tried (something) on
    T-shirt camiseta (*de manga corta*)
    tub tina
    tubeless tire llanta sin cámara
    tube of lipstick tubo de labios
    tuna atún
    tuna salad ensalada de atún
    tunnel of love túnel del amor

turkey pavo
turnip nabo
(to) turn (someone or something) loose soltar (a alguien o algo)
    turned (someone or something) loose
    turned (someone or something) loose
turpentine aguarrás
turquoise turquesa
tuxedo smoking
TV announcer locutor de televisión
twice dos veces
twins gemelos
twin bed cama gemela
two-story building casa de dos pisos
type tipo, clase, estilo
(to) type escribir en máquina
    typed
    typed
typewriter máquina de escribir
typing mecanografía
typist mecanógrafo

U

ulcer úlcera (*del estómago*)
umbrella paraguas, sombrilla
undershirt camiseta
undertaker empresario de funeraria
underwear ropa interior
(to) undress desvestir (se)
    undressed
    undressed
uneven disparejo

uniform uniforme
union sindicato, unión
university universidad
unless a menos que, a no ser que
(to) unload descargar
    unloaded
    unloaded
unpleasant desagradable
unusual poco común, raro

uphill cuesta arriba
upper berth cama alta
upside down al revés, lo de
   arriba abajo, volteado,
   invertido

upstairs arriba (*en una casa*)
up-to-date al corriente, al
   día; a la fecha, a la
   moda
usher acomodador

V

vacant desocupado, vacío
vaccination certificate
   certificado de vacuna
vacuum cleaner aspiradora
valley valle
vanilla vainilla
varnish barniz
(to) varnish barnizar
   varnished
   varnished
veal carne de ternera
veal cutlet chuleta de ternera
vegetable salad ensalada de
   verduras
veil velo
velvet terciopelo
Venetian blinds persianas
Venice Venecia
vest chaleco (*de traje*)

Vienna Viena
view vista; panorama
villain villano
vine vid, parra; enredadera
vinegar vinagre
violation infracción
violin violín
violinist violinista
virgin virgen
visa visa
vitamin vitamina
voile espumilla
volcano volcán
(to) vomit vomitarse
   vomited
   vomited
(to) vote (for) votar (por)
   voted (for)
   voted (for)

W

waffle waffle
waffle iron wafflera
wagon carreta
waist cintura
waiter mesero
(to) wait on despachar, atender
   waited on
   waited on
waitress mesera

wallet cartera
wall plug contacto
walnut nuez de Castilla
war guerra
warden encargado de la
   prisión
wardrobe guardarropa
warehouse almacén, depósito
washer rondana

369

washing machine lavadora
wash tub tina de lavar
(to) wash your mouth out
        enjuagarse la boca
        washed your mouth out
        washed your mouth out
    wasp avispa
(to) waste desperdiciar; perder
        (tiempo)
    wasted
    wasted
    watercress berro
    watermelon sandía
(to) water-ski esquiar (en el agua)
    water-skied
    water-skied
    water skies esquíes acuáticos
    wave onda; ola
    wavy ondulado
    wax cera
(to) wax encerar
    waxed
    waxed
    wealth caudal, riqueza (s)
    wealthy rico
    wedding boda; casamiento
    wedding band anillo de
        matrimonio
    wedding cake pasted de
        bodas
    wedding day día de la boda
    wedding gown vestido de
        novia
    wedding march marcha
        nupcial
    wedding present regalo de
        bodas
    wedding ring anillo de
        matrimonio
    weed hierba (mala)
    weekly semanal, semanalmente

    weeping willow sauce llorón
(to) weigh pesar
    weighed
    weighed
    weightlifter el que hace
        pesas
    weightlifting (el deporte)
        hacer pesas
    weights pesas
    well pozo
    well done bien cocido
    well-known (adj.) bien
        conocido
(to) wet mojar, humedecer
    wet
    wet
    whale ballena
    wharf muelle
    wheel rueda; rin
    whether si
    whipped cream crema
        batida
    whirlwind torbellino,
        remolino (de viento)
    whiskey whisky
(to) whisper cuchichear, susurrar
    whispered
    whispered
    whistle silbido; pito; silbato
(to) whistle silbar
    whistled
    whistled
    wholesale por mayoreo,
        mayoreo
    whole wheat bread pan de
        trigo entero
    whooping cough tos ferina
    widowed (adj.) viudo(a)
    width anchura
    wig peluca
    willow sauce

will power fuerza de voluntad
windmill molino de viento
windshield parabrisa
windshield wiper limpiador
(*de coche*)
wind storm tormenta de
viento
windy de viento (*día*);
ventoso
(to) wind your watch, clock
darle cuerda al reloj
wound your watch, clock
wound your watch, clock
wine guinda
(to) wink (at) guiñar el ojo
winked (at)
winked (at)
wire alambre
wisdom tooth muela del
juicio
witch bruja
(to) withdraw sacar, retirar
withdrew
withdrawn
withdrawal retiro
withdrawal slip esqueleto
para retirar
within adentro (de)
witness testigo
(to) wonder preguntarse
wondered
wondered
wool lana

work shoes zapatos mineros
worm gusano
wormy agusanado
(to) worship adorar, venerar
worshiped
worshiped
(to) wrap (something) up
envolver (algo)
wrapped (something) up
wrapped (something) up
wreath corona (*de flores*)
wreck choque fuerte
wrench llave (*herramienta*)
(to) wrestle luchar
wrestled
wrestled
wrestler luchador
wrestling (*el deporte*) las
luchas; luchar
wrestling match lucha
(to) wrinkle arrugar (se)
wrinkled
wrinkled
wrist muñeca
(to) write (something) down
apuntar (algo)
wrote (something) down
written (something)
down
writing escritura, letra
wrong number número
equivocado

X

x-ray radiografía
(to) x-ray sacar radiografía

x-rayed
x-rayed

Y

(to) yawn bostezar
yawned
yawned
yeast levadura
(to) yell (at) gritar

yelled (at)
yelled (at)
Yiddish dialecto hebreo-
alemán